The NEW Diabetes Diet

Control At Last (& Easy Weight Loss) with No Carb Counting
No Sugar, No Flour...AND BROWNIES!

Joyce and Robert Schneider, M.D.

NOTICE TO READERS

This book is intended to provide straightforward information about diabetes to readers everywhere, not as specific medical advice to any one individual. Diabetes varies greatly from person to person, and in any one person from day to day, hour to hour. There are many variables: different organ systems affected, different degrees of severity, different phases along the way. Diabetes is a moving target with no two targets exactly the same.

Only your doctor knows your particular mix of problems and can prescribe treatment for you. Whether you have diabetes or not, you should, of course, always consult with and be guided by your own physician before embarking on any new diet, eating or exercise plan. This applies as well to changes in medication, whether oral, injection, or over-the-counter.

ISBN: 1461065895
ISBN-13: 9781461065890

DEDICATION

. . .

[From a press release of the International Diabetes Federation, dated December of 2006, four years ago as of this writing]

"The International Diabetes Federation (IDF) has published new data indicating the enormity of the diabetes epidemic. Data published today in the Federation's Diabetes Atlas show that the disease now affects a staggering 246 million people worldwide, with 46% of all those affected in the 40-59 age group. Previous figures underestimated the scope of the problem, while even the most pessimistic predictions fell short of the current figure. The new data predict that the total number of people living with diabetes will skyrocket to 380 million within twenty years if nothing is done."

We dedicate this book to all who struggle against this epidemic: to researchers and health care providers…and especially to those who struggle alone, trying to understand it all and find their way back to health.

CONTENTS

Part One: A very new idea

Part Two: Miracle Recipes

INTRODUCTION

· · ·

From Joyce (the cook): In their e-mails, on blogs and forums, and via our website (thecookandthecardiologist.com), Facebook and Twitter – over 80,000 followers: @JoyceSchneider1 – people suffering with diabetes have made it clear:

"I've got all these books and they just talk about the science. Please – *what can I eat?*" Others describe nutritionists and diabetes educators "not agreeing with each other," and "diabetic" recipes that still cause sugar spikes. And here's the most common refrain: "Isn't there a meal plan somewhere, something for every day, where I don't have to do all this constant guesswork and counting?"

Yes, finally. It's here. In trying to manage diabetic health, we've figured out something totally new that will surprise and delight you, maybe even astonish you, whether you have type 1 or type 2.

From Robert: In over thirty years of Internal Medicine and Cardiology practice, I've cared for literally thousands of overweight, prediabetic, and diabetic patients. It has been frustrating, with the Holy Grail of making their lives better always just out of reach, despite a constant barrage of new drugs, new theories, and new diets.

Until now.

This book is vastly different from any other you've seen. We have listened to what people with diabetes have told us, and we see that they're still struggling. All those new drugs and new diets – how much have they accomplished? Do people with diabetes feel any more in control of their disease?

And are hospitals less full or more overwhelmed than ever with people suffering from the cardiovascular complications (heart attack and stroke) caused by diabetes?

The recipes in this eating plan consist of never-imagined innovations in ingredients, cooking, and baking techniques, developed in response to the obesity epidemic, and with particular emphasis on eating plans for both type 1 and type 2 diabetes.

We are Joyce and Robert Schneider, M.D., also known as the Cook and the Cardiologist. We work well as a team, since doctors (usually) don't cook, and cooks (usually) don't know medicine. We teach and learn from each other, with a love of food – especially chocolate – that we want to share with you.

Astonishing reports

First, in a report issued by the CDC (Centers for Disease Control), dated January 27, 2011, it was announced that over one third of adults in the U.S. (79 million people) have prediabetes, while the number of people with full blown type 2 diabetes has surged to 26 million (compared to 23.6 million in 2008).

Together, the most recent number of people with prediabetes or diabetes comes to 105 million – more than one out of three Americans!

Second, an editorial from *The Lancet*, dated June 26, 2010. The entire issue of this illustrious British medical journal was devoted to the global diabetes epidemic, and to coincide with the 2010 annual meeting of the American Diabetes Association.

(The editorial is written in medical language, which makes it a bit hard to interpret. What it's really saying is…we're getting nowhere. Current diets and treatments just aren't working. It's all getting worse. Somebody THINK of something!)

Now give *The Lancet's* editorial a read, noting especially the very last sentence, which was speaking to the most esteemed physicians and diabetes researchers from all over the world:

"Type 2 Diabetes—Time to change our approach"

"…Four articles in this edition [focus on] cardiovascular risk in people with type 2 diabetes, or describe new strategies in drug treatment. …But there is a glaring absence: no research on lifestyle interventions to prevent or reverse diabetes. In this respect, medicine is losing the war against diabetes.

"Type 2 diabetes, a largely preventable disorder, has reached epidemic proportion. A strong, integrated, and *imaginative* response is required, in which the limits of drug treatment and the opportunities of lifestyle interventions are recognized." *(The Lancet*, Volume 375, Issue 9733, Page 2193, 26 June 2010 *Editorial*

A new idea

Such an awful disease, and it all comes down to one little word: carbs. On one hand the key to controlling diabetes, on the other hand binding you to the drudgery of "carb counting," fretting that you may have eaten too much or too little. It is still a 24/7, exhausting battle for control of your blood sugar. It takes over your life.

How is that different from ten or twenty years ago?

We wanted desperately to help. We were also aware – since Bob is a cardiologist – of the double dilemma facing diabetes sufferers: Count every carb, but don't eat animal fats either because of the cardiovascular complications diabetes causes. There was the vicious circle, the Catch 22.

Because, *what's left to eat?*

Even yams, barley, other starchy vegetables and – yes – whole grains will metabolize into sugar in forty or so minutes. For us, they too were a no-no, because our mission was finding a way to keep people's blood glucose stabilized for longer and longer stretches.

Sweets. That bothered us too. Nearly everyone craves sweets, and wouldn't it be wonderful if people with diabetes could eat as many sweets as they wanted – without fear of getting into trouble? Without even the slightest blood sugar spike?

Now there was an impossible dream. Or was it?

We once asked a sixteen-year-old with type 1 diabetes what he wanted most in the world. "A brownie," he said. "Without having to stab myself with the bleeping insulin." He then said that he just wanted to give up, take a platter of brownies to the local hospital E.R., sit down, and eat them. "Think they could save me?" he asked.

An idea was born, and got bigger every day. We felt angry. Medicine had conquered polio, smallpox, tetanus, diphtheria, and whooping cough. Why couldn't it conquer diabetes?

There had to be a way. Every question prompted new questions. I asked and Bob, a great teacher, explained patiently, over and over. Clearly, people with diabetes needed some carbs to treat or avoid hypoglycemia, also known as low blood sugar with its shakes and feeling dangerously faint. But when those same people just feel hungry, they often eat more carbs than they should, which in turn provokes the wild swings of their blood sugar.

Protein, on the other hand, doesn't cause blood sugar spikes. But that protein should be lean, and cooked chicken breast can get boring, and animal fats are out.

Imagine, we would muse, not needing carbs *or* saturated fat to not feel hungry.

One day, I (Joyce) started experimenting with protein powder. First I just stared at it and played with it a little. It was white, fluffy, and certainly looked like flour. Add water and you could make nice, squishy softballs with it.

I experimented more, adding a bit more and then a bit more to baking recipes. Things like muffins came out tasting not too bad, but they fell apart.

Then I realized that it wasn't the protein powder's fault. Rather, the ingredients needed baking's bad boy old glue – sugar and egg yolks – to hold everything together. But sugar and egg yolks were no-no's too. Yes, they're in most "diabetic" recipes, which then describe a serving size that wouldn't fill a mouse.

I spent the next year experimenting, often getting extremely frustrated at yet another failure and storming around the kitchen like a crazy person. "Now dear," Bob would say. "Remember, penicillin wasn't built in a day."

I persisted while Bob wrote, researched, explained more, and did a loving, humorous job of keeping me calm (relatively speaking), and at it.

So, what's the end of the story?

Flourless, all-protein, no sugar pancakes, brownies, blondies, muffins, pizza, tortillas, pies and more that are just as luscious as their counterparts made the old way. Eat as much as you like with no sugar spikes. They'll make it easier for you to lose weight because they eliminate cravings.

Brownies for breakfast?

Yes! Have two or three, or muffins or pancakes – with no fear of sugar spikes!

A typical big brownie, for example, has 74 calories, 12 grams of protein, less than one gram of carbohydrate, two grams of fiber, 1.5 grams of mono-unsaturated fat and 4,666 antioxidants from pure cocoa. That's it! Nothing unhealthy. Zero guilt and zero worry.

It's the same with all our other baked yummies.

Healthy? Our new-way ingredients contain such large amounts of fiber, vitamins, calcium, and antioxidants that they can serve as any meal replacement.

Luscious, no fear, and no sugar spikes.

Sound good?

Read on…

"It's gonna take a lot of fireworks to clean this place up."
Homer Simpson

Chapter One

THE NEW DIABETES DIET

The Carbohydrate Connection

Until now, the diabetic roller coaster has been: too-low blood glucose (hypoglycemia: dizziness, fainting, "the shakes,"); too-high blood glucose (hyperglycemia, leading to heart, brain, and kidney damage), and the struggle to keep on an even keel between them. Carbohydrate intake is the single, most important key to controlling diabetes, and at the same time it has been the overwhelming stumbling block. The reason is that, until now carbs have been our main source of energy but at the same time, they metabolize into sugar.

Until now the only solution has been the drudgery of "carb counting," complicated food exchanges, glycemic charts, diabetes medications, insulin injections, multiple daily finger-sticks, and the anxiety of counting down the seconds on the meter until the blood sugar number pops up on the screen. Diabetes sufferers have kept notebooks, even Excel sheets, obsessively tracking every morsel they eat whether complex carbs like whole grains, which raise blood sugar in 30-60 minutes, or simple carbohydrates like sugar and white flour, which will quickly "spike" blood sugar within fifteen minutes..

Until now there has been little you could do to gain control over diabetes.

Why this book is different

This book's new concept is that "complex" carbs *aren't* necessarily "good" carbs, as they've been called for the past decade. Carbs are carbs. If they spike in fifteen or forty-five minutes, they're still what provoke dreaded blood sugar peaks and plunges.

We want to clarify the confusion and conflicting advice on diet, weight, fat, carbs, and sugar in what is fast becoming the world's leading health problem. Two thirds of Americans, including one third of children and adolescents, are overweight or obese. Very soon almost 30 million Americans will have Type 2 diabetes, and already 79 million more are prediabetic, a condition defined as having overnight Fasting Blood Sugar (FBS) levels of 100 – 125 milligrams of glucose per 100 cc of blood.

The combined current numbers of those with Type 1, Type 2, and prediabetes come to more than one out of every three Americans. So, you are not alone in this.

You're not alone, either, in the confusion.

People with diabetes tell us they don't trust what they read. They can just look at a "diabetic" recipe and tell you, "I can't eat that! It would kill me!" They are frustrated with recipes containing sugar in its sneaky forms (honey, molasses, dried fruit, and brown sugar), and with recipes containing flour (even carb-y whole wheat). They have gotten more savvy and know that "complex" whole grains and brown rice and barley and sweet potatoes are just carbs after all, giving them only thirty to forty minutes before they, too, zoom and then crash back down again.

From a diabetes website: "Nooo! How'd my blood glucose drop to 51? I just had whole wheat pasta 90 minutes ago! *I am so tired of not being in control.*"

And: "I just binged on a cupcake. How much insulin do I need to cover it?"

And: "Back in the 40's AGAIN? Didn't know I was this low!! Need a juice box. Somebody PLEASE explain?"

Hang on, friends. There's good news ahead.

Three surprises

First surprise: we have developed a 6-week (and ever after) eating plan that gets rid of flour, the major source of carbohydrates in food. Instead of flour we use white, fluffy protein powder (which has no carbs). We also use milled flaxseed which has more fiber than whole grains, no absorbable carbs, *and* can substitute for butter and margarine in baking. Milled flaxseed also has specific benefits for heart health and for insulin regulation and insulin resistance, which we'll soon tell you about in detail.

Second surprise: we don't use sugar in any of its sneaky, unsuspected forms, which means no honey, dried fruit, molasses, brown sugar, sugar alcohols, or agave. "Natural" or "organic" sugar is still sugar. Your body truly doesn't know the difference.

Flour and sugar gone? Kicked out completely? Is it possible? Yes, it is. And suddenly weight loss, controlling both types of diabetes, and avoiding prediabetes become a lot easier.

Third (and happiest) surprise: a feature of The New Diabetes Diet is its baked goodies. Say good-bye to cravings for brownies, muffins, blondies, cookies, pies, cakes, tortillas, pancakes, snack bars, bread, sandwich rolls, and more. The protein powder substitutes beautifully for flour. And protein's calories keep you feeling full and energized hours longer than any carb; also make it easier to stick to a diet if weight loss is your goal.

Our baked goods are just as luscious as those made with unhealthy, old-way ingredients, and they contain such large amounts of fiber, vitamins, calcium, and antioxidants that they can serve as any grab 'n run meal replacement.

Pancakes for breakfast? Sure, a stack of them! Or this eating plan's muffins, brownies, blondies – all of them. Once you've gotten your blood glucose to where you want it, keep snacking on these all-protein baked goods. They will keep you stable for longer and longer.

A big blondie with heart healthy Omega 3 walnuts, for example, contains 122 calories, 16 grams protein, less than 3 grams of carbs, 2 grams of fiber, less than 1 gram of monounsaturated fat, and 2,674 antioxidants.

That blondie's two grams of fiber, by the way, are the same amount that you'll find in a slice of whole wheat bread – which also contains 23 grams of carbs, 128 calories, and just 3 grams of protein.. (Source: FatSecret.com)

Whole wheat bread's nutritional data may vary slightly, depending on the brand.

But these blondies taste better, flavored with cinnamon, ginger and nutmeg.

And some whole wheat slices are quite thin. Not filling, not luscious, and certainly not worth the calories.

Recipes ahead, but first…

About hypoglycemia

If you're not on medications, transition should be easy. Simply substitute our recipes at your own pace, from one recipe a day up to three meals a day, whatever works best for you.

If you are on medication, whether insulin or oral medication, gradual modification of your drug doses should accompany these changes in your diet. Check with your doctor before any diet, medication, or exercise change.

Be on the safe side even after your transition period, and carry "fast carbs" such as glucose tablets with you. They are sold at all drugstores. Other good choices to have on hand are ½ cup (four ounces) of non-diet soda, ½ cup of regular orange juice, or portable juice boxes and even Gummi Bears.

But with your "fast carbs" eat lean protein: for example this eating plan's baked goodies. (Some only take 90 seconds in the microwave.) It's a good idea to have some always pre-made and in the fridge. By the time your "fast carbs" have flashed and crashed, energy from the slow metabolizing protein will be up and running, stabilizing your blood sugar for hours to keep you more permanently in control.

Gluten free too

Our baked goodies don't even use gluten free flour substitutes such as barley, corn, rice, amaranth, or buckwheat. These, too, are still carbs. And if you have diabetes (or are just trying to lose weight), a carb saved is a carb saved.

Wouldn't it be nice to get rid of most carbs?

Heresy! We *need* carbs you're thinking, right?

Yes, we need carbs. Our bodies run on glucose, and carbs are the fastest "glucose fuel." But they're not the only glucose fuel, and, with this new eating plan's goodies, you can now limit your carbs to the healthiest fruits, nuts and vegetables.

Protein and healthy fats – olive and canola oil – also convert to glucose; more slowly, true.

But protein causes no sugar spikes as it is metabolized, so you can feel safe eating to feel full, which is not possible with ordinary diabetes regimens. A bedtime snack of any of this plan's baked goods will also give you a better night's sleep, without having to set the alarm for three or four a.m. for fear that you may be dropping into hypoglycemia.

Heart health too

What is also critical about this eating plan, as opposed to others, is its avoidance of saturated fat and cholesterol, including oh-so-trendy "grass fed" red meat. (A classier kind of saturated fat?)

This is especially important because diabetes patients are twice as vulnerable as the general population to cardiovascular complications, such as heart disease, stroke, Peripheral Artery Disease (leg amputation), Retinal Disease (blindness), Nerve Disease (nerve damage and loss of sensation in limbs), and – rarely – CKD (chronic kidney disease.). All of these cardiovascular complications are due to arterial narrowing caused by saturated fat and cholesterol deposits, and then clots, blocking arteries inflamed and damaged by fat particles.

This is the crucial point that many diabetic eating plans miss.

In their efforts to stay low carb, they anticipate people's hunger, so they include large amounts of animal and dairy saturated fat and cholesterol. Diabetes sufferers may at first be happy with the results. They get their blood sugar down and may even lose weight.

But blocked, gunked-up arteries are a dangerous price to pay.

We do use Mediterranean-healthy olive and canola oil, both high in MUFAs and PUFAs – mono- and poly-unsaturated fats which improve arterial health.

We will also show you how to remove cholesterol from fish and chicken. Did you know that fish, chicken, and beef all contain the same amount of cholesterol –70 milligrams per four-ounce serving? What fish and chicken don't have is saturated fat.

Brownies, muffins and pancakes? Really?

The discovery that protein powder can substitute completely for flour is so new that you may just be finding out about it here. We especially like to use soy protein powder. It adapts marvelously to cooking and baking, and is a miraculous, pure protein: vitamin rich, containing as much calcium as fat free milk, with no carbs, cholesterol, or saturated fat, and many more B vitamins (B6, B12, Niacin, Riboflavin, Folic acid, and Thiamin) than in any whole grains.

But is soy protein powder okay for men?

Yes, definitely. Soy may even protect men from their own human estrogen. Male bodies do produce small amounts of estrogen as well as testosterone. Belly fat further increases a man's estrogen levels. But soy's phytoestrogens (weak estrogen from plants) may help by occupying estrogen receptor sites in the male body and blocking their more powerful and potentially problematic human male estrogen, which has been associated with prostate cancer and other health issues.

Further, the Chinese and Japanese have eaten soy for over 3,000 years. In the long history of both cultures there have been no stories, anecdotal or otherwise, of males having problems with their masculinity.

If you've been hearing that a plant-based diet is better for you, soy is one of the many reasons why. But no one dreamed that it was so adaptable! Yes, you can make more than smoothies with it!

Does "plant-based diet" sound dreary to you? Get ready to smile.

You can make, for example, your own easy Homemade Protein Bread – no yeast or waiting required – each slice containing **92 calories, 19 g protein, *0 g carbs*, 2 g fiber, & 1,500 lignan antioxidants.** Two slices for a sandwich contain 184 calories, 38 grams of protein, 4 grams of heart healthy fiber derived from milled flaxseed– and still zero carbs! You can fill your sandwich with peanut butter and sugar-free preserves, or salad … anything! A whole, jam-packed sandwich with 38 grams of protein – and carbs just from the veggies! Or make elegant, fun paninis. Or grilled cheese sandwiches. Or dice the bread for poultry stuffing or croutons to pop into soup and salads. Pure protein croutons! Imagine!

- Imagine stuffed tortilla wraps or banana nut bread or pancake and tortilla rollups that are healthier than anything advertised as "healthy?" Here's a partial list:
- **Pancakes**, each 98 calories, 15 g protein, 3 g carbs and 2 g monounsaturated fat
- **Blondies,** 122 calories, 16 grams protein, less than 3 grams carbs, 2 grams fiber, less than 1 g saturated fat, and 2,674 antioxidants
- **Tortillas**, each 61 calories, 11 grams protein, 0 g carbs, 3 g monounsaturated fat, and 36,000 lignan antioxidants
- **Quesadillas**, each 59 calories, 10 grams protein, 2 grams carbs, 1 g monounsaturated fat and 12,000 lignan antioxidants
- **Banana nut bread**, each slice 110 calories, 11 g protein, 7.6 g carbs, 2 g fiber, 1.7 g monounsaturated fat, 2,250 lignan antioxidants, and 975 Omega-3 acids

- **Pizza,** each slice (one sixth of a pizza) 161 calories, 23 g protein, 3 g carbs, 2 g fiber, 1,000 lignan antioxidants, 1.5 g monounsaturated fat,
- **Burger rolls**, each 177 calories, 36 g protein, 0 g carbs, 2 g fiber, and 11,502 antioxidants

Note: If saturated fat isn't listed, it's because there isn't any.

Those are just a few examples. Not of this eating plan's chicken, fish, fruit or vegetable recipes, but of the formerly most craved but carby treats which you can now have – as much as you like – using this book's new kind of recipes.

And if you've been using insulin, you likewise won't have to bolus; i.e. cover treats with insulin injections. Imagine that. With zero worry or guilt, ever again.

Diabetes – Type 1 and Type 2

Our eating plan can help both Type 1 and type 2 diabetes, even though they are different diseases. This is possible for the most part because it keeps carbohydrates at the absolute minimum necessary for your blood glucose stabilization.

Type 1 diabetes is primarily an autoimmune disease, in which the pancreatic cells that produce insulin are destroyed by the body's own immune system. The cause is thought to be partly genetic, partly due to some previous viral infection. Symptoms usually first occur in childhood or adolescence. Insulin and blood glucose control have so far been the only way to control the disease, as well as to delay its complications, including those that affect the kidneys, eyes, nerve pathways, and blood vessels.

However, significant problems can arise with intensive insulin therapy.

Insulin dosage is tricky because it pushes blood sugar down, sometimes too far, resulting in a greater risk for hypoglycemia; also, in many cases, weight gain. This may be because, until now, hypoglycemia with its lows, shakiness, and blackouts, could only be counteracted with "fast" carbs, which could get the type 1 sufferer up and running again, but which could quickly start a vicious cycle of highs and lows, by increasing the need for more insulin, and then more fast carbs to deal with the excess insulin. All those carbs and calories can result in weight gain, which in turn affects blood pressure, cholesterol levels, and cardiovascular health.

Up, down, up, down, a 24/7 frightening seesaw. The yearning of every person with type 1 is to be less anxious about carbohydrate intake, and less dependent on insulin.

We believe that Type 1 diabetes sufferers who follow our eating plan can reduce their insulin dosage, and improve their daily control.

Type 2 diabetes is much more common, comprising about 95% of cases. It is associated mainly with diets high in calories and carbs, and by physical inactivity. There may also be genetic factors in some cases, exacerbated by weight gain.

When you eat, the pancreas releases the hormone insulin into your bloodstream. The circulating insulin then acts to escort sugar (i.e. glucose, the active, metabolized form of sugar) into special receptor sites on the surface of your muscle cells. But with weight gain and lack of exercise, the cells become overloaded with sugar and resistant to insulin. The pancreas tries to compensate by increasing its insulin production, which wears it down, and its insulin production drops.

Insulin and the muscle receptor sites also regulate the amount of sugar in your blood. Receptor sites are like gates, and insulin is the gatekeeper, admitting sugar into muscle cells when they need it, and letting it stay in the blood when they don't. But in type 2 diabetes this regulation process doesn't work well, and glucose accumulates in the blood, harming other organs and the whole cardiovascular system. Still the pancreas struggles on, pushing out insulin only to have it "rejected" by the sugar-overloaded receptor sites. Finally, the pancreas becomes exhausted.

When that happens, you have advanced from prediabetes to diabetes.

Fat is another big player in this process. All that accumulated excess blood sugar from carbs converts into fat, and usually lands in the belly. Belly fat is Poison Central, since it *mainlines* fat particles right back into the blood stream, inflaming and injuring arterial inner walls, provoking cholesterol deposits and clots which block circulation.

It's hard to believe that this whole harmful cycle starts with just carbs, whether oatmeal and whole wheat, or flour, sugar, and that pretty cupcake…but it does.

The term, "Insulin Resistance" is misleading

So the picture clears: it isn't insulin that resists; it's the receptor sites on muscles and tissues that resist.

But the good news is that *when you move or exercise,* muscle and other tissue cells sense that they need more glucose for energy, and "open up;" i. e. increase their number of receptor sites for your glucose to "land." Muscle and tissue cells function best with only a certain amount of sugar in them. Not enough? They'll need and welcome more. Too much? They'll reject it. So if you're taking in more carbs (which break down to sugar) than muscle and tissue cells need, they shut down their receptor sites against this "assault," and your blood sugar rises.

Can type 2 diabetes be reversed?

Yes, but…

Anyone who has ever been type 2 diabetic is still more vulnerable to being diabetic again than someone who's never been diabetic. The condition, once you've had it, is always there, latent.

Say you've just lost 50 or 100 or more pounds, and you're now on maintenance. Your weight loss has gotten you off meds, you're even having normal FBS (Fasting Blood Sugar) numbers, and you're feeling thrilled, terrific.

Should you still consider yourself diabetic and be super careful about carbs?

Yes. Stay on a daily maintenance plan of 1,800 to 2,000 calories if you're a woman, 2,000-2,200 if you're a man, but no carb or sugar binges and avoid weight gain, or your insulin resistance will kick in again and you'll be heading back to diabetes.

The condition, again, is always there, latent.

Your health is wonderfully restored, and cardiovascular risk averted, but it doesn't hurt to continue "thinking like a diabetic." That is, to be super careful about carbs and to choose a good maintenance eating plan....

...which would still consist of the New Diabetes Diet's brownies, muffins, pancakes, blondies, pizza, tortillas, pumpkin pie – everything you love to eat anyway – so that's okay, isn't it? With flour (all kinds) and sugar (all kinds) banished completely, losing weight and controlling both types of diabetes become a lot easier.

Why this eating plan is healthiest for everyone

This eating plan is not just for people with diabetes. It's the healthiest new way for everybody because:

- We use primarily plant based protein, an excellent source of calcium, vitamins, and minerals, plus some fish and chicken. Recent studies (cited in this book) endorse plant based protein diets as best for your health.
- It is low in carbs *and* saturated fat and cholesterol. And it is high in good fats (mono and poly unsaturated) which lower bad LDL cholesterol (think L for Lousy) and increase good HDL cholesterol (H for Healthy).
- It is high in Omega-3 Fatty Acids (in fish, milled flaxseed, and walnuts) which also increase good HDL, plus decrease triglycerides, inflammation of the arteries, arterial clotting, atherosclerosis, and cardiovascular disease.
- It is high in antioxidants, particularly herbs and spices which have spectacular amounts of antioxidants to combat arterial inflammation (the first dangerous step on the way to cholesterol deposits which narrow arteries).
- It is high in pure, *non-alkalinized* cocoa, which is also a powerful anti-inflammatory. (Alkalinization, also known as Dutch Process, destroys the antioxidants.) Cocoa also has the amazing power to dilate arteries in *seconds,* lowering blood pressure and allowing more oxygen and nutrients to reach every organ and tissue, including the heart, brain, kidneys, and extremities. This helps to prevent heart disease, strokes, peripheral arterial disease, and retinal arterial disease.

Is the "Glycemic Index" any longer even necessary?

Maybe. For a while, yes. See how this plan works for you. Discuss it with your doctor, then decide. For sure you'll find yourself largely free of the obsessive, night and day drudgery of pounding your calculator and counting every carb. And you'll be free of those strangling "Rules for Diabetic Control:" Monitor! Medicate! Test! test!, test!

If you've been using insulin, imagine a life with no more "Carb up, Shoot up."

Imagine fingertips that don't hurt.

Imagine the never ending coping …gone.

Do continue with your careful foot and eye care, although this eating plan should stop any progression of symptoms if they've started. Try to keep your days consistent, consistent, consistent. Eat, snack, and take your meds (if you still need them) at the same times daily.

And, again, consult with and be guided by your own physician before making any changes in medication, whether oral, injection, or over-the-counter. This is especially true for people with diabetes, whose needs can very greatly from one person to another.

What are your objectives?

Will you want to lose weight, go on maintenance, or both? Doing either is just a matter of portion size.

If you are a woman of average height and you weigh between 180 to 210 pounds and want to lose weight, aim for 1400 – 1500 calories a day, which is exactly what this diet provides. At your current weight (and depending on your physical activity), you burn about 2,000 calories a day. Limiting yourself to 1500 calories daily will mean a 500 daily calorie deficit. Multiply those 500 daily calories times seven days and you get 3,500 calories, which equals a pound. You will lose one pound a week, but with good, steady consistency. You will lose even more – up to 1½ pounds – if you exercise.

However, aiming for daily calories lower than the amount just cited is not recommended, and runs the risk of a hypoglycemic reaction.

(People often report that four, five, or more pounds come off in the first week. That is mostly water. Especially if, as this eating plan urges, you've stopped using salt.)

Now let's say you're that same woman mentioned above, and you've successfully lost 50 pounds, and from now on just want to maintain your weight. Chances are (if you're Type 2), your weight loss has gotten you off drugs like metformin and you're feeling terrific.

Should you still consider yourself a "diabetic" and be super careful about carbs?

Yes. In large part it depends on what your overnight FBS is (Fasting Blood Sugar). If it's 125, that's pretty good, you're right on the cusp between prediabetes and diabetes. But you still have to watch your carbs and stay on maintenance. For that you can go up to 1800 to 2000 calories a day, but – no sugar or carb binges, and avoid weight gain, or your insulin resistance will kick in again and you'll be heading back to diabetes.

But let's say your FBS numbers are below 100 (normal), and now you're really thrilled. Does that mean that at last you can go back to cupcakes and binges? No, it still doesn't.

Anyone who has ever had type 2 diabetes, even after weight loss and getting off meds and having normal FBS numbers, is still more vulnerable to having diabetes again than someone who's never had diabetes.

Remember, the condition, once you've had it, is always there, latent.

Your health is wonderfully restored, and cardiovascular risk averted, but it doesn't hurt to continue "thinking like a diabetic." That is, to be super careful about carbs especially, and to continue exercising, and to choose a good maintenance eating plan.   But that would still consist of this eating plan's tacos, sandwiches, chocolate mousse, pumpkin pie, and everything you love anyway – so that's okay, isn't it?

Your future won't hold the cravings that other diets imposed.

Everything just described also applies to men, except that the average man needs about 200 calories more daily than women for maintenance. Which also means that men can lose weight on more calories; say 1600 calories a day, as opposed to 1400 or so for women.

Men burn on average 2,200 calories a day, and exercise makes that number higher. A 500 calorie a day deficit (1,700 calories) will easily lose a pound a week for you. And if you lower your daily calories to 1,600 calories a day, that makes a 600 calorie a day deficit, which plus exercise will melt off 1 ½ pounds a week or more.

Whether you're a man or a woman, take it slow at first, to see how you react and feel. The calories of each recipe in this book have been individually calculated – in addition to the meal plan's daily tallies – so if you find favorites you can switch around and still keep on track.

Eat our recipe brownies all day if you like! Another fascinating thing about protein is that its slo-mo breakdown has the opposite effect of carbs, which make you want to eat more, more, more, even if the carbs are "complex." Whereas, it is actually hard to eat too much protein; it will keep you feeling full for so long you just won't feel hungry.

For people with diabetes, individual needs and reactions can vary considerably, especially when two or more medical conditions co-exist. Type 2 diabetes and obesity often come together, for example, making exercising painful. Your own physician knows your particular mix of health issues, and should be the final overseer of what is your best health management.

Find what works for you, and the calorie level you're most comfortable at. See how far protein's slow-release glucose energy carries you, and helps you sleep through the night without fear of hypoglycemia.

We sincerely hope that this book brings big change to your life, reducing or ending your dependence on medications to the extent possible, in tandem with your diet change.

And if you must be on medications, we also hope to improve and simplify your life by decreasing or eliminating the need for constant carb counting, finger sticks, low sugar crashes, and high sugar organ damage.

Exercise: so important, and how it works

Exercise lowers the sugar level in muscle cells. The cells respond by needing more sugar; i.e., increasing and opening more of their receptor sites. Insulin can then "escort" and move sugar from the blood into the cells.

Without exercise, the opposite happens. Sugar builds in the cells; they become "all full up;" their receptor sites close down, and insulin can't move sugar into them. Sugar in the blood rises, and then rises more. The more carbs you eat, the more this process worsens.

Exercise has a special bonus in that its benefits last for nearly twenty-four hours, meaning that all those extra insulin receptor sites "stay open" for that long. That is why exercise is urged for every day.

Exercise is important for everyone, but for people with diabetes it is right up there with carb restriction in removing excess glucose from the blood.

But what if exercise is hard or painful for you, or you're just starting out and feel weak?

The good news is that exercise can be cumulative, meaning that you can break it up into small sessions and still get the good effects. Three brisk ten-minute walks instead of one 30-minute workout have been proven to provide the same health and weight loss benefits. Ditto six five minute walks each day, every time you get the chance to get up, stretch and move. Even little things, like pacing while you brush your teeth or talk on the phone or wait for the microwave will cumulatively help lower your blood sugar and enhance your muscles' ability to remove sugar from your blood; i. e., lower your insulin resistance. If the weather's bad and your living space is small, place an empty wastepaper basket upside down and "power walk" around it. Work in ten minutes here, ten minutes there, so that your total adds up to 30 minutes a day.

Every step taken counts.

The goal is simply to move in every ordinary little way that you can think of. Did you just take a can down from a shelf? Put it back, then take it down again. Or use two cans, one in each hand, and do a whole minute's worth of alternate up-downs, kind of like milking a really big cow. One minute! – and you've just opened a whole lot of receptor sites happy to pull glucose from your blood for the next twenty-four hours.

Walking, incidentally, is the best exercise for everyone for another reason. Because of gravity, blood pools in your leg veins. But walking gets your leg muscles – the biggest in your body – working like powerful pumps for the best return blood flow to your heart, then from the heart to circulate throughout the rest of your body.

Working your leg muscles is therefore a great help to your circulation.

For diabetes sufferers, carb restriction and exercise are your dual handles to control.

Cocoa, the miracle drug

We use cocoa – the healthy kind – in a lot in our recipes, and urge you to have at least two cocoa or chocolate recipes a day. Why? Because cocoa is more than a wonder drug. We consider it practically a fountain of youth.

Research published in November of 2008 in the *Journal of the American College of Cardiology* provides evidence that cocoa's spectacular antioxidant, epicatechin, is anti-inflammatory and significantly helps prevent damage to blood vessels, which is a leading cause of cardiovascular complications. Epicatechins' action also helps to prevent damage to other organs, and to your feet, and even to your skin. Epicatechins are powerful health and anti-aging agents.

In a later chapter we will show you how this works. For now though, make a note that only cocoa in its unsweetened, non-alkalinized form can perform this magic. (Alkalinization, also known as Dutch Process, destroys the epicatechin antioxidants.)

Good brands of pure, non-alkalinized cocoa are Trader Joes and Hershey's, the little brown box in bakery aisles. Most supermarket chains carry their own brands of unsweetened, non-alkalinized cocoa. These are also available on Amazon.com. No need to spend more on "fancy" brands.

Commercial chocolates, even the much advertised dark kind, unfortunately aren't nearly as healthy as their ads claim, especially if their labels say that their cocoa has been Dutch Processed, or "partially Dutch Processed." What you want is those true-cocoa epicatechins. Commercial chocolate also contains sugar or sugar alcohols, and saturated fat.

One of our favorite recipes is easy-to-make fudge sauce on berries, sliced banana and chopped walnuts. But there are other chocolate recipes; *lots* of them. Have big portions, including cocoa or chocolate drinks; they're healthy for any time of day, and there's no need to wait for dessert to enjoy them.

Say a permanent good-bye to cravings. With flour (all kinds) and sugar (all kinds), banished completely, suddenly weight loss, controlling both types of diabetes, and avoiding prediabetes become a lot easier. The New Diabetic Diet will work superbly to help you feel happier and much more in control of your life.

Definitions List:
1. Normal fasting (overnight) blood sugar, called FBS or Fasting Blood Sugar, is about 70-100 milligrams of glucose per 100 cc of blood.
2. Prediabetes is 100-125 milligrams of glucose per 100 cc of blood.
   - Over 125 FBS is diabetes.
   - Another measure you should know is the HbA1c (A1c for short). The A1c measures your average blood sugar during the preceding two to three months. Normal A1c is about 5.0-6.0. The American Diabetes Association advises a target of no more than 7.0 for people with diabetes. There is controversy about whether intensive therapy to lower A1c further reduces cardiovascular disease or not.

Salt and your health

Before ending this chapter, a word about salt. What's that got to do with diabetes? A lot. High Blood Pressure (hypertension) is often a partner with diabetes in the assault on your blood vessels, heart and brain. Salt (sodium) in your diet is the main villain in increasing your blood pressure. One teaspoon of table salt has 2300 milligrams (mgs) of sodium, the maximum amount anyone should consume in a day.

People with high blood pressure should stay below 1500 mgs per day.

How, exactly, does salt hurt us?

Picture a crimped garden hose with its water turned on full force. That is high blood pressure, aka hypertension. It pounds and throbs against the inner lining of the arteries, creating conditions for cholesterol and calcium to clump, narrow your arteries, clot, and lead to heart attack and stroke.

Excess salt also causes increased thirst and fluid intake to keep blood and body fluids at the right dilution. The vascular system (arteries, veins and capillaries) is a closed system, like that garden hose. Put more fluid into it and its pressure rises. That's how high blood pressure happens.

The three main target organs for habitually eating too much salt are the brain (stroke), heart (hypertrophy [enlargement] leading to congestive heart failure), and kidneys (leading to renal disease, kidney failure, and a life on dialysis machines).

All the sodium we need exists naturally in food, vegetables, and fruits. We don't need a salt shaker. Especially since a lot of salt is added to processed foods (canned, bottled, frozen, or packaged). As with sugar, food manufacturers know that salt makes their product taste better. This applies to fast foods too: a single cheeseburger and fries may contain more than a day's worth of sodium. Read Nutrition Facts labels.

Even a can of healthy beans – pour off the liquid, there are around 1400 milligrams of salt in it. If you have hypertension, rinse the beans. Are you making healthy stir fry? Teriyaki has huge amounts of salt. Try watering it down or, even better, use just ginger and garlic in your sauce. Restaurant food, all condiments, pickles, and processed meat are also high in salt.

Here's a good rule of thumb: if you didn't make it yourself, it has salt in it.

Especially don't trust "Reduced Salt" labeling on the package, bottle, or can; that often means a trivial reduction. Food manufacturers know people enjoy the taste of salt, and they don't want to lose sales.

The choice is yours. And recipes to thrill you are ahead.

Good luck!

"I don't care *what* you call it! If I can eat brownies *and* lose weight, I'm in!" From a Facebook friend

Chapter Two

THIS DIET WILL SIMPLIFY YOUR LIFE

No more "double life"

Until now, you may have felt that you were living in a different world from your friends and loved ones. They may (or may not) have been helping you stay on a healthy path. At a gathering full of great eats, there's always that offer of something dreary with the well meaning but unintentionally embarrassing, "Here, I made this just for you."

Or: "Oh have this one little cupcake. You can cover it with insulin – isn't that what you've *been* doing?"

Some may not be fully aware of your risks, or possibly are struggling with and denying their own overweight and unhealthful habits. (Who's thin these days?) There may also be family members who keep reminding you to "keep their food separate," which means double kitchen duty for you. Balky children can be a problem; also, sometimes, spouses or significant others. They may even be, to your dismay, overweight themselves, but insist on "regular food" and even bring tempting junk into the house.

It is often so hard to deal with the loneliness of the condition, the feeling of deprivation, that many diabetes sufferers admit giving in to ordering "diabetic gift baskets" online. "Worry free!" claim the sellers, whose very expensive products include "sugar free chocolates, candy bars, cookies, jelly beans, fruit candies, and crackers, peanuts, and pretzel sticks. Those "sugar free" goodies are usually made with sugar alcohols, which are no free ride for diabetics, and not uncommonly cause gastric distress. The salt in those crackers, peanuts, and pretzel sticks only harms people's blood pressure, and the prices of these prettily-wrapped confections range from forty to ninety-plus dollars.

"I couldn't help it," writes a woman named Patty. "I so needed something for when I was feeling bad."

Then her daughter started to buy gift baskets for her. Each woman gave up other things in order to be able to afford the "treats."

Those days are over. Now you can make your own sweets safely (fudge truffles, no spikes!). And no more "double duty, double life," struggling to manage your condition while simultaneously coping with the "regular" world. Because this eating plan may well be the healthiest, not just for you but for everyone you care about.

What you're eating, they should be eating too. The bonus is that they'll *like* it, even if they don't have diabetes!

Latest discoveries

Recent findings spotlight the updated diabetes eating plan as the best for anyone wanting to avoid stroke, heart disease, and cancer - all of which are overwhelmingly caused by overweight. These days, with the soaring rates of overweight and obesity, the risks apply to most of us: children and adults.

We're all potentially in the same boat. If not today, a year or a few years from now.

The National Institutes of Health, the Centers for Disease Control, and the U.S. Health and Human Services Agency have all called for an increased emphasis on treating weight, high cholesterol and high blood pressure (hypertension) both in those with diabetes and in the population at large – children included – before these conditions develop more serious complications.

In pediatricians' offices, the epidemic of overweight kids has become an urgent concern. And you've seen the bellies of friends, neighbors, people just walking down the street. Overweight alone, even without the presence of diabetes, can cause cardiovascular disease, cancer, hypertension, and stroke.

It's a win win! So much for "keep my food separate!"

Diabetes and the Plant Based Diet

In 2010, former President Bill Clinton happily reported that he had saved his life by his special diet and dramatic weight loss. In a short time he shed twenty-four pounds, getting back pretty much to the same weight he had been in high school. How did he do it? A strict diet of vegetables, low-sugar fruit, and protein powder. He had not been diabetic; just overweight, but given his history of coronary artery bypass surgery, he decided to radically change his diet or see his health deteriorate further. Often pictured in the past with a thick middle consuming cheeseburgers and fries, he now looks younger, more energetic, and healthier, and has undoubtedly improved the condition of his arteries.

Our eating plan is far less radical, using fish, chicken and gorgeous desserts (in which plant protein powder is substituted for flour). But it does follow the principles of the plant based diet in its prevention and treatment of disorders that were once thought to be a "normal" part of aging.

They are not. Rather, they are due to the 20th century lifestyle: fast food, processed food, sitting at work, sitting at home, expanding waistlines, little exercise, and smoking. You could say, therefore, that cardiovascular disease, high blood pressure, high cholesterol, obesity, cancer, and type 2 diabetes are overwhelmingly 20th century diseases.

•   •   •

Consider again that Bill Clinton was not diabetic; his problem was heart disease. But people with diabetes are more than doubly vulnerable to heart disease than the general population.

Additionally, according to a January 2011 report from the Mayo Clinic, type 2 diabetes in children is on the rise; and children as young as six or seven are also increasingly being diagnosed with high blood pressure, in large part because of the high amounts of salt in junk, fast, and commercial food.

A good rule of thumb: if you didn't make it yourself, it has salt and bad fat in it. .

But here is the disconnect. In the "regular" world, most people still eat the unhealthy old way because they often can't help it. Most of us are often rushed, or have to travel or eat on the run. What do nutrition specialists eat when they're in airports or on the highway? What's in your average vending machine? Fresh oranges and apples and this plan's fudge brownies with 20 grams of protein and 4 grams of carbs?

Wouldn't that be nice.

But let's be honest too. Most of us are at home most of the time. And home is where you *are* in control of what you eat and fix for your family.

The National Institutes of Health recently reported findings that plant based foods are high in disease-preventing properties, and low in disease-causing substance such as saturated and trans fats, cholesterol, and sugar.

In a study of 500,000 subjects, the NIH also studied the opposite kind of diet – animal fats – and reported that consumption of red meat was associated with increased cardiovascular (CVD) and cancer mortality.

Plant-based diets also have a beneficial effect on something called telomeres, the ends of chromosomes, which are associated with increased longevity.

Another important study, "The Effect of a Plant-Based Low-Carbohydrate Diet," was reported in the *Archives of Internal Medicine* issue of June 8, 2009. The study's researchers examined the effect of using protein and healthy fats from vegetable sources only, instead of those from animal sources. They emphasized soy, nuts, fruits, vegetables, and vegetable oils. The researchers' goal had been mainly to lower heart disease, but to their surprise they did more than that; they succeeded in helping patients achieve weight loss, reduce bad LDL cholesterol, lower their blood pressure, and lower their risk for type 2 diabetes and its complications.

Crucial findings, to be sure. But these esteemed studies and their researchers still had a problem. *What recipes to use?*

We posted the studies on Twitter and got some interesting responses.
"Sounds boring," the typical reply.
"But I *need* carbs!" from people with diabetes.
"I use soy protein in smoothies. Should I now munch on bamboo shoots?"
Meanwhile we had discovered that soy protein powder isn't limited to smoothies; you can make practically anything you see in a bakery window with it! As for the cholesterol in fish and chicken, you can get it out. It's easy.

Surprise everybody
For how long have you heard people say that the diabetic diet is a dreary grind with special foods?
Tell them not any more. Not with pancakes, pies, muffins, brownies, blondies, pizza, burgers and more. This is because we've devised a brand new cooking and baking technique that we call No BEFS (no **B**utter/margarine, **E**gg yolks, **F**lour, or **S**ugar in any form.)
So, you're rushed in the morning. No time to make anything healthy for yourself or school lunch or a commuting spouse. This eating plan's protein baked goods or bread or rolled up pancakes filled with sugar-free preserves and chopped walnuts are a joy to have stacked and ready to grab in the fridge.
The only thing about this book's recipes is, you'll have to make them yourself – but they're easy. In fact...

Some goodies take only ninety seconds in the microwave!
This Apricot Mighty Muffin, for example, contains 121 calories, 17 g protein, 10 grams of carbs (from the sugar free fruit preserves), 0 g cholesterol, 3 g fiber, 2.3 g monounsaturated fat, 23,055 antioxidants (including 3,000 lignan antioxidants), and 1,300 Omega 3 acids (The fiber, Omega 3s, and lignan antioxidants are all from the milled flaxseed. Compare this muffin's 3 grams of fiber to the 3 grams of fiber in one cup of cooked oatmeal; or the 1.9 g of fiber in a slice of whole wheat bread. And *they're* loaded with carbs.)
Here is the recipe:

cooking spray
1 scoop Soy Protein Powder
1 tbsp milled flaxseed
1 ½ tsp cinnamon
½ tsp baking powder
1 tbsp + 1 tsp Splenda
2 tbsp sugar free apricot preserves
2 tsp water
2 tbsp liquid egg whites

Spray inside of Pyrex measuring cup. In it mix all ingredients. Stir well, blending in the sugar free preserves. Scrape down the sides, gently pushing mixture down in cup. Microwave for 90 seconds, cool slightly – and pop out!
*Note: To make muffin less moist, use a bit less water.

Now for recipes that take longer than ninety seconds. If you can find a spare thirty or forty minutes from somewhere – they say we watch too much TV anyway – you can make a whole pan of twenty protein brownies or blondies to last you a week. Bring some to work too, or to any gathering. Listen to the howls go from "Oh, I shouldn't!" to "No *carbs!?* You're kidding! THANK YOU, bless your heart!"

Breakthrough recipes

Each slice of homemade protein bread has 92 calories, 19 g protein, 0 g carbs, 2 g fiber, & 1,500 lignan antioxidants). A dinner-sized roll has 92 calories, 19 g protein, 0 g carbs, 2 g fiber, & 1,500 lignan antioxidants); your homemade healthy mayonnaise substitute, per ¼ cup serving, contains just 30 calories, 5.5 grams protein, no bad fat whatsoever, and just two grams of carbs.

The list goes on. A standard hamburg, by the way, contains just 12 grams of protein (and then there's its all-carbs roll), compared to this plan's 19 protein grams in a single slice of bread.

For lunch, picture filling sandwiches, rolls and tortilla wraps all high in blood-sugar-stabilizing protein, with the only carbs from the vegetables and whatever else you choose to put in them. (We even have a sandwich called the Inside Out Sandwich – the protein's on the outside!)

And dinner will no longer be a hassle for you with our safe-and-healthy-for-all recipes, plus cooking tips that may be quite new to you. For example, a quick trick to get the cholesterol out of chicken and fish.

Here, for example, is how to make Chicken Stroganoff, comfort-food creamy but without the saturated fat of Beef Stroganoff. This recipe makes 4 servings, each 184 calories, 27 grams of protein, and 5 grams of carbs.

4 boneless, skinless chicken breasts
1 tbsp olive oil
black pepper to taste
1 medium onion, chopped
1/2 pound fresh mushrooms, sliced
¾ cup chicken bouillon, salt-free
1 tsp garlic powder
3 tbsp tarragon, dried
4 oz Fat Free Sour Cream

Cholesterol melts at 325 degrees Fahrenheit (162 degrees Centigrade). To get it out, first parboil the chicken in about two inches of water for about three to four minutes. Then carefully carry the skillet to the sink. Under lukewarm water from the tap, pour off all the pink-gloppy drippings (the cholesterol). Even rinse and clean the chicken under the water, with the chicken still in the skillet.

That's it. Most of the cholesterol is out, gone.

Now return the skillet containing the chicken to the stove, and add olive oil. Toss chicken in the oil, sprinkle with pepper, and cook over medium-high heat until golden. Turn, sautéing and cutting chicken into smaller pieces. As those pieces turn golden, push them to the far side of the skillet.

Add the onions and mushrooms; cook until golden. Stir in the chicken broth, garlic and tarragon; stir, and lower heat. Add sour cream last, and stir chicken back into the rest of the mixture, covering chicken with sauce. Simmer for 5 minutes, stirring occasionally, and serve.

Another tip? Toss some spinach into the mix (fresh or frozen) and – presto – it's Chicken Florentine!

Sauteed slivered almonds and green beans make a crunchy, healthy side dish, and then for dessert….fudge sauce poured on brownies? Put them in front of the most finicky young eaters and see what happens. The brownies especially will wow them: "Oh boy, I thought we couldn't *have* these!"

Tell them how healthy it all is. Kids love having it both ways too. They'll brag to their friends. Even very young ones are aware that it's bad for them to be overweight. Not to mention the pain of being teased.

Couldn't even the busiest parents teach their children how to make their own healthy bread, pancakes, or muffins (reassured by the fact that soy protein powder has more B vitamins than whole grains, as much calcium as fat free milk, and more additional vitamins than in any other single food source)? The bread recipes are fast and easy; no yeast or waiting for it to rise. Kids could fill their sandwiches with salad or peanut butter and sugar-free preserves…or anything that's salt free and *not* bologna, pepperoni or other processed meats. They'd be proud to know how to do it themselves; think it's funny and cool that the protein's on the outside!

Now you and everyone get pizza, or (turkey) burgers, or creamy comfort food, with Key Lime pie or pumpkin pie (healthy crusts!) or fudge fruit sundae for dessert. Low carbs, the heart-healthiest fats, luscious snacks and desserts – with every recipe just as delicious as its old-way counterpart.

Good-bye to counting, worry, and trying to please everyone.

And hello to the whole family changing together. There is no reason for anyone of any age to continue eating high carb and sugary foods, or those loaded with salt or saturated fat and cholesterol.

Lose all the bad stuff and still have goodies? Even a child who hates spinach might well like this eating plan's creamy spinach or broccoli snuck into spicy Tex Mex.

This eating plan's pizza also stands a good chance of keeping older kids out of the pizza joints. What teen wouldn't prefer to look thin and sexy? Given a choice, they'll choose having it both ways: looking good *and* having pizza. Yours. Homemade.

Or…they can make it themselves?

Have quiche (with crust!) or quesadillas tonight. Followed by gooey warm chocolate cake with fudge sauce and whipped topping. You won't believe it's safe for diabetes. Your loved ones and friends won't believe it's "healthy." They'll be wanting seconds, and maybe you will too, with no worries about your blood glucose spiking, or about you or your family gaining weight.

Make brownies for the neighborhood! Have a bake sale! Watch the news spread and everyone around you get excited and motivated!

Last tip: cook just two or three times a week.. Put the baked goodies in the fridge and dinner leftovers into plastic bags to freeze. Then, on some busy day when there's absolutely, positively no time to cook, just toss them in the sink to thaw and be ready later just to heat and eat.

Note: If any frozen entree has been thawing for hours, make sure it's still cool to the touch before re-heating and serving it.

The best thing about home cooking is that you know what's going into your body. Cooking is a huge ego booster. It's also the only art form you can eat!

You, at parties and during holidays

At parties, turn the tables. Have them clamoring for what *you* eat.

Bring your own homemade goodies – lots because they'll go fast. People will be incredulous. "You're kidding! No carbs?" you'll hear. And: "I've got to lose weight too, it's just been so hard!"

First, for politesse, give your hostess a call and, after the usual, awkward "Don't worry I'll have something for you," tell her not to worry; offer to bring something yummy that will please everyone. She'll be delighted – and curious.

If it's a barbecue, show up with any of these:

- Crunchy flaxseed crackers (each 14 calories, 1.3 g protein, 0 g carbs, 0 g saturated fat, 3 g fiber, and 3,840 lignan antioxidants) as a choice for the inevitable Cheetos, Doritos, and Fritos. Guess what will disappear fastest?
- Homemade Cheddar Biscuits
- Low Salt Bruschetta on toasted sweet roll slices (one sweet roll, unsliced, contains 10 calories, 2 g carbs, 0 g fat, 2 g fiber, and 4 g protein.)
- A big bowl of Mixed Green Salad with Toasted Almonds (each serving 130 calories, 17 g protein, 3 g carbs, and 5,500 antioxidants) … plus you can add walnuts and artichoke hearts to be even more filling.
- Vinaigrette for dressing… Per 1 ½ tablespoon 63 calories, 5 grams protein, 4.5 g carbs, and 2 g monounsaturated fat (Even "low-fat" mayonnaise still has a lot of bad fat.)

- And Key Lime Pie – bring two! – for dessert. (Each big pie, with *crust*, makes six servings, each containing 63 calories, 5 grams protein, 4.5 g carbs, 1 g fiber, and 2 g monounsaturated fat.

Other recipes are delicious and diabetic-perfect for other holidays: healthier Pumpkin Pie; stuffing made from all-protein bread croutons; Frosted Chocolate Layer Cake with each piece containing 270 calories, 10 g carbs, 46 g protein, 5 g fiber, 2.5 g monounsaturated fat, and 4,665 antioxidants)…

You get the picture. Who *needs* animal fats and extra carbs? Nobody! And they know it, and will be grateful to you.

Who's going to say no to having it both ways – taste *and* health?

You and restaurants

In restaurants, forewarn yourself because you're much less in control. Which is a pity because we all enjoy a night out on the town without doing too much damage to our progress. So what's the answer? We all need fun.

But there are ways around the problem.

First, think international, such as Italian, Chinese, and Japanese. In the cultures of those countries, there has always been an important emphasis on vegetables. And their food is usually made to order, so don't hesitate to request a dish just as you would like it.

To an Italian restaurant you could even bring your own box of Dreamfield's pasta. That's the one available at most supermarkets that has only 5 grams of digestible carbs per serving. Call ahead to be sure, especially if you re planning to go during busy time. The chef will be happy to cook it up for you or your whole group if you re with friends and family. If others order cheese and meatballs with it, that s fine; you can order Pasta Primavera with vegetables sautéed in olive oil folded into the pasta. It s a beautiful and filling dish.

In Chinese and Japanese restaurants you can order steamed and savory vegetable main dishes made with tofu. One thing about teriyaki, though: it is very salty. If you are concerned about hypertension, request that your sauce be placed in a small bowl next to your main dish, and water it down a bit. It tastes just as good; no taste is lost.

Note too that, even in supermarkets where teriyaki is advertised as having "less sodium," it still has a lot.

Salt is a big problem because all restaurants use it. If that is a concern, be nicely firm about requesting that your dish be made with "no salt, please." You probably won't even get an odd look from your waiter (not that you should care), because these days salt's harmful effects on blood pressure are widely acknowledged.

(This is not meant as an endorsement for the "food police." But really, salt is as dangerous as cigarettes. Probably even more so. More people die of hypertensive heart disease than lung cancer. Salt, like sugar, makes everything taste better, and unfortunately is so bad for us.)

Which brings us to that last category of restaurant, American restaurant chains. You know, the ones with thick cheeseburgers or batter-fried shrimp in Alfredo sauce advertised all the time on TV? Oh boy, where to begin? They make everything ahead by the barrel, especially their fatty salty sauces and their fatty salty breading. Even if you see entrees at "under 600 calories" on their menus, they're not worth it with their load of salt and bad fat.

And yet, if your friends and family insist on going to one of them, there are still ways to have fun and leave feeling full. Many of these places have salad bars. Bring a plastic bag full of your protein bread croutons, maybe too some fat free shredded cheese, add them in, and toss it all in vinaigrette. Or, if they offer hot (healthy) vegetable plates and have pasta too on the menu, request that the two be combined. A chain restaurant Pasta Primavera. Very filling and pretty.

Ask too if they use olive oil, and look the waiter hard in the eye when he answers.

You could even try bringing your own Dreamfield's

"Insulin is natural isn't it? But it's a hormone!"

Chapter Three

COMMON DIABETES MYTHS

Diabetes is a serious, potentially deadly, and complicated disease. To make matters worse, there are mistaken beliefs that make it hard for people to understand the true facts of diabetes. Commonly held myths will here be explained and debunked, in order to create a more understandable, manageable picture of the disease.

Myth: **Diabetes isn't that serious a disease.**
Fact: Diabetes causes more deaths than breast cancer and AIDS combined. Two out of three people with diabetes die, not from the disease itself, but from the cardiovascular complications it causes, such as heart disease and stroke.

Diabetes is not only serious; it can be unstable, hard to control. Its complications, in addition to heart attack and stroke, include large artery disease of the legs, peripheral neuropathy (small artery disease of the feet), retinal, and kidney disease.

The latest numbers show that one out of three Americans are diabetic or prediabetic. In Canada it's one out of four; in the United Kingdom it's one out of seven. In the past single year, the number of people in the U.K. diagnosed with diabetes jumped by more than 150,000. Health care systems around the world have been overwhelmed.

It has been estimated by health insurer United Health Group Inc. that by 2020 more than half of Americans will have diabetes or be prediabetic. The cost to the U.S. health care system will be $3.35 trillion.

Myth: **Only overweight or obese people develop type 2 diabetes.**
Fact: Being overweight is overwhelmingly a risk factor for developing diabetes, but age over forty and family history also play a role. Do you have close blood relatives with the disease? Children? Parents? Siblings? Ethnicity plays a role too. People of African-American, Hispanic, South Pacific and Native American background, even if relatively thin, are at a much higher risk. The reasons for this are not clear.

Myth: Glucose only comes from carbs

Fact: All foods fall into just three categories: protein, fat, and carbs. Glucose comes from all of them. True, the fastest glucose fuel comes from simple carbs. "Complex" carbs can take a bit longer to metabolize and convert to glucose, and protein's glucose energy can take 45 to 60 minutes to kick in – but it lasts hours longer. If you're feeling hypoglycemic, have some fast-acting carbs such as orange juice, regular soda, or even Gummy Bears which are portable. The important thing is to simultaneously eat lean protein. By the time your carbs have flashed and crashed on you, the protein will have metabolized into glucose. Its energy will stabilize you for hours and will not cause sugar spikes.

Myth: Eating too much sugar is what causes diabetes.

Fact: No, that is a huge oversimplification. The very definition of what, exactly, *is* "sugar" has been under-explained and may come as a surprise to you.

All carbs – even "complex" carbs – metabolize into sugar in your body. Therefore, consider carbs and sugar as the same thing.

How much sugar is in those carbs? How can you "translate" the grams of carbs you're eating into the equivalent number teaspoons of sugar those carbs will metabolize into?

Easy. Divide by four.

That is, divide the number of carbs you're eating by four and that's the number of teaspoons of sugar those carbs will metabolize into: in about 40 minutes if they're "good" carbs, faster if they're "bad" carbs...but it's still the same divide-by-four.

If food labels or recipes list only their number of grams of carbs, take that number and divide by four. For example, a granola bar admitting to 24 grams of carbs on its label – divide those 24 grams by 4. That granola bar contains the equivalent of 6 teaspoons of sugar! No different from six teaspoons of white sugar from your old sugar bowl!

And if a cereal label lists 22 grams of carbs per cup? Same thing. Divide those 22 grams by 4. That cup of cereal contains what will quickly metabolize in your body into five and one half teaspoons of sugar.

A typical slice of whole wheat bread contains twenty grams of carbs. Those twenty divided by four equal five teaspoons of sugar. It's so much healthier to get your fiber from milled flaxseed, which contains no carbs, and has other huge health benefits.

Myth: Honey is a good substitute for sugar

Fact: Honey is not a substitute for sugar; honey *is* sugar. In fact, honey metabolizes even faster than white sugar because it's already in solution (liquid form). Honey is Number One in the deceptive list of "sugar alternatives" which are really just sugar in another form. Your body recognizes them as sugar, and is not fooled. On the rest of that Deceptive List, after honey, are molasses, brown sugar, and dried fruit (dates are a favorite). They're delicious, true, and work beautifully in recipes ... because they're sugar. Yet you'll find "substitute honey!" in so many "diabetic" recipes; you'll even hear that Deceptive List recommended by some nutritionists, and certainly by TV folk anxious to please their sponsors. This is wrong and damaging.

"But honey is *natural!*" you'll often hear in protest. The words "natural" and "organic" mean ... not a whole lot. Most of the world's poisons are natural and organic: arsenic and strychnine, for starters, not to mention nicotine, booze, cocaine, opium, saturated fat, and cholesterol.

If you still enjoy a little honey in your tea "instead" of sugar, and then you get a sugar spike minutes later, at least now you will understand why your body is reacting the way it is. And you can re-adjust according to your needs.

Myth: **Only older people get type 2 diabetes**.

Fact: In the past few years, children as young as age 5 are being diagnosed with type 2 diabetes. The disease in children and adolescents is surging, fueled largely by the obesity epidemic. This is a crisis. Too many kids don't exercise anymore; they just eat and sit in front of their computers and video games. Children under ten also have rising rates of high blood pressure (hypertension), largely due to the huge salt content in fast and junk food. The change in today's children's health would have been unimaginable to a pediatrician of ten or twenty years ago.

What to do? Parents should encourage good eating habits for children as well as for the entire family; kids copy what they see. You can also encourage them into more physical activity (walk to school?), and eating smaller portions. There's only so much the schools and communities can do. Maybe try giving your children *chores*. Hard-work chores. They'll sweat off a lot, and...be proud of themselves. It's an old-fashioned concept, but...try it?

Myth: **People with diabetes have to eat special foods**.

Fact: Healthy meal plans for people with diabetes are now considered by physicians to be the healthiest for everyone: high in protein, low in carbs *and* bad fat (saturated fat and cholesterol). Additionally, so many adults and children are overweight these days that there is also renewed emphasis on limiting salt as much as possible. Like sugar, salt makes food taste good, but the general population's rise in high blood pressure makes limiting salt a good idea for everyone, not just for people with diabetes. (Beans are healthy but pour off the liquid; that's where they hide the salt.) Lowest sugar fruits (strawberries and blueberries) are healthiest for diabetes sufferers as well as for everyone else. Formerly "good," starchy vegetables (barley, brown rice, and yams) are best avoided because they, too, are carbohydrates.

"Diabetic" foods really offer no special benefit. Most of them will still raise your blood sugar levels, and are usually more expensive.

Myth: People with diabetes don't have to worry about high blood pressure
Fact: Two out of three adults with diabetes have high blood pressure (hypertension). Diabetes increases your risk of developing high blood pressure because it adversely affects the arteries, predisposing them to atherosclerosis (hardening of the arteries), and kidney disease. Atherosclerosis, if not treated, can lead to blood vessel damage, stroke, heart failure, heart attack, or kidney failure.

Having normal blood pressure is as important to managing diabetes as maintaining good control of your blood sugar. And limiting your salt intake plays an important role in controlling your blood pressure.

Too much salt exacerbates high blood pressure, which (picture a crimped hose) pounds the inner lining of arteries, creating inflammation (abetted by fat particles) where cholesterol and calcium clump, narrow your arteries, then clot, and cause heart attack or stroke.

One quarter teaspoon of salt equals 580 milligrams. A pinch. It doesn't sound like much, and it isn't if your blood pressure is normal. If not, it is advisable to avoid salt as much as possible. All processed, fast, or commercial food contains salt, so home cooking is best. Try substituting zesty, savory spices for salt.

Myth: Sugar alcohols are ok to eat or even binge on if you have diabetes
Fact: Sugar Alcohols are processed from sugar molecules, and include names like sorbitol, mannitol, xylitol, lactitol, maltitol, and others ending in -ol. They still have calories of the sugar type (though fewer: two or three calories per gram as opposed to four calories per gram of standard sugar), and they still affect your blood sugar. Their benefit is that they metabolize more slowly than regular sugar, so they last you longer, hold off those need-sweets-again-crashes.

Products containing sugar alcohols may be marketed as "no sugar added" – but beware. They often cause bloating, gastric distress, and diarrhea. There is also the commercial deception that sugar alcohol-containing products are "sugar free." Plus products like that also contain significant amounts of carbs which quickly break down to sugar. Either way, sugar alcohols are no free ride for people with diabetes.

Myth: Diet soda makes you fatter and your diabetes worse
Fact: That notion just doesn't make sense. Zero calories are zero calories; our brains and bodies can't be "fooled." Further, if someone who drinks diet sodas gains weight, the question is really: What *else* is that person eating?

Myth: Insulin is natural. It's not made in the lab

Fact: Even so-called human insulin is made in the lab. Decades ago, insulin was extracted from cow and sometimes pig sources. Unfortunately this insulin process included impurities and many allergic reactions, plus it became impossible to make in the amounts needed to meet the rapidly surging demand. Now synthesizing human insulin is a multi-step biochemical process that depends on recombinant DNA techniques that can only be done in laboratories.

Also made in the lab are medications such as metformin, Lantus, Byetta, and other drugs to treat diabetes. Ditto vitamins, aspirin, antibiotics, and virtually all other medications. When did "made in the lab" become a negative term? Can you picture life before Pasteur's anti-rabies vaccine? Salk's polio vaccine? Alexander Fleming's penicillin discovery? Connaught's diphtheria anti-toxin? Until the mid 1920s diphtheria ranked first as a cause of death for children under 14.

The medications discovered by these heroic scientists were all made in the lab.

Myth: You'll know when you have diabetes type 2

Fact: Typically, diabetes type 2 may be present for several years before becoming symptomatic. There are estimated to be six million Americans who have diabetes type 2, and don't know it. It may be discovered accidentally when a blood sugar test is done as part of a routine checkup. If you are overweight and think you have no other symptoms, it is still strongly advised to see your doctor.

Myth: If no family member has diabetes, you can't get it.

Fact: Diabetes type 2 can and does occur in the absence of any family history. If you do have blood relatives with Diabetes type 2 you are, it is true, at higher risk. But even without a family history of diabetes, if you're overweight you are at increased risk and should be evaluated by a physician.

Myth: Whole grains are good for diabetics.

Fact: More false than true. Whole grains are still carbohydrates, and are converted into sugar by the body although a bit more slowly than white flour. People with diabetes should be careful about consuming whole grain products such as bread, cereal, and pasta, although a small amount in combination with more slowly metabolized lean protein will give smoother control of blood sugar levels.

Myth: All fruits are good for diabetics

Fact: Fruit, especially whole fruit with its fiber, should be good for you, but it's an area where you have to be careful. Some fruits are very high in sugar. Dried fruit, of course, is crammed with sugar, and except for the purpose of treating hypoglycemia, should be avoided. The same goes for recipes that deceptively tell you to "substitute sugar" with dried fruit. Dried dates are popular with such recipes. Ack! One cup of dried, pitted chopped dates contains 130 carbohydrates, which will quickly metabolize into thirty-two and one half teaspoons of sugar! (Divide the 130 carbs by 4.)

Fruits lowest in sugar are blueberries, strawberries and cranberries. A double boon here is that all three are high in antioxidants.

Fruits low to medium in sugar are casaba melon, watermelon, peaches, nectarines, cantaloupes, honeydew melons, and apples.

Fruits high in sugar are plums, oranges, pineapples, and pears.

Fruits very high in sugar are grapes, cherries, tangerines, pomegranates, non-dried dates, and bananas.

Myth: **People who have "borderline" diabetes needn't worry about it**

Fact: Either you have diabetes, or you don't. The lay term "borderline" probably refers to prediabetes and insulin resistance. That should be treated seriously, with an initial focus on weight loss and exercise, often prescribed for three to six months, depending on your overall clinical status, before starting on medication.

Physicians define prediabetes as having an overnight Fasting Blood Sugar (FBS) between 100-125; below 100 is normal, and over 125 is full blown diabetes. Prediabetic individuals are definitely at risk for full blown diabetes, and the complications of diabetes including cardiovascular disease (heart attack and stroke).

Myth: **People who diligently follow their treatment plan can stay in control.**

Fact: Diabetes is very hard to control. Sometimes, someone diligently following all his or her doctors' orders may experience the odd high reading for which there seems no explanation. Sometimes too, the usual insulin dosage will cause a reading that's too low, leaving a person bewildered besides feeling faint or shaky. Stress, infections, exercise or the lack of it, and even slight variations in diet play a role. Plus, as we age, our bodies are constantly changing and needing possible adjustment. It often seems that our blood sugar doesn't want to cooperate. It is a hard, hard disease to manage.

But don't let an occasional "off" reading make you want to throw in the towel. Overall, your glucose control will be managed. Hang in there, and know that the occasional "odd" day is part of the fight.

Myth: **Only an Atkins-type diet works for people who can't tolerate carbs**

Fact: Such diets – low carb, high animal fat – have caused a lot of damage.

There are people with diabetes who swear by them, pointing to the fact that dieting on bacon and sirloin has helped them lose weight and get their blood sugar down.

Those two - weight and blood sugar down - are good news. But those people's arteries are at increased risk of being sick, clogged, gunked up.

All that saturated fat has raised their LDL cholesterol (the bad one). This directly causes fatty cholesterol deposits inside arteries and narrows them, which in turn causes heart attack and stroke. Lost weight and lower blood sugar - again - are good, but only half the full trip to health.

It is interesting that online, Atkins-type diabetic adherents refuse to disclose their LDL numbers. ("It's fine! MYOB!)

The American Diabetes Association says, "Since people with diabetes are at an increased risk for heart disease, it's also important to limit the bad-for-you fats that lurk in full-fat milk products, meats, and processed foods. Saturated fat ups your risk for heart disease and stroke, so begin replacing foods like whole milk, regular cheese, butter, shortening, bacon, and bologna with low-fat versions such as skim milk, low-fat cheese, olive oil, and lean meats or fish."

Some fats, however, are good for you. Olive and canola oil reduce the risk of stroke and coronary disease because they are high in MUFAs and PUFAs (mono- and polyunsaturated fat) and very low in saturated fat. Both also have high levels of antioxidants to counteract inflammation of your arteries and further bolster your health.

The protein you enjoy can be replaced by this diet's protein pancakes, or recipes like chili made with fat-free ground turkey, or creamy chicken stroganoff, or Tex Mex made so that it tastes just like the made-with-beef version. Within these pages there are many recipes that substitute chicken for beef, and are just as tasty. Soon you might not even miss red meat.

Myth: **Diabetes is catching.**
Fact: Diabetes is not contagious. It can't be caught like a cold or flu, or by coming in contact with someone who is diabetic. This being said, keep in mind that family history and genetics can play a role.

Myth: **If you have diabetes, medicine works better than diet and exercise**
Fact: No matter what stage of diabetes or prediabetes you're in, and regardless of what other treatments you may be following, exercise is still a "miracle drug."

A sixteen year study by the Mayo Clinic Proceedings, September 2009, reported that among three thousand people, all either prediabetic or diabetic, there were striking differences in health and mortality based on physical fitness.

Those with low exercise capacity (get tired easily), as measured on an exercise treadmill, had a 50% higher mortality rate than those with high or even moderate exercise capacity.

Similarly, those who were overweight or obese and physically unfit had more than double the mortality rate of those physically fit and normal weight.

Becoming fit by regular exercise lowers blood sugar, blood pressure, and bad cholesterol (LDL), improves arterial function, inhibits clotting, decreases arterial plaque deposits, and improves good cholesterol (HDL; think H for Healthy). Exercise thus lowers your chances of succumbing to cardiovascular disease (heart attack and stroke). Overweight/obesity and lack of exercise go hand-in-hand when it comes to causing early disability and a shortened lifespan.

Check with your own physician before embarking on any exercise program. Do it for life. Start at any age. It works.

Myth: People with diabetes are more likely to catch cold or the flu.

Fact: You are no more likely to catch cold or get the flu than the general population. However, people with diabetes are advised to get flu shots. Any additional illness can make diabetes harder to control, and people with diabetes who do get the flu are more likely than others to develop serious complications.

Myth: People who have only a "minor" heart attack, a complication of overweight and diabetes, need not be concerned.

Fact: There is no such thing as a minor heart attack. Any heart attack, medically known as a myocardial infarction, or MI, has damaged the individual's heart muscle. Damaged heart muscle gets replaced by scar tissue, resulting in a decrease in the heart's pumping capacity and an increased possibility of abnormal heart rhythms.

Exceptions to this may be *thin* adults who have type 2 diabetes for some genetic or other reason. Their hearts are in less danger because they don't have belly fat feeding irritating fat particles into their blood streams and damaging their arteries.

Myth: High blood sugar is more dangerous than low blood sugar.

Fact: Both are dangerous. High blood sugar levels (hyperglycemia) are damaging to body tissues, such as all body organs and blood vessels. High sugar in the blood is converted into fat and deposited in the belly, which – this cannot be emphasized enough – is the worst place for fat to be. It is called Central Obesity, aka Poison Central, and it *mainlines* fat right back into the blood stream, causing inflammation of the arterial lining. This leads to cholesterol deposits, narrowing of the arteries, clots, and arterial blockage.

Low sugar levels (hypoglycemia), on the other hand, can cause loss of consciousness, falls, injury, coma, and even death. Low sugar can also damage body cells, particularly in the brain.

Myth: Drug companies exploit diabetics because they won't make insulin you can take by mouth.

Fact: Drug companies have tried, and so far, it can't be done. Insulin is a hormone, and gets broken down, digested, and destroyed in the stomach. It never reaches the blood stream where it can help control your blood sugar.

Unfortunately there's no way around it. Insulin at present cannot be taken by mouth.

Myth: Type 2 diabetes is not as serious as type 1.

Fact: When poorly controlled, type 2 diabetes is just as serious as type 1, each leading to the same cardiovascular complications such as heart attack, stroke, nerve damage, kidney failure, blindness, and amputation.

Myth: Frequent finger sticks are necessary.

Fact: It's a mostly intangible question. True, people with unstable type 1 diabetes will feel the need to check their numbers often, but after a while they'll pretty much know what affects them and how. At some point, for many with type 1 and type 2 diabetes, finger sticking becomes obsessive. "I can't feel my finger tips anymore!" is often heard. And: "I don't know how different foods will affect me. I check my numbers before and after every morsel I eat."

If you're feeling hypoglycemic, check your numbers immediately. Eat fast carbs and protein together, then follow through until you have stabilized. To help, here is the conversion order speed of all foods as they metabolize: Glucose tablets and honey are the fastest to enter the blood; next comes table sugar (sucrose); then white flour, rice and potatoes, and – scant minutes later – starchy vegetables and whole grain products.

The last and slowest to metabolize is protein. It will not cause sugar spikes, even if eaten in high amounts.

Myth: You can have diabetes for a long time and it won't cause damage.

Fact: Diabetes, like high blood pressure (hypertension), is silent for many years before causing symptoms. Over the long run, diabetes will double your risk of cardiovascular disease (CVD). That includes heart attack and stroke. Symptoms means body organs undergoing harm and crying out for help. Other long term consequences of diabetes include disease of your leg arteries resulting in amputation, retinal damage resulting in blindness, and serious nerve and kidney disease.

There is still time to make the necessary changes: diet, weight control, exercise, medical supervision, and medications if necessary.

Myth: It's ok to use natural diabetic remedies online

Fact: Ads like this have been appearing everywhere online lately. Be very skeptical of them. Unfortunately, they are often scams, always asking for money. There is no magic bullet for diabetes. There is no "natural remedy" yet discovered, and unfortunately no quick fixes. If there were, diabetes type 2 would not be the global epidemic that it is.

Myth: Women with diabetes shouldn't get pregnant.

Fact: This is an old myth which still troubles many women. The good news is that nowadays, diabetes education and self management if followed carefully enable the mother-to-be to monitor her blood sugar so that it comes as close to normal as possible. Pre-pregnancy, a woman should also try to get herself into the best general physical shape as possible by means of diet and exercise. It is also recommended that she work under a physician's care starting around three to six months before conception, so that not only her blood sugar, but also her blood pressure, heart, and vascular health are ready for a healthy pregnancy and delivery.

The less good news is that problems can arise if these preparatory measures are not followed – especially if the woman is overweight. Type 2 diabetes and overweight too often go hand in hand.

The disease is called toxemia of pregnancy, which includes pre-eclampsia, characterized by fluid retention, high blood pressure (hypertension), and kidney problems during pregnancy; and then eclampsia, meaning seizures and coma during labor. This disease occurs more with overweight and extra salt intake Even in young women, once labor has begun eclampsia can lead to cerebral hemorrhage (stroke) in the mother and stillbirth for the child.

According to a report from the Agency for Healthcare Research and Quality, dated December 15, 2010, one in sixteen U.S. women who give birth – more than 250,000 each year – has diabetes. The epidemic of type 2 diabetes has surged among adolescents and young adults, also increasing, in pregnancy, the risk of miscarriage, preterm birth, and low blood-sugar and jaundice in the infant. Babies born to mothers with diabetes also appear to have an increased risk of developing the disease later in life.

So, pre-moms, safety involves more than just keeping the blood sugar controlled. It's also about trying to get your weight down and reducing your salt intake. It's that simple and that hard.

Diabetic women *can* have healthy pregnancies and healthy babies. Here's hoping that getting ready for this so important event becomes much easier for you from here on.

Myth: If you're type 2 diabetic, you won't have to take insulin like type 1 people do.

Fact: It is true that type 2 diabetics have many, years-long chances of dodging the bullet, whereas type 1 patients require insulin immediately after diagnosis because the insulin producing cells in their pancreas have been destroyed. But in type 2, when diet, weight control, and exercise can no longer keep blood sugar below 125, it means those insulin producing cells have been exhausted. At that point, oral medications such as metformin may be indicated. There are a variety of other oral medications too, which act via different mechanisms: for example, preventing release of sugar from storage in the liver, coaxing a little more insulin from the pancreatic cells, and improving the uptake of insulin by the muscle cells.

Sometimes, however, these mechanisms will no longer keep blood sugar in an acceptable range, at which time a type 2 diabetic will require insulin.

Myth: If both your parents have type 2, you're going to get it.

Fact: You are at greater risk, but your odds are greatly improved by your lifestyle. Once again, the trio of diet, weight and exercise will play a vital role. Now is the time to be on a diabetes-like diet, stay thin, and exercise regularly. You can greatly reduce your risk despite the genetics you inherited.

Myth: **It's okay to binge on carbs and "cover" it with insulin**

Fact: Many do it, but it's not a good idea. Eat, "cover" it with insulin, aka bolusing, is also known as "Carb Up, Shoot Up." But the "up" will only last for a short time, and then you'll find yourself back down again; sometimes too far down, as insulin corrections can be inexact. You may fall, you may lose consciousness. If you are driving a car or using machinery it could be dangerous. Have the cupcakes, then bolus? It isn't good for you in the long run. This is not to say that an infrequent variation from your usual discipline can't be done.

Anyway it should hopefully no longer be necessary. With the goodies in this book you can enjoy every craving without fear. Have some brownies! Make a stack of pancakes or tacos! As the recipes in this book will show, "bolus worthy" goodies need no longer tempt you. It's time to enjoy life and stop worrying.

"My new diabetes educator doesn't agree with my old one. All I want to know is, what can I *eat?*" From an online diabetes web site

Chapter Four

DIABETES PATIENTS' MOST ASKED QUESTIONS

We've received many emails and questions, and have also seen questions asked on online diabetic sites. The common thread from all quarters seems to be confusion, fear, and a lack of information. What follows are real questions from people struggling with diabetes.

You should, of course, first consult with and be guided by your own physician. This applies as well to changes in medication: oral, injection or skin patch, prescription or over-the-counter. It is especially true for diabetes, a moving target, affected not only by diet, weight, exercise, and diabetic medications, but also by infections, fever, stress, other disorders and the drugs used to treat them. "No one size fits all:" goes the refrain of every diabetes web site.

I just had my first crash

Sean M.: I had my first crash this morning. Woke up at 5 shaking and weak. Did a finger stick and my blood sugar was down to 53. I drank orange juice and ate toast, but I was petrified. The doctor just increased my meds a little. Could that be the reason? This experience I've only heard described was horrible. My blood sugar numbers have come down alright, but that experience was hell. Is it worth it?

Answer: You need to tell your doctor about your reaction. You said s/he increased your meds just a little, but different people can have different reactions to even a slight change. Discuss the possibility of going back to your old dosage, but your doctor will also likely advise adjustments in your diet and exercise routine.

A diet very low in carbs, no bad (saturated/animal) fat, and protein from fish, skinless chicken and plant sources, along with walking 20-30 minutes a day will help you decrease your drug needs, blunt the spikes and cushion the crashes so they are a rare if ever event. Exercise can be *cumulative*, by the way: ten minutes brisk walk here, 10 minutes there; try to get in close to 30 minutes daily, but it doesn't have to be all in one rigorous workout. Additionally, avoid sugary fruits and starchy carbs including all flours, potatoes, rice, brown rice, and corn. The carbs in vegetables and low-sugar fruits (blueberries, strawberries) along with plant protein like soy will give you an orchestrated release of glucose into your blood as each of these food types has a different mouth-to-blood time span, and you will keep blood sugar on a more even keel.

The dream of every person with diabetes is to get off meds. Sometimes they cause as many problems as they solve. Ultimately, weight loss, diet, and exercise really are the best medicine. They are hard, but they're the surest way to find real control.

Can stress affect my blood sugar?

Betty D. I've tried so hard to lose weight and do all the right things, but there's so much stress in my life I often lose control, fight, and binge eat. We have financial worries and a nasty relative who lives with us and is always criticizing me. Lately my finger sticks have been giving me worse and worse news. Is this nerves? Can all this stress be affecting my blood sugar?

Answer: Stress can definitely increase your blood sugar. Our stress reaction comes from our ancestors, and is called the Fight or Flight response. Ancient man confronted with a wild beast or human enemy had two choices: fight or run like crazy. Nowadays, we might find ourselves confronted with everything from financial worries to stalled traffic or troubled relationships, but modern stress triggers the same reaction: a spike in adrenalin, which tells our liver to pour sugar into our blood so we can take action.

But too often we can't, and that makes it worse. You still *want* to move, throw things, act out. This is normal - and counter-productive. Fighting just produces more stress. So do emotional eating binges, in addition to raising your blood sugar.

Still, try letting your mind and your muscles do their adrenalin thing, which is to *move*, to *act*. Use your anger or frustration as fuel for something that's good for you: Exercise. Take a good, stormy walk and breathe deeply. Within minutes you'll start feeling proud that you didn't do anything self-harmful. And feeling proud is the best stress reliever.

How low is too low?

Amy G.: I am type 2. I was happy to lose 12 pounds and that my blood sugar numbers were dropping, but lately it's gotten scary. How low is too low? Yesterday I woke up at 4 in the morning to check my fasting blood sugar and it was 132. I figured that was pretty good. Unfortunately I fell back to sleep without eating! Woke back up at 7, had to rush around helping my husband with something because he was late, and by eight I was famished and shaky. I didn't check my sugar because I knew it was low. So I had bacon with eggs, toast and milk, also took my pill, but I was still shaky for the whole next hour. Then I tried to do chores, but started feeling weak again, so I had a banana. Felt better, but less than two hours later as I walked upstairs I got the shakes again and almost fainted. Decided finally like a dope to check my sugar, and it was only 70. This scared me so I made spaghetti with whole wheat noodles and tomatoes, but I had to stay in my chair depressed and shaky with my head in my arms and again it took an hour for the shakes to stop. Then two hours later I tested again and it was only 75!

Sorry to bore you with this long story…but what is happening to me? Should I snack more often? I know orange juice is a quick fix but it doesn't last and the shakes just come back. What can I do? I feel so desperate.

Answer: Amy, you were right about an overnight Fasting Blood Sugar (FBS) of 132 being good, and if you averaged that all the time you'd be fine. Instead, you ran into the rollercoaster of up and down blood sugar readings

Head off symptoms by having breakfast earlier, no matter what. One idea is having healthy snacks already made so you can just grab them on the run.

Also, have you heard of the Dawn Phenomenon? Around 4 or 5 a.m., our bodies automatically get ready for waking: your adrenalin kicks in, and your liver starts to release more blood sugar to get your brain and muscles ready for action. But by 8 AM that blood sugar is dropping again. If there's no time for a sit down breakfast, have already-made healthy eats ready, and have them earlier. Also, chores or any exertion drops your sugar. For exertion try prepping again with a snack.

In a later chapter you will find more information on the Dawn Phenomenon. Please don't feel alone. It is a common problem.

Your key question was, "Should I snack more often?" Yes, but here's a wonderful trick: Use carbs as a "starter dose" to get your levels back up, but combine them with protein, which takes longer to metabolize but is also your longest-lasting fuel. When protein slowly converts in the liver into glucose energy, it can keep you going strong for hours. In the meantime, continue snacking on low-fat protein. This carbs-as-starter, then protein, is a good combo: fast-release followed by slow, longer lasting control. A fast carb, plus a medium speed carb (yams mashed with cinnamon?), and protein work well too.

The banana you mentioned is crammed with sugar, almost as much as the quick-fix glass of o.j. These hit home too fast: sugar spike, then insulin spike, then sugar crash. And…those whole wheat noodles? They may take 30 minutes longer than "bad carbs" to metabolize, but they too will soon be sugar and their fuel won't last you like protein's does. Even fat-free milk contains 13 carbs (equals 3 ¼ teaspoons of sugar; divide by 4).

For breakfast and snacks try smoothies made with soy protein powder. There are many other recipes for SPP in this book. One scoop of soy protein powder contains 12 ½ grams of protein, as much as in a hamburger. But soy protein powder is pure protein (no carbs, saturated fat, or cholesterol), with more nutrients than other food sources including milk, citrus fruits, and whole grains.

Lastly, your doctor might want to slightly lower your medication or spread it out during the day. You only mentioned one dose in the morning. Also keep the carbs you do eat to non-sweet fruits, and non-starchy veggies (avoid corn, all flours, rice and potatoes of any kind). Beans and nuts are high in both fiber and protein, and nuts such as walnuts, unsalted almonds, and pistachios are also high in monounsaturated (good) fats.

With these adjustments you will notice far fewer episodes of hypoglycemia and hopefully find that you are blood testing much less often or not at all. Control of diabetes will be in your hands, not the other way around!

How much protein can I have?

Janet R.: Your protein idea sounds good and I'm excited about it. I've always failed at diets, and I'm still 180 pounds because other diets left me so hungry. My only question is, is there any limit to how much protein I can eat?

Answer: If your kidneys are normal, and over 97% of diabetics have no kidney problems, you can have up to 162 grams of protein a day.

Generally, protein consumption depends on height, weight, and moderate regular physical activity. If friends ask you how much protein they can have, they or anyone can easily figure their numbers. Multiply your weight in pounds by 0.9. That's all. For example, someone weighing 180 pounds should multiply that number (180) times 0.9 to get 162. That person can eat up to 162 grams of protein a day. Which sounds like a lot, but it's really less than one gram of protein per pound of body weight. In metric units, this gives you about 2.0 grams of protein per kilogram (2.2 lbs) of body weight. Usually 2.0-2.8 grams of protein per kilogram of body weight is given as the daily *maximum* limit.

Let's say you have another friend who weighs 200 pounds. S/he should multiply 200 times 0.9, which equals 180 grams of protein a day. That would be that person's upper limit.

The *minimum* adult requirement is 50 grams of protein a day, but most people have no problem with eating more than that. Most adults in the U.S. normally consume much higher amounts of protein. A typical American diet of bacon and eggs for breakfast, a cheeseburger or turkey sandwich for lunch, a mid-afternoon snack of nuts or a hot dog, a chicken or meat dish at dinner, and a raid on the refrigerator at night contains up to 150 grams of protein per day (plus saturated fat, sugar, carbs and calories in unhealthy doses). This is well within normal kidney capacity to process, especially so in a predominately plant-based protein diet.

Our recipe plan provides up to 125-150 grams of protein per day and 1400-1500 calories per day without all the animal protein baggage.

Plus the meals and recipes are individually tallied and can be switched around, the amounts of protein varied up or down to suit your needs.

Remember too that for decades diabetics trying to lose weight and avoid carbohydrates were put on the Atkins Diet, which, for purposes of comparison, was high in protein (up to 150 grams per day), but that protein came from animal sources burdened by harmful saturated fat and cholesterol.

It's actually hard to eat more than 150 grams of protein a day. That amount would make you feel so full for so long that you wouldn't feel hungry again for hours.

I'm a Type 1. Will your plan work for me?
Jill H.: It's really nice, all your efforts for curing T2 and your concern for "obesity and the diabetes epidemic," but I'm a Type 1 diabetic. Type 1 isn't caused by obesity and I didn't get it from eating too much candy. I hate that people lump us with the T2s. T1 you're practically born with because of some genetic or auto-immune screw up, and it's a life sentence, 24/7, every day of the year with no vacations and horrible nights where we're always afraid we're going to die because lows that are practically comas may happen during our sleep. I set the alarm clock for 2 and 5 to wake up and eat candy to get my blood sugar back up, and then I bolus it. You keep saying to avoid carbs and sweets, but they and insulin are the only things keeping us T1s alive! So how can your plan work for me? We NEED those fast carbs! Without them we'd be dead!

Answer: Jill, we understand the anger that type 1 sufferers feel. Diabetes type 1 and type 2 are different illnesses that never should have been given the same name.

Still, why not give this eating program a try? By all means keep raisins and glucose tablets with you and by the bed. For hypoglycemia definitely use fast-acting carbs, but with them eat, say, one of this program's protein brownies or blondies. The calories from those forty grams of protein have the kind of slo-mo energy that will last you and stabilize your blood sugar for hours longer than carbs, even "good carbs." In the past – understood – there weren't many choices for lean protein, and who wants to eat cold chicken breast at four in the morning? Plus, you mentioned that you bolus, cover the carbs with insulin, when you eat the quick carbs. That means injections. Those are painful. With protein you'll likely be able to decrease your frequency of insulin injections. Protein's slo-mo energy can even carry you through the night so you can get a better night's sleep.

We hope you try out this new approach, after checking with your doctor. If it doesn't work, you still have your raisins, fruit juice, or glucose tablets by the bed, but you may be surprised. You may not need them.

I'm a guy. I'm not going to eat soy!

Ted M.: I'm Type 1 and a weight lifter, usually just in shorts when I do my thing, and no way am I going to touch all that estrogen in soy. Too bad, your program sounds great. For women.

Answer: Surprise, Ted: men actually benefit from soy. The weaker plant estrogen of soy may in fact protect men from their own human estrogen. Did you know that men's bodies produce small amounts of estrogen? They do. Surprise again.

As mentioned previously, the Chinese and Japanese have eaten soy for over 3000 years. In the long history of both cultures there have been no stories, anecdotal or otherwise, of males having problems with their masculinity.

Which is good news because soy is probably the most pure protein, with very high amounts of vitamins and minerals (higher than skim milk and whole wheat bread put together). Additionally, soy has no saturated fat, trans-fat, cholesterol, sugar, or carbs - a double win where health and nutrition are concerned.

About male estrogen: Males normally produce small amounts of estrogen as well as testosterone. Belly fat and/or too much alcohol further increase a man's estrogen levels. But soy's phytoestrogens (weak estrogen from plants) may help by occupying estrogen receptor sites in the male body, and blocking their more powerful & potentially problematic human male estrogen, which has been associated with prostate cancer and other health issues.

From the medical literature: Clin. Sci. 100 (6): 613-8. Mitchell JH, et al: "There was no observable effect on endocrine measurements, testicular volume or semen parameters over the study period. This is the first study to examine the effects of a phytoestrogen supplement on reproductive health in males. We conclude that the phytoestrogen dose consumed had no effect on semen quality or secondary sexual characteristics."

More research: Fertil Steril. 2009 Oct 9: "Consumption of soy protein of low or high isoflavone content does not adversely affect semen quality or reproductive anatomy or function in a sample of healthy adult men."

J. Nutr. 133: 2874-2878. September 2003 Zhang, X, et al   Lower risk of coronary heart disease associated with soy consumption.

Mol. Nutr Food Res. 2009 Feb;53(2):217-26. Lower risk of prostate cancer associated with soybean consumption.

Help! I get conflicting info on what I can eat.

Donna L.: Recently I had to change doctors. The new one sent me to a new diabetes educator who practically scolded me and told me my other diabetes educator was wrong. She kept talking about which good carbs are best, starting with oatmeal for breakfast and using Wheat Thins for snacks. I told her oatmeal gave me spikes. She said so have half a bowl and my body will adjust. But I'm starving! My next appointment with her is next week and I dread it. So I am trying to figure out for myself why the list she gave me of good carbs has a negative affect on my blood sugars when she says they traditionally shouldn't.

Answer: ALL carbs are still carbs. Period. Try to keep them as low as absolutely possible, with the exception of low-sugar fruits and non-starchy veggies. The starchies include corn, brown rice, all kinds of potatoes and all kinds of flour. There are still corn and brown rice etc. in "diabetic" diets, which will only hinder attempts to control one's blood sugar. Stick to lean protein too, with low or no saturated fat & cholesterol. By the way, a small amount of oatmeal is ok, but not a whole or even a half bowl.

Are you surprised that you get all the carbs you need from low-sugar fruits and non-starchy veggies such as apples, blueberries, strawberries, broccoli, zucchini, and green leafy vegetables? Consider a medium-sized apple. In it there are 21 carbs. Now, how do you translate the number teaspoons of sugar those 21 grams of carbs will metabolize into? Easy: divide by 4. That apple's 21 carbs divided by 4 will quickly metabolize into over 5 teaspoons of sugar! But apples and other healthy fruits and veggies are important, both for their fiber and for the antioxidants in their darkly pigmented skin.

Your best diet should include: ample protein (no saturated fat or cholesterol); low carbs (the healthy fruits & veggies mentioned); and good fats such as mono- and poly-unsaturated fats. These are found in olive and canola oils; also in certain nuts such as walnuts and unsalted almonds and pistachios.

I was just put on Metformin. What is it?

Wesley A.: My doctor just put me on metformin, but didn't really explain why or what it is. It seems like half the people in my office are on it, but nobody really seems to know what it does. How does it work?

Answer: Physicians' usual treatment approach is 3-6 months of diet, weight loss, and exercise. If these don't work or are too difficult for the patient, medication may be needed. Metformin is often the drug of choice. Metformin is the generic name; there are several brand names such as Glucophage, Glumetza, and Fortamet.

Metformin works in three ways: it decreases gastrointestinal absorption of sugar, decreases formation of sugar by the liver, and increases insulin sensitivity. It does have side effects, however, and interactions with other drugs. Almost all drugs do. Metformin's main side effects are nausea, vomiting, diarrhea, and headache. There is also a serious side effect called lactic acidosis which fortunately is rare. It has been reported in about 1 out of every 30,000 patients.

In 2008, 40,000,000 prescriptions for the generic form alone were written in the US, so it is no surprise your office is a metformin-intense zone. Remember, though, that with diet, weight loss, and exercise many people with type 2 diabetes can still get off it. Every pound lost brings you closer to that.

You're wrong about red meat!

Ron A.: I'm a type 2. Five years ago I weighed three hundred, had out of control blood sugar, and was starting with organ damage. I tried to lose weight, but my blood sugar stayed a mess, and I was always dying of hunger. Then I started the Caveman Diet, ate like my ancestors did and like *we are supposed to*! Thanks to steaks, bacon, egg yolks and all that other great stuff YOU say not to eat, I lost one hundred and thirty pounds, got off meds, and got my blood sugar under control. Permanently. My blood sugar now stays around 85, I'm on zero meds, and I feel GREAT! What do you say you to that?

Answer: First off, do you really think cavemen enjoyed red meat every day? They didn't. They mostly starved throughout their short lives, and were lucky if they made it through the winter on nuts and berries. People of even one hundred years ago would not believe the abundance of food we have today; food that doesn't even require calories expended to catch and cook it.

Diets like the one you describe, have done a lot of damage. Some people like yourself swear by them, pointing to the fact that dieting on bacon and sirloin has helped them lose weight and get their blood sugar down. Well, those two - weight and blood sugar down - are good news. But...

Their arteries are sick. Ticking time bombs for heart attack or stroke.

They may look thinner on the outside, but all that saturated fat has raised their LDL (bad) cholesterol. This *directly* causes fatty cholesterol deposits inside arteries and narrows them, which in turn causes heart attack and stroke. Lost weight and lower blood sugar - again - are good, but only half the full trip to health.

Gunked-up arteries are a serious price to pay, especially since people with diabetes have more than double the risk for heart disease.

You didn't state your age, but it's never too soon to limit the bad for you fats that lurk in full fat milk products, meats, and processed foods. This means replacing foods like whole milk, regular cheese, butter, shortening, bacon, and bologna with low fat versions of these foods such as skim milk, low fat cheese, olive oil, and lean meats or fish. Olive and canola oil, instead of butter and "healthy" margarine (they aren't) reduce the risk of stroke and coronary disease because they are high in MUFAs and PUFAs (mono- and polyunsaturated fat) and very low in saturated (bad) fat. Both also have high levels of antioxidants to further bolster your health.

We understand the either/or dilemma that both dieters and diabetes sufferers had to deal with in the past. If you didn't want to spend weeks (or a lifetime) feeling ravenously hungry, your diet was EITHER high carb/low protein, or low carb/high protein, with the protein in each case carrying the extra burden of saturated fat and cholesterol.

If someone told you to keep both your carbs and your protein low, you'd be fully justified in saying "Well what in the world can I eat?" But with this book that's no longer a problem. You can have it both ways: low carb and low (bad) fats, the kind found in animal-sourced foods.

So, Ron, go have a big, filling pile of pancakes. Surely you like pancakes? They'll have zero affect on your blood sugar, and deliver a more pure and healthy kind of protein than even the leanest cut of red meat could.

Or if you're not in the mood for pancakes, try our chili recipe made with ground fat free turkey, or Tex Mex made with chicken but tasting just like the same thing made with beef. Give these and other recipes a try.

Courage often consists of letting go of the familiar.

Can I eat peanut butter?

Tom L.: People I know with diabetes swear by peanut butter and say it's an okay snack, but my doctor told me to stay away from fats. Isn't peanut butter fat? I'm confused.

Answer: We get this question a lot, Tom. Peanuts and peanut butter alone are great tasting and good for you, since they contain mostly mono-unsaturated fat. Read the labels, though. Some peanut butters contain added sugar; others contain added sugar and salt. Trader Joe's is an excellent brand, it's just pure ground-up peanuts. If you don't have a Trader Joe's near you, there are good sugar-free peanut butters available on Amazon.com.

How much coffee and tea can I drink?

Marge D.: I've had type 2 for almost a year. I cannot start the day without coffee, and still enjoy it during the day, but diabetic friends tell me it's bad to drink it. They say it's better to switch to tea, but I've heard that isn't good either. Are both bad if you have diabetes?

Answer: The problem is caffeine, Marge, although coffee has more caffeine than tea. Drinking regular coffee stimulates the adrenal glands, which in turn leads to increased blood sugar levels, and potentially to the development of insulin resistance. Diabetes sufferers who drink coffee frequently are at higher risk of undermining their efforts to bring their condition under control.

A study conducted in early 2008 by Duke University researcher James D. Lane, PhD, followed the impact of caffeine consumption on ten patients with type 2 diabetes as they went about their lives. Doctor Lane and his colleagues put continuous blood-sugar monitors on the patients, who were managing their disease through diet and exercise but with no extra insulin.

On one day, each patient took capsules containing caffeine equal to four cups of coffee; on other days the patients were given identical capsules containing a placebo.

Despite the fact that the patients were free to eat whatever they wanted, the researchers found that, on coffee drinking days, the patients' blood sugar rose higher after every meal than it did on days when they had no caffeine.

"Coffee is such a common drink in our society that we forget that it contains a very powerful drug – caffeine," Dr Lane said. "It increases blood glucose by as much as oral diabetes medications decrease it. For people with diabetes, drinking coffee or consuming caffeine in other beverages may make it harder for them to control their glucose," he added.

Following are comparisons between coffee and different kinds of tea:

- Coffee (a 5 ounce cup) contains 80 milligrams of caffeine
- Black tea (one tea bag) contains 40 milligrams of caffeine
- Oolong tea (one tea bag) contains 30 milligrams of caffeine
- Green tea (one tea bag) contains 20 milligrams of caffeine
- Decaff tea (one tea bag) contains 2 milligrams of caffeine
- Herbal tea (one tea bag) contains 0 milligrams of caffeine

People with diabetes are all different, however, and react in varying ways to different foods and beverages. See what works for you. If you still miss coffee there should be no problem with drinking it decaffeinated. Green tea is still very good for you for its antioxidant properties, and as you can see it contains only one quarter the amount of regular coffee's caffeine.

Can I drink alcohol?

Terry M.: I was recently diagnosed. My diabetes educator told me I shouldn't drink at all, but I hear differently from people who have had diabetes a lot longer than me. On the other hand they say they never get the big D under control, so I'm afraid. How bad could one glass of beer be?

Answer: You have to be careful with alcohol, Terry. It lowers blood sugar because it prevents the liver from releasing its stored sugar into the blood. If you are diabetic but *not* taking medication, alcohol will lower your blood glucose somewhat; more or less depending on the individual. However, if you are on insulin or other diabetes medications that also lower your blood sugar, the alcohol and medications together can provoke hypoglycemia.

If you're low to begin with or if you haven't eaten, you should not drink at all. Hypoglycemia caused by alcohol can last for up to twelve hours after drinking.

If you want to have a drink, be sure to check your blood glucose before you do. Then limit the amount and have it with food. It is also important to check your blood glucose before you go to bed. If it is low, have some carbs to raise it quickly, plus some lean protein to keep you stabilized even longer.

For general safety concerns, it is also advisable to wear an I.D. that states "I have diabetes." The symptoms of too much alcohol and hypoglycemia can be similar. You wouldn't want people to confuse hypoglycemia with inebriation, because they might not give you the proper kind of assistance.

If you are female, or over 65 with a thin muscle mass, you can drink one or fewer alcoholic beverages a day. A more muscular man can drink two or fewer alcoholic drinks a day.

A drink is defined as 12 ounces of beer, 5 ounces. of wine, 1.5 ounces of 80 proof spirits like gin or vodka. Cocktails or after dinner liqueurs are high in sugar and should be avoided.

Helpful tips include sipping slowly, and having a glass of water near your drink to quench your thirst. Distrust alcohol's initial "feel good" feeling, as it might make you more easily tempted and lessen your resolve.

Most people with type 1 or type 2 diabetes can have a drink. But care and common sense are important.

Are artificial sweeteners all bad?

Andy C: I tried artificial sweeteners to help me with my sweet tooth cravings but I had to give them all up! They either raise my blood sugar (sorbitol, mannitol, Splenda) or messed up my stomach something awful. Meanwhile I'm re-gaining the weight I lost, so help please? What am I getting wrong? They seem to work for other people. P. S. What about Stevia or Truvia? They are natural, at least.

Answer: Andy, many or most people share your confusion on this topic. First, like apples and oranges, you've lumped together sugar alcohols with Splenda (sucralose). These two are completely different.

Sugar alcohols, a consumer-friendly name, are processed from sugar molecules, and include names like sorbitol, mannitol, xylitol, lactitol, maltitol, and others ending in -ol. They still have calories of the sugar type (though fewer: 2-3 calories per gram as opposed to 4 calories per gram of standard sugar), and their supposed benefit is that they metabolize more slowly than regular sugar so they last you longer, hold off those need-sweets-again-crashes.

For sure it was the sorbitol and mannitol you mentioned that raised your blood sugar and "messed with your stomach;" sugar alcohols often cause bloating, discomfort and diarrhea. It is misleading for sugar alcohol-containing products to be labeled "sugar free." These products still contain significant amounts of carbs, which still break down to sugar and – yes again – can cause weight gain.

Splenda (sucralose) has no calories, and a decades-long track record of confirmed-safety studies and control group studies done by 80 countries. Doctors call it a godsend. It has been long approved by the FDA with, as physicians say, "no red flags."

You mentioned Stevia and Truvia being "natural." We feel that the word "natural" has largely become a food industry scam word. Most of the world's poisons are natural: strychnine, arsenic, snake venom; ditto animal (saturated) fat, heroin, cocaine, booze, nicotine, on and on. Conversely, insulin, metformin, vitamin pills, antibiotics, and many other substances that help you are all made in the lab.

I heard Splenda contains chlorine

Dana C.: I was all excited about trying some recipes that use Splenda, but a friend told me that Splenda contains chlorine. Is this true? She says she read it online.

Answer: Dana, this is a great question to follow the one preceding, and a good example of the stuff posing as "information" online, usually from someone trying to sell you something else.

The answer is, heavens no, Splenda does not contain chlorine; it contains chlo*ride*, which is completely different. Chloride is in salt, also known as sodium chloride, and in everything else you eat: fruits, vegetables, chicken, and meat. This is because salt occurs naturally in everything, and, along with it, its chloride component.

By the way chlorine itself – remember? – is added to all our drinking water and to irrigate our crops, and to animal feed, and consequently to all the food we eat. Still, no need for concern there. Chlorine itself is an atom. When it becomes part of a molecule (two or more atoms), its properties change completely.

Coconut and palm oil are healthy too, aren't they?

Frank D: I've been using coconut oil for years in my restaurant. People seem to like the food, but lately a lot of them ask what kind of oil I use. When I tell them, some of them go ape and say it's bad. Why?

Answer: You meant well, Frank. But the truth is that coconut and palm oils are the two exceptions among plant oils in that they are high in saturated fat. They are cheap for food manufacturers to use, and are in thousands of food products ("all vegetable oils!" spin the labels). Until the government catches up with the powerful food lobby, if ever, you're best off sticking to olive & canola oil. Sunflower and safflower oil are also good, or most vegetable oils – as long as they stay liquid at room temperature, and aren't palm or coconut oil.

Can I use agave nectar as a sweetener?

Cassie T: I'm afraid of artificial sweeteners, but agave is natural and it's supposedly a lower glycemic sweetener. A lot of my friends love it, but somebody else told me it's bad. Which is true? Everyone says different things, it's all so frustrating and confusing!

Answer: Important question! Because agave is 92 % harmful fructose. (High Fructose Corn Syrup is "only" 55% fructose.) Agave does have a lower glycemic index than table sugar, but its huge amount of fructose can cause weight gain, increased insulin resistance, and metabolic syndrome (central obesity, high blood pressure, high cholesterol, and cardiovascular disease).

The fact alone that it immediately increases insulin resistance makes it especially harmful to diabetes sufferers.

Just another member of the sugar family, fructose is the biggest bait-and – switch gimmick out there. A derivative of honey, berries, tree fruits, and sweet potatoes, fructose has been commercialized into a refined sugar which – true, absorbs more slowly, but also damages the body far more. Fructose and HFCS (high-fructose corn syrup) have been added to many, many processed foods, beverages, and, more ominously, so-called "diet yummies," telling people they can "cheat and eat" as much as they like.

Irony: fructose, with its longer shelf life and the fact that it's cheaper, has become the trans fat of the sugar family. Read every label. If there's even a hint of fructose in a product, you don't want it.

Consider again the astonishing fact that High Fructose Corn Syrup is "only" 55% fructose, while agave nectar is 92% fructose! This issue is so important; few people suspect how many commercial products contain even "only 55%" fructose. There are hundreds and hundreds of them, ranging from cereals, breakfast pastries, crackers, cookies, cakes, and condiments to poultry stuffing, bread, some dairy products like sweetened yogurt and frozen whipped toppings, plus ice cream and many juice drinks.

These products are mostly found in the center aisles of supermarkets.

As always, check the labels.

"I feel great! Okay, I could lose fifty pounds, but why should I get my blood sugar checked?" Said by a friend. He thinks denial is a river in Egypt.

Chapter Five

MEDICAL ASPECTS OF DIABETES

Are you prediabetic and don't know it?

Almost sixty million Americans are prediabetic, on the brink of type 2 diabetes. Many of them don't know it, or are in denial. Which is easy because prediabetes is insidious. It usually has no symptoms. Most people diagnosed with diabetes have had it for years without knowing. Others hear the stories and worry; but too often they just dither and decide to do nothing, which still leaves them fretting.

All it takes is a simple lab test. Alan Mertz, President of the American Clinical Laboratory Association, says it can help get a real grip on what's happening.

"Ask your doctor about an easy lab test called hemoglobin A1c. The test can tell you if you have diabetes or are close to developing it – a silent and serious condition called prediabetes," says Mertz.

The A1c test is quick, easy, and does not require you to fast before getting it. Because it measures the average amount of glucose in your blood for the preceding 2-3 months, it is not affected by what you've eaten recently. The American Diabetes Association has added the A1c test to its list of recommended tests for identifying diabetes, urging it especially for people who are overweight.

Overweight is overwhelmingly the main risk factor for prediabetes and type 2 diabetes.

Prediabetes is the "in between area" where blood glucose levels are above normal but have not reached those of diabetes. A normal A1c number is between 4 and 6. A prediabetic number would be 6 to 6.5. Above 6.5 is diabetic. These numbers may vary slightly, depending on which lab or physician you've been to. But very slight differences don't mean a lot. The A1c test will tell you generally what your blood glucose number is, and it will usually parallel your fasting blood sugar number (FBS). And the fact that the A1c is easier than people think, says Alan Mertz, "will help consumers' willingness to get tested – and help us battle a deadly and dangerous disease."

Roughly forty percent of people with prediabetes will become fully diabetic in as little as three years if they don't act. They are already in danger: individuals with prediabetes also face a much greater chance of cardiovascular disease like stroke, heart attack, kidney and neurological problems than those without similar risk.

Occasionally prediabetes will have symptoms, which include increased thirst, frequent urination, weakness, fatigue, poor healing of wounds, and blurred vision. Some of these symptoms are attempts by your body to shed excess or poorly utilized sugar; they may also be discomfort from tiny nerves with early impaired circulation.

Consult your doctor if you notice any of these warning signs.

If you do, and if your A1c comes out a bit high...it is now time to make a second appointment, and fast for eight hours overnight, and get what is called an FBS test. This means Fasting Blood Sugar. It means having a venepuncture – a small amount of blood drawn from a vein, usually from the inside of your elbow – and that's it. It doesn't hurt. It usually feels like a pin prick or slight stinging sensation. Your doctor will send your blood specimen to a lab, and you'll usually have the result back within hours, or at most overnight. (This test can also be done on a finger prick drop of blood.)

If your Fasting Blood Sugar number is between 70-100, that's normal. If it's 100-125, that is the prediabetes range. A number over 125 is full blown diabetes. The doctor may want to repeat this test in a week or two, to be sure of the result.

Clear risk factors for diabetes include: being overweight with a body mass index above 25; being physically inactive; having a family history of type 2 diabetes, and being African-American, Hispanic, American Indian, Asian-American, or Pacific Islander.

Family history is very important. If close blood relatives like your parents, siblings, or children have diabetes, you may have it too. Uncle, aunts, cousins with diabetes are also a warning signal.

It all comes down to blood sugar. Prediabetes means the body is not utilizing sugar well, usually because the muscles resist allowing sugar to enter them and be used for energy, so sugar (glucose) accumulates in the blood. Over a long period of time high amounts of sugar in the blood damage the body's arteries that supply blood to the heart, eyes, kidneys, and nerves.

This, again, can be happening when you feel fine. That's why it's so important to see a doctor, get a checkup, and have at least the A1c.

It is recommended to have a doctor's visit every year or two. It may not be necessary to have a comprehensive history, physical, and lab tests every time, but you should have the basics tested: blood sugar, blood pressure, cholesterol levels, urine analysis, and possibly more depending on your age and symptom history.

If you are diagnosed as prediabetic you *can* turn it around, but the three most important things are your diet, weight loss, and exercise. If you've been sedentary, consider starting with five to ten minutes of daily exercise and gradually increase to at least thirty minutes almost daily. Your doctor will give you specific guidance that fits your situation.

Amazing facts to motivate you.

1. Your blood sugar drops with just a one-pound weight loss. In fact, with just the first ounces off, you've made yourself immediately healthier. (Overweight is also a huge risk factor for breast and ovarian cancer in women, prostate cancer in men, and colon cancer in both men and women.)

2. Your heart, which is the size of your closed fist, is a small, hard working muscle, pumping 24/7. And for every extra pound of fat you carry, your body has to grow seven new miles of blood vessels – primarily capillaries but also small arteries (arterioles) and small veins (venules) – and your heart has to work that much harder. Put on two pounds and that's fourteen new miles of blood vessels; fifty extra pounds requires 350 miles of new blood vessels. On and on...

3. But good news: the opposite is true. For every pound of fat you lose, your body sheds seven miles of blood vessels. They just re-absorb, break down, and get excreted. Lose two pounds and that's fourteen miles of blood vessels gone, lightening your heart and body's load.

Know that even a little weight lost is a lot. Repeat that out loud to yourself: even a little is a lot. Let it be your mantra.

Weight loss is a slow process, a bit like watching the grass grow. Try to accept that, and the next time you catch yourself groaning, "Oh it's almost a week and I've only lost two pounds" – understand that that's *good*. You've already brought valuable change to your body; taken a literal load off your heart.

Try this too for reinforcement: take a can off the shelf that weighs one or two pounds, and heft it. Or, in the supermarket, keeping your elbow straight, lift some wrapped meat weighing two pounds. *It's heavy*. And you'll think, Wow, I lost this much?

The body has astonishing powers to self-heal. Its owner just has to help it. Just begin. Don't be afraid. There are prediabetics without number who balked for a long time before getting themselves seen. Here's one:

"I finally stopped duckin it and got myself in there. Doc said my blood sugar is 117. He was grinning and wanted to know what finally got me to listen to the wife and show up. I said it wasn't the wife, it was my grandfather. He's a type 2. Last Sunday I watched him pull a rusty nail out of his foot that had been pierced clear through for hours without him ever feeling it. That got my attention, so I showed up."

Lap Band surgery

Lap band surgery has become a booming business, largely since it's been touted as a way to cure obesity and avoid type 2 diabetes.

This procedure, which has only been licensed in the U.S. since 2001, has offered hyped hope of an "easy fix" to the rising numbers of overweight people who desperately want to lose weight, and have tried every diet without success. The marketing by "rubber band docs" has been aggressive and everywhere, including in steady streams on Twitter. People, usually women (and possibly paid) re-tweet hourly about how wonderful the procedure is. ("Made me sexy again!") One health company has filed with the Food and Drug Administration seeking permission to market the procedure to teenagers. If the company gets approval, there will be greater numbers of teenagers signing up for the surgeries, having heard only the rosy sales talk, and unaware of the risks.

The "cure" in question is laparoscopic gastric banding, or lap-banding. Unlike the even riskier gastric bypass surgery (a complete restructuring of the digestive tract) in lap-banding surgeons fit an inflatable band around the top of the stomach to pinch it smaller. The band works like a belt, with notches to tighten or loosen the "pinch." The result? Patients feel fuller faster, and lose weight.

True, weight loss surgery has advanced considerably in the past few years, and modern lap band surgery has become mostly safer, carrying fewer complications than early forms of gastric bypass surgery.

But there is no such thing as a "simple" operation. There is always risk, pain, and some complications more serious than others. There are also extra risks which accompany any surgery involving overweight patients.

These risks should be discussed with people other than your surgeon, who too often wants to do the procedure. Google "complaints about lap band surgery," and do some serious reading. Join online groups that discuss their experiences post-op, and for many months afterward.

Lap band surgery, like any surgery, should be a last, last, last resort.

Most complications occur *after* lap band surgery, and most patients – as high as 88% – will experience some degree of mild to severe complications in the weeks and months following surgery:

- Roughly half of all patients will suffer varying degrees of nausea and vomiting.
- About one-third will suffer from burning regurgitation of acid stomach contents, which can lead to esophageal cancer.
- Another post-op problem is a slippage of the band, and
- roughly one patient in seven will experience a blockage of the passage between the two pinched off sections of the stomach.
- Other moderate to severe problems following lap band surgery can include erosion of the band into the stomach, and

- twisting or leakage of the band's tube, resulting in fluid leaking into the abdomen and causing inflammation including peritonitis.
- Difficulty in swallowing, constipation and diarrhea are also quite common.

One "bander" from an online Lap Band site reports her experience: "I got my lap band in May of 2010. Right after the surgery I couldn't even drink. The doctor said to just sip clear fluids. I still could barely keep any fluids down, even when he loosened the band that was still sticking out of my stomach. No improvement. I'd take a sip, and it would come right back up tasting horrible, like stomach acid. It was fourteen days before I was able to drink normally, the doc had to reopen my tube and loosen it more. He said I was "sensitive to the swelling." Well, who DOESN'T get swelling?

At his office, after three weeks of incredible misery, a nurse almost casually said that "maybe my band had slipped." One doctor wanted to do an x-ray or fluoroscopy, and then another doctor said no. I have had incredibly bad follow-up care from them. It's a group, and they always seem to be in a hurry. I've heard they do twenty lap band surgeries a day. They didn't pay attention when I said it was days before I was able to drink normally, and they still don't pay attention when I say food gets stuck and comes back up tasting of acid. They don't care once they've done you. Some woman doctor lectured me that there's a difference between throwing up and regurgitation, and that regurg is to be expected! Nobody talked about that before the operation! All they talked about is how much weight I was going to lose in just a few weeks. Now it's five weeks later and it's still hard to eat or drink.

In the last fifteen days I have lost 21 pounds, not because of the operation but because the operation starved me. I could have lost the same amount if someone had shut me in a cell and starved me. Looking back, that would have been better. I can't say I'd recommend this operation to anyone. The post-op is torture, and I'm still not out of the woods."

Another "bander," seven months post-op, says that although the worst is behind her, she still can only eat "mush" and that her tummy "looks funny, dented, with wrinkly skin."

There have been a rising number of Lap Band lawsuits.

Diabetes and Celiac Disease

Celiac Disease, an intestinal disorder, is triggered by gluten, a protein found in wheat, barley, and rye. Five to ten percent of type 1 diabetics also have celiac disease, compared to less than one percent of non-diabetics. Celiac disease and type 1 diabetes are both auto-immune diseases.

According to The Annals of Medicine, December, 2010 issue, "Celiac disease symptoms include diarrhea, intestinal bloating and stomach cramps. Left untreated, it can lead to malabsorption of nutrients, damage to the small intestine, and other medical complications."

Good news: The New Diabetic Diet is gluten free as well as low carb. Moreover, whatever "gluten free" products you've heard of *still use carbs*, consisting of flours made from rice, corn, barley, buckwheat and so on.

You don't need those carbs. You can get "fast" or needed carbs from fresh fruit, vegetables, and heart-healthy nuts like walnuts, almonds and pistachios.

With this book's recipes, you can have *gluten free and carb free* rolls, bread, brownies, blondies, pizza and piecrust, muffins, cookies, banana nut bread – you name it. This is because we completely substitute soft, white, protein powder for flour. The resulting baked goodies are just as tasty, and keep you feeling full longer with no sugar spikes from the protein. And the soy protein we use is so nutrient-rich that it's healthier than whole wheat slices and skim milk combined. (Soy protein powder contains more than three times as many B vitamins as whole grains.)

Additionally, instead of butter or margarine our recipes use milled flaxseed, which bakes beautifully, is heart-healthy, disease-preventing, and contains more fiber than whole grains or a cup of broccoli or oatmeal.

It's pretty exciting, isn't it? Gluten free, carb free, and more fiber and nutrients than whole grains?

This nutritional breakthrough is well timed, because recent studies report that the incidence of glucose intolerance is rising.

The Annals of Medicine, December, 2010 issue reports: "Working to solve the puzzle of when people develop celiac disease has led researchers from the University of Maryland School of Medicine Center for Celiac Research to some surprising findings. They have found that the autoimmune disorder is on the rise, with evidence of increasing cases in the elderly.

"Since 1974, in the U.S., the incidence of the disorder has doubled every 15 years. Using blood samples from more than 3,500 adults, the researchers found that the number of people with blood markers for celiac disease increased steadily from one in 501 in 1974 to one in 219 in 1989. In 2003, a widely cited study conducted by the Center for Celiac Research placed the number of people with celiac disease in the U.S. at one in 133.

"As the people in the study aged, the incidence of celiac disease rose, echoing the findings of a 2008 Finnish study in *Digestive and Liver Disease* that found the prevalence of celiac disease in the elderly to be nearly two and a half times higher than the general population. The recent findings challenge the common speculation that the loss of gluten tolerance resulting in the disease usually develops in childhood."

The epidemic of type 2 diabetes, added to increasing numbers of celiac disease cases in the elderly and in patients with type 1 diabetes, makes this eating plan's eliminating both gluten and carbs seem like a good idea.

Gestational Diabetes

Gestational diabetes occurs only during pregnancy and is self-limited to the duration of the pregnancy. It occurs in approximately up to eight pregnancies out of every one hundred in America. Usually, the patient has had no prior history of diabetes, but is found to have an elevated blood sugar during pregnancy, which then returns to normal soon after giving birth. Future pregnancies may re-ignite the blood sugar rise, which once again disappears after giving birth. Women with gestational diabetes should have their blood sugar checked at least annually in the future as they do run some risk of developing type 2 diabetes.

In some instances, undiagnosed insulin resistance prior to the pregnancy will predispose a woman to gestational diabetes.

Because the high blood sugar only lasts for the duration of the pregnancy, it ordinarily does not create lasting problems or organ damage for the mother. The newborn, however, is often of high birth weight which may make vaginal delivery difficult and result in delivery by Caesarian Section.

Infrequently excess thirst or urination may occur for the pregnant woman, but more often the diagnosis is made when the blood sugar is checked, a routine test during pregnancy.

One theory as to why women develop gestational diabetes is that the hormones produced in the placenta to support the pregnancy may provoke insulin resistance. The onset of elevated sugar tends to be in the last half or last trimester (three months) of pregnancy, and sugar levels return to normal soon after delivery as hormone levels return to their pre-pregnancy levels.

There are well known risk factors for the development of gestational diabetes. These include being overweight or having prediabetes, having a family history of diabetes, having had gestational diabetes during a previous pregnancy, or having given birth in the past to a baby weighing nine pounds or more. Ethnic issues also play a role, similar to type 2 diabetes: if you are African-American, Hispanic, Native American, or Asian American, your risk is higher.

Prediabetes due to overweight before becoming pregnant has become an increasingly prevalent risk. The definition of prediabetes is having a Fasting Blood Sugar (FBS) of 100-125.

In addition to large birth weight requiring Caesarian Section, the newborn may experience problems with low blood sugar. This is due to excess insulin production by the newborn's pancreas in response to maternal glucose, continuing for a short time after delivery. If the newborn is born prematurely, Respiratory Distress Syndrome may also occur. There is also an increased risk for yellow jaundice due to immaturity of the newborn's liver and its inability to process bilirubin, a substance normally excreted by the liver. This usually does not create any long lasting problems, but if the blood bilirubin level reaches excessive levels, blood exchange transfusion may be needed to avoid brain damage.

Children of mothers who experienced gestational diabetes are at higher risk for developing type 2 diabetes later in life. As infants and toddlers they may experience difficulty with motor skills and with hyperactivity.

For the mother-to-be, pre-eclampsia may also occur. This is a condition in which blood pressure is elevated and protein (albumin) is present in the urine. Without treatment, blood pressure can reach very high levels at the time of delivery, causing serious risk for maternal seizures and a stillborn fetus.

Additionally, a study published in February of 2011 in the journal Obstetrics and Gynecology found that women who gain weight (over 3-4 pounds) in the first three months of pregnancy were at higher risk for gestational diabetes than women who did not gain weight.

Obstetrical care of the future mother should best be augmented by consultation with a diabetes specialist. The needs of both the mother and fetus need to be carefully monitored. Weight control, diet, exercise, and in some cases, treatment with insulin should be addressed. Growth and development of the fetus should be followed via ultrasound tests. Obese women who gained weight during the first three months were especially at risk.

A pediatrician or a neonatologist, a physician who specializes in high risk infant care, is often present at the births of gestational diabetes babies to handle any potential complications.

A woman planning pregnancy should get into the best shape possible: lose excess weight, eat a healthy diet, and do regular modest exercise.

The Dawn Phenomenon and Diabetes

"My life feels like one continuous dawn phenom." From a Twitter friend.

For everyone, the Dawn Phenomenon is a natural part of daily human body rhythm. However, it can wreak potential havoc on diabetes sufferers.

Around four or five in the morning, our bodies start getting ready to wake up. Triggered by the pituitary gland's hormones, the adrenal gland starts pouring adrenalin and cortisone into the blood stream, and that increases pulse and blood pressure. (This might explain why many people have their most intense dreams at this time.)

At the same time, the liver starts breaking down more glycogen into sugar, which enters the blood stream insuring a supply of fuel in anticipation of muscle action. The problem is, these hormones that get the body ready to start the day also increase insulin resistance, which in turn causes your blood glucose to rise.

This is why people with diabetes are often confused to wake up and find their FBS (Fasting Blood Sugar) number higher than it was when they went to sleep, even after having not eaten all night. But if you fall back to sleep and re-awaken an hour later, your triggered insulin response may have pushed your blood sugar way back down again.

And another up-and-down day has begun.

If you have diabetes and experience the Dawn Phenomenon, it is understandably frustrating. You might not understand what is happening to you, or know what to do about it.

The higher-than-bedtime blood sugar doesn't cause discomfort, but it's important to eat soon after you wake; otherwise your body's insulin response to that Dawn Phenomenon upsurge of sugar will do its roller coaster thing, and soon cause your blood sugar to crash, resulting in feeling shaky and ready to faint.

What can help?

Avoid carbs late in the evening, and if in the morning things are hectic in your house have pre-made snacks ready to grab. The best snacks or quick breakfasts include a mix of relatively fast-acting carbs and lean protein. One popular choice is shakes made with blended protein powder and berries. (Frozen berries are fine.) Another choice could be any of this eating plan's baked goods with whole orange segments.

There are stories of people who didn't eat because of very minor emergencies: a child who couldn't find his snow boots, a spouse frantically hunting for his or her cell phone. "Crazy little things," writes one woman who in her rushing around forgot to eat, and then experienced her worst crash ever. She learned from the experience of that awful day.

Desperate to "get back up fast," she drank a full glass of regular orange juice and ate several pieces of toast with real jam. That quick fix "took" quickly, then crashed quickly, and then she repeated the process by eating last night's leftover spaghetti she had made for her children.

Ninety minutes later, driving, she had to pull over and barely made it to the side of the road. Later she would dimly remember a cop trying to talk to her through her car window, and then nothing more until she came to in the hospital.

It is a harrowing story, and as the saying goes, every person with diabetes is different and learns from experience.

Now the happy news is that that woman has lost nearly seventy pounds, is nearly off her medications, and is very careful about what she eats and when. Her breakfasts now include a mix of short, medium and long-acting sources of energy, and she "coasts" for the rest of the day on lean protein snacks that last her for hours. Fat free cheese slices are her favorite, she says, and they're portable. She peels off the cellophane wraps while the cheese slices are still cold, and then stacks them with chopped, heart-healthy walnuts between the layers. She still wonders how she could have made the mistakes of that frightening day, but it can happen to anyone.

Diabetes can be scary, and most people with diabetes have had one experience or another which has taught them the hard way.

It is important to set your timing for each day. The key is consistency. Eat and snack at the same times; also take your medication and do your exercise at the same times, so that you are balancing all your sugar-lowering activities with whatever it is that raises your sugar.

Exercising in the evening can also help. Thirty minutes of brisk walking, or whatever exercise you can manage, will literally remove glucose from your blood and help to keep your sugar levels lower during the night.

You can manage the Dawn Effect. A protein snack at bedtime will last you hours longer than a carbohydrate snack, and can ease your waking to the Dawn Phenomenon if it does occur. There is no way to stop this natural part of waking, but you can greatly ease its impact.

If you're on insulin or oral diabetic drugs, work with your doctor to control timing and dosage along with your management of correct diet and exercise. As your weight (hopefully) comes down and your ability to exercise increases, your need for medication will decrease, and concerns about potential run-ins with the Dawn Phenomenon will hopefully be a thing of the past.

Diabetes foot care: nerve pain, neuritis, neuropathy

"It feels like a thousand bees stinging my feet. Can't sleep from the pain. Just lie there crying."

Nerve pain, neuritis, and neuropathy all mean the same. They describe a change in or loss of nerve function. This loss may be loss of feeling, or a pins and needles feeling, or the loss of movement ability.

In diabetes, neuropathy strikes especially in the feet. Diabetes makes you more vulnerable to injury and infection by damaging your foot nerves. This may begin as a stinging sensation, and in time may cause you not to notice a cut or blister, for example, or a sore from a pebble in your shoe, until these become large sores. This happens because there is diminished blood flow through the large arteries that run down from the hip area all the way to the toes, and then through the small arteries that supply oxygen and nutrients to the nerves in the feet. Both kinds of arteries are narrowed by atherosclerosis, the process of fat deposition inside the arterial walls. This process becomes much worse in diabetes. Carbs convert to blood sugar; high blood sugar converts to fat, and fat ultimately lands in arteries and arterioles throughout the body. The tiniest vessels will make their problems known first.

Neuropathy is painful. At the same time, without temperature sensation in the feet, a hot water bottle or electric blanket will not be felt as hot, causing serious burns. Another aspect of neuropathy is a loss of position sense, the awareness of where your feet are. This can cause injury to toes, or dangerous falls. Loss of ability to move the feet or walk can further impair the usual activities of daily living, including exercise or just plain walking.

Foot pain is an issue seen by every doctor who takes care of patients with diabetes. While in the last few years drugs have reached the market which your doctor can prescribe to give some relief of symptoms, the ideal treatment is of the underlying disorder, which is the diabetes nerve damage itself.

A valuable home remedy to add to your doctor's foot care prescriptions is the use of cocoa.

Pure, non-alkalinized cocoa's special antioxidants cause vasodilation – magic word! – which dilates your arteries in *seconds*, immediately sending more oxygen and nutrients to every organ, tissue, and blood vessel in your body – right down to the tiny arteries (arterioles) in your feet. This promotes better circulation, healthier nerve function, happier feet...and no side effects as there often are with drugs.

Here are some important foot care tips to follow:

- Take good general care of your diabetes. Keep your blood glucose in target range.
- Check your feet daily, looking for warning signs of diabetes complications. Check your bare feet for cuts, red spots, swelling, and blisters. If you can't see the bottoms of your feet, it helps to use a mirror.
- Every day, wash and dry your feet carefully, especially between the toes.
- To keep your skin soft, rub a thin coat of skin care lotion over the tops and bottoms of your feet, but not between your toes.
- Avoid walking barefoot. Wear comfortable shoes and socks that protect your feet. Before putting on your shoes, check their insides to make sure the lining is smooth and there are no small objects inside.
- Protect your feet from hot and cold. Test hot water before putting your feet into it. Avoid using heating pads or electric blankets. You can burn your feet without realizing it.
- Careful cutting toe nails, or see a foot doctor.
- Put your feet up when sitting. Several times a day, wiggle your toes and move your ankles up and down for five minutes. Avoid crossing your legs for long periods of time.
- Don't smoke.

Set a specific time every day to check your feet. Mornings might be a good time, when you are dressing.

Hypothyroidism and diabetes

"First my feet were cold, just freezing all the time, even when I wore heavy socks to bed. Since I have diabetes I assumed it was peripheral neuropathy. Then my skin got dry and itchy, and I couldn't even feel my heart beat. I knew something else was happening and got seriously scared. The doctor told me I was hypothyroid."

What is the thyroid? It is a small gland in the front lower part of the neck. It manufactures essential hormones that help regulate cell activity in our bodies, including metabolism.

Thyroid problems are not a complication of diabetes, but do occur more often in people with diabetes.

Problems can occur if this gland makes too much thyroid hormone (hyperthyroidism), or too little thyroid hormone (hypothyroidism). Diabetes patients who develop either hypothyroidism or hyperthyroidism often find it harder to manage their diabetes.

Although thyroid disease does occur among the general population, diabetes patients have it more frequently.

The glands in our bodies all depend on one another to function properly. The thyroid gland, for example, depends on the pituitary gland to help control the production of thyroid hormones. The pituitary gland produces what is called thyroid stimulating hormone (TSH). Normally, this hormone promotes thyroid hormone production and release into the blood stream. When the thyroid hormone level is low, the pituitary gland senses this deficit and releases TSH, which in turn tells the thyroid gland to make and release more thyroid hormone into the bloodstream.

This process works rather like a thermostat. If the thermostat senses cold air, it prompts the furnace to produce heat. If the air is too warm, the thermostat tells the furnace to shut off. The thyroid and pituitary glands have the same kind of signaling relationship.

Hypothyroidism

Hypothyroidism occurs when there is too little thyroid hormone circulating in the body. Its symptoms include:

- Fatigue
- Weakness
- Feeling cold (when others around you don't)
- Weight gain or increased difficulty losing weight
- Dry, itchy pale skin
- Depression and irritability
- Memory loss
- Coarse, dry hair
- Muscle and joint pain
- Constipation
- Husky voice
- Heavy periods (in women)

A patient may have any number of these symptoms, which will vary with the severity of the thyroid hormone deficiency and the length of time the body has been deprived of the hormone. You may sometimes have just one of these symptoms as your main complaint, while another patient will not have that problem at all but will be suffering from an entirely different symptom.

Most people will have a combination of these symptoms, and will need to discuss them with their doctor.

Potential Dangers of Hypothyroidism

Your body expects a certain amount of thyroid hormone. If it's not forthcoming, and your pituitary gland keeps pushing out additional thyroid stimulating hormone (TSH) to try to get the thyroid to produce more of its hormone, this constant barrage of high levels of TSH may cause the thyroid gland to become enlarged and form a goiter; what is also called a "compensatory goiter."

Symptoms of hypothyroidism will usually worsen if left untreated. Complications can rarely result in severe depression, heart failure, or coma.

The good news is that hypothyroidism can often be diagnosed with a simple blood test. Sometimes it's not so simple and more tests are needed. A good endocrinologist will definitely be needed, and will know how to care for you.

Hypothyroidism is completely treatable. Many patients need only take one pill a day. For other patients it's less simple, but there are several types of thyroid hormone preparations which will result in the best therapy. There is often a medical mix of issues, and treatment can be different for everybody.

Hyperthyroidism and diabetes

Hyperthyroidism is a condition in which too much thyroid hormone is being produced.

In a person with diabetes, hyperthyroidism may be the cause when blood glucose levels rise without explanation. If this condition is untreated and becomes worse, the person's diabetes can become increasingly unstable and harder to manage. Too many ketones (the end result of fat breakdown) may begin circulating in the blood, and more insulin or medication will be needed to lower blood glucose levels.

Women older than 40 are more likely to develop this condition, although men are not entirely excluded.

Hyperthyroidism can also speed up the body's metabolism. Increased metabolism can cause medications given in their usual dose to wear off more quickly, leaving the individual visibly sweating and trembling. This condition is often misinterpreted as low blood glucose, and an individual will try to eat "fast carbs" in an attempt to compensate. This in turn can reverse weight loss into weight gain, and further diabetes complications.

Common symptoms of hyperthyroidism include:
- Weight loss
- Extreme fatigue
- A pounding heart
- Feeling hot (when no one else is)
- Tremor of the hands
- Hair loss
- Diarrhea

- Feelings of nervousness and irritability
- Insomnia or restlessness
- In women, light or decreased periods

While fatigue may be indicative of other conditions, these symptoms with an existing diagnosis of diabetes should be given prompt attention by a physician.

Risks for hyperthyroidism include:
- Having a family history of thyroid disease
- Already having a condition that affects the immune system such as type 1 diabetes or rheumatoid arthritis
- Being female over age of 40
- Being male over the age of 65
- Having recently given birth

Hyperthyroidism can be treated with medication, radioactive iodine or surgery. Your doctor will do blood tests, regular Thyroid Stimulating Hormone (TSH) blood screenings during physical exam, and assess your symptoms in order to help you get corrective treatment.

Diabetic eye disease

Eye problems are among the long-term complication of diabetes. High blood glucose damages the eye's lens, retina, and optic nerve. Diabetic retinopathy, glaucoma, and cataracts are the most common eye problems found in diabetics.

Diabetic retinopathy is a main cause of blindness in adults. It is damage to the arteries of the retina, the lining at the back of the eye that senses light, and has fragile blood vessels that are easily damaged by high blood sugar and high blood pressure. Small hemorrhages on the retina may be seen by the eye doctor, and earliest treatment possible is recommended. As retinopathy worsens, its symptoms may include blurred vision, small black spots or cobweb-type "floaters" in the vision. The sooner the condition is diagnosed and treated, the better the chances of preventing permanent blindness.

Glaucoma is another condition common in diabetics, who are twice as likely to get it as non-diabetics. Glaucoma is caused by pressure building up in the eye. If left untreated, the pressure eventually damages the retina and optic nerve. This damage due to pressure results in gradual loss of vision. If glaucoma is diagnosed early it can be treated, and permanent damage or blindness can be prevented. An ophthalmologist (eye specialist) can perform a simple test to check the pressure in the eye.

Cataracts affect the lens of the eye, a structure behind the cornea that bends light entering the eye and focuses it on the retina. Cataracts occur in many people as they get older, but people with diabetes are at risk for cataracts at younger ages. The eye's lens gets cloudier, and double or blurry vision occurs. Stronger eyeglasses may help, but eventually the lens will have to be removed. Fortunately, cataract surgery with lens replacement will usually result in good return of vision. Cataract operations are quite common, and usually the patient goes home the same day the surgery is done.

When diabetes is the cause, there is one important similarity between these three different eye disorders. Early detection can make the difference between permanent visual loss and preservation of sight. At least annually, more often in some cases, an eye exam by an ophthalmologist is vital. The exam should include much more than a refraction, the process of determining how well you see at different distances, usually done in order to prescribe eye glasses.

The exam should include an exam with a slit lamp, an instrument that permits a close look at the lens itself. The retina should be examined after the pupils are dilated to allow a good look at the entire retina including the optic nerve, the macula (the central vision portion of the retina), the retinal arteries and veins, and the periphery of the retina. The eye pressure needs to be determined to test for glaucoma. In some cases where glaucoma is suspected, a visual field exam is done, a test that maps out any blind spots on the retina.

Many eye problems in diabetics are hard to prevent. But permanent blindness can be avoided with early treatment. To prevent eye problems you should also:
- keep your blood sugar levels and blood pressure under control
- don't smoke
- report any changes in vision immediately
- have eye exams yearly or more often, if necessary

Don't wait for any vision change to see the eye doctor. Schedule a yearly eye exam that checks for 1) diabetic retinopathy, 2) glaucoma, and 3) cataracts.

Especially see an eye doctor immediately if you experience: any blurred or double vision; one or both eyes hurt; eye pain or pressure, spots or floaters in the vision, trouble seeing out of the corner of the eye, or vision affected by rings, flashing lights, or blank spots.

Vegetarianism and diabetes

Well, are we talking potatoes or ratatouille? Strictly speaking, a vegetarian diet is certainly better for you than our traditional Western diet with its carbs overload and high amount of animal fats. On the other hand, there are carbs and bad fats in vegetarian diets too, such as starchy vegetables and dairy products such as cheese that are high in saturated fat.

Vegetarians also seem to have divided into three groups:
- **Vegans** eat only plant-based foods. They don't eat foods from animals, including meat, poultry, fish, milk, eggs and cheese.

- **Lacto-vegetarians** do eat milk and milk products along with plant-based foods. They don't eat eggs, meat, fish and poultry.
- **Lacto-ovo vegetarians** do eat eggs, milk and milk products, such as cheese and yogurt, in addition to plant-based foods. They omit red meat, fish and poultry.

All three groups eat "plant-based" foods – which, again, include potatoes, grains, rice, and that whole bunch of sugar-spikers. And all three groups avoid fish and poultry, which is used quite a bit in this eating plan – as long as you first melt out the cholesterol! Overall, these vegetarian diets are good, since they are centered on fruit, vegetables, legumes, nuts, seeds and, in the second two groups, some dairy products. There would still be those starchy vegetables (without which you'd be intolerably hungry), and egg yolks which are very high in cholesterol, and...substitute "low fat" for those dairy products, and you'd have a pretty good diet that is low in cholesterol and saturated fat, and high in fiber.

But where diabetes is concerned, "pretty good" isn't good enough.

Vegetarian diets as a whole are touted as low sugar, with its proponents forgetting or not realizing that all carbs become sugar. A vegan yam compote will metabolize fairly fast into glucose. Ditto the green pea and barley soup, and the oatmeal and quinoa scones. And since your goal is to control your blood sugar, recipes like that are not really what you want.

On the other hand, lest we forget, soy protein is a plant! A miraculous, carb-free, fat-free plant which The Federal Drug Administration (FDA) has enthusiastically endorsed, saying that twenty-five grams of soy protein daily help to lower LDL (bad) cholesterol, and to prevent complications of heart disease, cancer, and diabetes.

Yes, soy specifically helps in diabetes care. It also contains as much calcium as fat free milk, more B vitamins than are found in whole grains, plus other nutrients such as: vitamin D, the sunshine vitamin; selenium, an important antioxidant; iodine, which is essential for thyroid hormone manufacture; and iron, which helps to prevent anemia.

A new vegetarian diet for diabetes?

Have we just stumbled onto a new kind of vegetarian diet, something wonderful for people with diabetes – and for anyone else who wants to lose weight and get healthier by avoiding starchy carbs, saturated fat and cholesterol? That third group of vegetarians do eat a lot of egg yolks (300 mg of cholesterol in each), and groups two and three include full fat cheese in many of their recipes.

However, all of that cholesterol and saturated fat should be avoided by diabetes sufferers, with their extra vulnerability to cardiovascular disease.

Anyway, who would want to use wheat or barley flour to make pancakes when you can make them just as luscious with soy protein powder – and eat all you want with no danger from sugar spikes?

If you're still tempted to switch to a vegetarian diet, the recipes in this book might well be your best bet. Just skip the chicken and fish, that's all. You'd be getting your protein – the best and purest – from soy, and since the Lacto-ovo group do eat eggs, this eating plan's use of egg *whites* would be perfect!

You could call yourself…what? A Lacto-ovo Soytarian?

Some of the recipes in this book are all-veggie, delicious, and contain none of the starchy bad boys. That would include quesadillas, cheese blintzes, crepes, tacos, tortillas, stuffed sandwiches and rolls, and of course all the baked goodies. As for main courses try sautéed crunchy almonds with green beans and broccoli, or zucchini sautéed with filling milled flaxseed and other goodies, or ratatouille! Now there's a gorgeous colored, filling treat you'll love and maybe even want twice a week. Make extra; bring it to work in a plastic bowl or stuff your protein-bread sandwiches with it. There must also be a ton of antioxidants in it!

Here's the recipe:

Ratatouille, from Provence. This Mediterranean vegetable stew is also delicious served as a cold salad. Quick and easy to make, each serving contains 256 calories, 4 g protein, 15 grams carbs, 9 grams monounsaturated fat and over 17,000 antioxidants.

4 tbsp olive oil
1 lg. onion, chopped
6 minced garlic cloves
1 1/2 cups green, red, and orange peppers, coarsely chopped
large eggplant, cubed, skin on
2 medium zucchini, sliced
1 tsp. fresh black pepper
1 tbsp. dried basil
1 tbsp. dried oregano
½ cup sun-dried tomatoes

In a heavy skillet, heat oil over medium heat. Sautee the onions and garlic. Add chopped peppers, zucchini, & eggplant (does not need to be soaked or salted before).

Blend all together well, mixing & adding the spices.

Add sun-dried tomatoes last. Cook ten minutes over higher heat, stirring.

Let the ratatouille cook down to the consistency you like.

P.S. Have you seen the movie, "Ratatouille?" If you have, maybe see it again? If you haven't, it's a must. The sheer making of ratatouille is fun. It's pretty colors: purple, red and orange. It's the epitome of Mediterranean healthy.

When you serve it, your plate will look like a magazine cover.

"Every time you smile at someone, it is an action of love, a gift to that person, a beautiful thing." Mother Teresa

Chapter Six

TIPS FOR A HEALTHY LIFE STYLE

"Eat right! Stay active!" So goes the advice on every diabetic fitness site. Did you ever get the feeling that those sites were written by people who *don't* have diabetes? If they did, they would realize that the hardest part of getting yourself motivated (daunting word) is the emotional part. Having diabetes can be overwhelming, depressing, and when you're feeling like that it's often hard to do anything.

Feeling better thus comes first and foremost in the three best tips for a healthy life style: 1. emotional, 2. nutritional, and 3. fitness. It's so much easier to take on the second two if you've gotten over the first hurdle.

• • •

1. Emotional

If you've just been diagnosed, you're likely feeling stunned and scared. If you've been living with the disease, you're likely feeling worn down by the 24/7 struggle for control. Feelings of hopelessness weaken the energy needed to manage your diabetes and blood sugar, and become an exhausting, vicious circle.

The good news is that there are ways to break free, take charge.

First, talk to your doctor as soon as possible. Friends and family are also hopefully helpful – although if they don't have diabetes, it may be hard for them to really understand. The usual advice also includes starting right out with exercise for its feel-good endorphin benefits, or volunteering, or trying to schedule "fun" activities every week. But what if the harried, too-busy doctor doesn't call right away and then sounds rushed, and your friends and family aren't all that helpful, and you're feeling too down to exercise or volunteer or do anything?

Know that you're not alone

There's something else you can do "for ignition" that's quick and easy.

Surprise – go to Facebook. There are many, many people with diabetes on Facebook, and you'll find wonderful relationships there. "I LOVE my computer, my best friends are in it!" writes one man with type 2. Sometimes virtual friends become the most supportive of all. They trade stories and tips and send love and hugs and are in the exact same boat as you.

Open an account on Facebook.com, if you don't already have one. Take a few minutes filling out the basic info for your Profile Page (that's what they call it), upload your picture if you wish… and you're done. Congratulations, you now have a Facebook account! Now, to get an idea of how many diabetes friends Facebook has waiting for you, look at the top of your page. See that wide white Search box? Into it, type "Diabetes," and then click the magnifying glass over on the right. The list that comes up is the beginning of over 8,000 Facebook pages for diabetes organizations, groups large and small, and individuals.

Next, type "Joslin Diabetes Center" or "American Diabetes Association" into the search box. With so many thousands of Facebook diabetes pages, they're two good places to start. When you find the pages, scroll down to either Joslin's "Friends" box or the ADA's "People Like This" box, on the lower left. Click on anyone's photo or icon. When you come to that person's page, click the "Add as Friend" box to the right of the photo. A box will pop up. You can click the "Send Request" button directly, or fill in the "Add a personal message" with a friendly hello, and then click "Send Request." That's it! You've made your first friend! Go back to the page where you were and do it again. You'll hear back from those people very soon in your email. Click on the link in your email to confirm your new friends, and you're in motion, you're acquiring a whole new community of support.

Visit your News Feed often. That is your village square, with its "What's on your mind?" box to fill in at the top. You can also post your thoughts at the top of your Profile Page, and they'll automatically appear in your News Feed, where you'll find a constant, encouraging exchange of insights, tribulations, hope, and company. ("My dad's having surgery." "God bless! Prayers to you both!")

Add friends daily. Through them you'll find other groups, individuals, and discussions. As your friends' list grows, your News Feed will get busier. It's like a party line, everyone with the same concerns as yours.

If you have any questions, just ask one of your new Facebook friends, either by writing directly on their "wall" (their page), or by using the more Direct Message function which is located, almost invisibly, above their photo, to the right of the white word, Facebook. Hover your mouse over those three icons, Friend Requests, Messages, and Notifications. Click the Message one, and then, to the right, "Send new message."

For beginners, just writing on someone's "wall" is easiest.

Twitter is also good for finding friends with similar interests, but the beauty of Facebook is that you can write long letters to each other, as opposed to being limited to Twitter's 140 characters.

Through such communication, which is often better and more openly emotional online than in "real" life, you'll find the comfort that comes from sharing, caring, and empathizing, and with finding others who will respond to you in the same way. Did you just say something that made someone else feel better? The irony is, having comforted that other person will make you feel better too.

Happy, even.

And from happiness comes energy.

How are depression and stress different?

Depression and stress are quite different (and stress affects your blood sugar). Depression paralyzes, stress assaults. External stress is something like losing your job; internal stress is being chronically unhappy with your job. Either way stress leads to anxiety, something everyone experiences as feeling tense, upset, angry and frustrated.

Chronic stress leads to anxiety, which then leads to depression.

Stress starts a chain reaction assault on our bodies, which release cortisone in response. Cortisone then tells the liver to pour some of its stored sugar into the blood as fuel for our muscles, the long-ago reaction described as fight or flight. But modern people can't flee the nasty boss or the traffic tie-up, so this extra sugar is not used by the muscles. It peaks and accumulates in the blood, provoking an insulin response from the pancreas which pushes sugar too far back down, and soon there is a sugar crash.

How to beat stress? There really are ways.
- Notice what makes your feelings leap out of control.
- Recognize angry feelings as something that can hurt you.
- Define what *really* matters to you. The rest...just...doesn't...matter.
- Downplay the rest.

Depression keeps us down; stress wears us down. The way out of both is: *action*. And action is sometimes just the littlest thing. Like forcing yourself to call an old friend, or smiling at someone in the street, or offering help to a stranger. You'll be surprised at how the smallest thing can cheer you.

Sometimes action is just making a decision: I am *not* going to fret over the missed bus, or so-and-so's criticism, *because that will hurt me.* It is sooo not worth it.

Let that be your mantra.

When you're feeling better emotionally, you can tackle the other challenges.

2. Nutrition

There is much that is new and exciting about nutrition, which we'll come to in a minute...but first, the basics.

A. The main thing is to <u>keep down carbs _and_ saturated fat and cholesterol.</u> This is true for everyone, but more so for people with diabetes who are twice as vulnerable to the cardiovascular complications (stroke and heart attack) caused by these animal fats.

B. Next, <u>consider carbs and sugar as the same thing</u>, because all carbs become sugar. (Try to stick to low-sugar fruits and non-starchy veggies.) Even "good" carbs metabolize into sugar, maybe not immediately like "bad" carbs from white bread, white rice, and sugared sodas - - but "good," "complex" carbs will also soon metabolize into sugar.

How much sugar? How many teaspoons' equivalent? Easy to figure: Divide by four.

That is, divide the number grams of carbs you're eating by 4, and that's the equivalent number teaspoons of sugar those carbs will metabolize into: in thirty to sixty minutes if they're "good" carbs, faster if they're "bad" carbs…but for all carbs it's the same divide-by-four.

If food labels or recipes list only their number of grams of carbs, take that number and divide by four. For example, a granola bar admitting to 24 grams carbs on its label – divide those 24 grams by 4 … That granola bar contains the equivalent of 6 teaspoons of sugar!

A cereal may list 22 grams of carbs per cup. Divide those 22 grams by 4: That cup contains what will become, in thirty to sixty minutes, 5 ½ teaspoons of sugar. And a medium-sized apple containing 21 grams of carbs 21 divided by 4 comes out to over 5 teaspoons of fast carb sugar. Sweet! A quick, high-energy snack.

That isn't to say don't eat healthy apples (if a whole apple's sugar content is too high for you, eat half an apple.) This divide-by-four technique is just a way for you to be aware of exactly how much sugar any kind of carbs will quickly metabolize into.

C. Fiber comes next. It is so important to help you lose weight, reduce your risk of heart disease and cancer, and feel full longer because it breaks down slowly in your bloodstream. But the fiber in whole grains isn't worth it since grains carry heavy loads of carbohydrates. Better sources of fiber are lower in calories and carbs and higher in vitamins. Think spinach, carrots, broccoli, asparagus, peppers, kale and…

…mighty milled flaxseed, which is vastly healthier for you than whole grains. At the beginning of the next chapter, "Exciting new ingredients," are listed some of the important reasons why this is so.

D. Soy foods have been shown to decrease blood glucose levels in all diabetes sufferers, and to increase insulin sensitivity in people with type 2 diabetes. Foods rich in soy also lower cholesterol and help to prevent cardiovascular disease. Studies of soy's health benefits are increasing at a furious rate. One fascinating study was published in September 2009 in the Journal of Nutritional Biochemistry by Doctor Y-C Kim. Dr. Kim, a molecular nutrition researcher, found that soy's special isoflavones activate the same receptor sites as the insulin-sensitizing effects of diabetes drugs. Considering the fact that some diabetes drugs have side effects, this is exciting news.

E. Cinnamon is also a powerful diabetes-and-heart-disease-fighting antioxidant. One teaspoon contains *five times* as many antioxidants as one half cup of blueberries or a cup of pomegranate juice. Cinnamon's anti-inflammatory properties prevent damage to the interior of arteries, thus avoiding cholesterol deposits, blockage and clotting of the arteries. Studies also show that cinnamon helps to lower blood pressure and bad LDL cholesterol, prevent complications of diabetes, and regulate blood glucose.

Ordinary cinnamon from your supermarket is fine. Store it in a dry place for up to six months. There's no need to buy expensive "cinnamon tablets" and supplements.

F. Cocoa, the pure, non-alkalinized kind, is another new, major star in the field of nutrition. It is a daily must for its ability to dilate your arteries and arterioles (tiny arteries). This helps to prevent, in addition to heart attack and stroke, peripheral neuropathy, which is severe pins and needles type pain and then loss of feeling in the feet. Big arteries in the legs also benefit from pure cocoa, which helps to avoid Peripheral Artery Disease (insufficient blood supply through narrowed large arteries), and the need for leg amputations.

Non-alkalinized cocoa contains a special antioxidant called epicatechin, which activates nitric oxide in your arteries. (That's not nitrous oxide, the old-fashioned laughing gas.) *Within seconds*, nitric oxide dilates your arteries and arterioles, increasing the flow of blood, oxygen, and nutrients to every organ in your body, including your skin. Cocoa thus helps to prevent aging, inside and out.

But what if peripheral neuropathy has already started or intensified in your feet? Can cocoa's amazing vasodilation (glorious word!) properties still help you? The answer is yes. Almost as soon as you eat non-alkalinized cocoa, it dilates and brings oxygen and nutrients to your foot arterioles which had previously undergone diminished blood flow. The nerve endings begin to repair. Help starts to happen, and from there will grow. Anything in our bodies needs time to mend, but the process begins right away.

As for chocolate regular candy, it's delicious of course, but it also contains fat and sugar. You can head off cravings for it by making your own fudge truffles, or thick, rich fudge sauce for other swoony goodies from this plan's recipe.

Where can you get this pure cocoa?

It does bear repeating if you missed it earlier in the book. Two good brands of unsweetened, non-alkalinized cocoa are Hershey's (the little brown box in bakery aisles), and Trader Joes. Pure cocoa is also available on Amazon. com. Alkalinization, also known as Dutch Process, destroys the epicatechin antioxidants. If the product even says "partially Dutch Processed," it doesn't contain the magic.

Cocoa, soy protein, milled flaxseed and cinnamon are all super cheap and found at your local supermarket. They are like wonderful medicine with no side effects, and there's no need to pay more for any of them.

Nutrition tip:

Cinnamon sprinkled heavily onto a two tablespoons mound of milled flaxseed (a serving) can be placed on the side of your dinner plate, or even mixed into nearly whatever you're eating. Try them blended into chili, or salad, Tex Mex, or practically anything. Flaxseed's nutty grain taste and cinnamon's great flavor also go well mixed into your side dish of vegetables.

Have hot cocoa or a cold chocolate drink during the day and then, for dessert, have something chocolate from this book's recipes. The easiest and quickest recipe is fudge sauce on blueberries, strawberries and sliced banana with chopped walnuts for their heart-healthy Omega-3 acids.

Foods to avoid are:
- processed and fast foods
- sugar in its many disguises (honey, molasses, brown sugar, dried fruit, and agave which is 92% dangerous fructose)
- flour of all kinds including whole grains (flaxseed is better!)
- starchy vegetables like potatoes, barley, white rice, brown rice, and corn.

This book's recipes will more than make up for those former "bolus-worthy" sugar spikers. And how likely are you to miss barley and sweet potatoes if you can have cupcakes and pancakes?

Needless to say, don't smoke!

What about supplements?

People often ask about vitamin and minerals. Soy in particular is crammed with both, as are most other ingredients in this eating plan's recipes. Very little if any supplements are needed.

Different vitamins have come in and out of favor over the decades. Virtually all are found in ample quantities in any average diet, and excess vitamins have proven to be toxic in high doses. More is not always better. Vitamin D may be useful especially in northern climates, since sunlight plays such a large role in converting Vitamin D in the skin to its active form.

Research has just begun on investigating whether Vitamin D plays a role in preventing or improving diabetes. Low levels of Vitamin D are found throughout the population, in both people with diabetes and in the general population. It is not even clear what an optimum blood level of Vitamin D should be. There have been, however, short term studies involving small numbers of diabetic people, correlating low Vitamin D levels with poorer diabetes control. But there are other possible explanations for this, such as the presence of nutritional deficiency in general.

Vitamin D is found in fish, fortified milk, and vitamin supplements which are discussed above. Surprisingly, two scoops of soy protein powder (one third cup) contain more vitamin D (35 %) of an adult's Minimal Daily Requirement than do eight ounces of fat free milk (just 25%).

But vitamin D is certainly no cure-all for diabetes, a multi-faceted disease for which diet, weight and exercise remain the focus of prevention and treatment, along in some cases with insulin and oral medications.

Grapefruit has also been causing excitement, but it is much too early to know if naringenin, grapefruit's compound that may help increase insulin sensitivity, will have any real benefits.

More importantly, people should know that substances in grapefruit can cause too high levels of statin drugs like Lipitor, widely used by diabetic patients for cholesterol control.

3. Fitness

Exercise is vital, but it should be simple, something you can do almost every day with a minimum of inconvenience, cost, or time taken from the other things you need or want to do. Elaborate equipment is not necessary, but a treadmill, stationary bike, or gym-type gadgets can certainly be used if you like. The important thing is to start.

Pace often, even while doing the most mundane things. Do a silly little step-step-step, like marching in place, as you cook or fold laundry or check the carburetor. The point is just to *move* at every opportunity. Every single step counts.

Walking is low-impact and works for most people. Aim for twenty to thirty minutes a day, almost every day, totaling at least two hours per week. In good weather it can be done outside, in a safe area like the mall, a parking lot, or the local school track. It can also be done indoors in a small space. Furniture can be moved to create a small ring or track. Do figure eights around two chairs, or any other routine that gets you moving. Play some music, it helps. Or have the TV on. (No, skip that; the TV distracts, and will stop you.) Walking with a buddy is also a good idea.

Just five minutes helps

Walking can also be done just five or ten minutes at a time; do that several times a day and the daily, accumulated benefit is just as healthful. Keep track; aim for a thirty minute daily tally.

Exercise of any type or duration is now considered a miracle "drug" for health and longevity.

If you must sit for work, just getting up and taking more breaks is also good for you. A study published in the European Heart Journal, January 12, 2011, reported that the *number* of breaks you take from sitting at your desk or on your sofa can make a big difference. Stand, stretch, move around as you straighten papers or talk on the phone or just pace a bit: breaks of as little as one minute can make a big health difference.

An amazing British study followed a large, multi-ethnic population to examine the correlations between total amount of time spent sitting and breaks taken, paying special attention to indicators of risk for diabetes, heart disease, and inflammatory processes that can play a role in atherosclerosis (blocked arteries).

Findings showed that prolonged periods of sitting, even among people who hit the gym two or three times a week, were associated with worsened cardio-metabolic function such as belly fat, lower levels of HDL ("good") cholesterol, higher triglycerides (blood fats), and higher levels of C-reactive protein (an important marker of arterial inflammation).

The study also found that, even in people who had to sit for long stretches, the more breaks they took, the smaller their belly fat and the lower the levels of their C-reactive protein and arterial inflammation.

Conclusion: Gym or no gym, the longer-sitters were healthier if they just took frequent breaks!

What else is great about walking?

Your leg muscles are the largest in your body. When you walk, your leg muscles help pump blood back to your heart. Since we spent so much time sitting, this pumping function of leg muscles prevents pooling and clotting of blood in your legs, and greatly helps circulation.

A report of the Mayo Clinic Proceedings, September, 2009, described a sixteen-year study of three thousand people, all either pre-diabetic or diabetic, with striking differences in mortality based on their physical fitness. Those who tired easily, as measured on an exercise treadmill, had a 50 percent higher mortality rate than those with high or even moderate exercise capacity. Additionally, people who were overweight or obese and physically unfit had more than double the mortality rate of those who were physically fit and of normal weight.

Becoming fit by regular exercise also lowers blood pressure, blood sugar, and bad cholesterol (LDL), while on the other hand it improves arterial function, inhibits clotting, decreases arterial plaque deposits and improves good cholesterol.

But what if walking is painful?

Arthritis affects more than half of people with type 2 diabetes, and becomes a barrier to getting more physically active.

It is a conflict, but one that can be overcome by doing aerobic exercise, strength training, and swimming or other forms of water exercise. Swimming defies gravity, so there aren't any jolts or painful pressure to sensitive joints. This is particularly helpful to those who have experienced degeneration of the joint cartilage, commonly seen in people who have type 2 diabetes which is often associated with obesity, a risk factor for diabetes. For many years the extra body weight has been an added strain on the weight-bearing joints.

Try, too, sitting and lifting hand weights, which weigh from one to five pounds. Yet another kind of easy-on-the-joints exercise is lying on your back on a soft surface and using resistance cords, or – here's a friend's clever idea: She filled a pillow case with bags of play sand, then sewed the pillow case shut, then lay on a soft surface on her back raising and lowering her six pound "pillowcase." She built up her arm strength, worked out with her "pillowcase" daily while dieting on 1600 calories a day – and she lost twenty-one pounds.

Now, even though she says her knee joints are "still shot," the mere fact that she weighs so much less has enabled her to "graduate" to walking, which she now does twice daily for fifteen minutes each time at a steady pace.

"The prevalence of arthritis is astoundingly high in people with diabetes," says Dr. John H. Klippel, president and CEO of the Arthritis Foundation. Dr. Klippel also speculates that obesity is a risk factor for both osteoarthritis and diabetes. "Many people with arthritis don't exercise because it hurts them. But they have to understand that if they exercise, it will actually reduce their pain and prevents the disease from progressing,"

If it hurts, still try to find a way. A healthier weight will place less pressure on your joints, particularly the knees. What a relief that would be, as opposed to being overweight which causes you to tire more quickly, tempting you to give up on your exercise program.

If your weight-bearing joints are in fairly good shape, consider exercise like boot camp: it will ache at first. Then you'll get stronger, develop endurance. As the weight comes off you will be able to exercise more vigorously. Your joints and whole body will feel better. In as little as six weeks you will feel like a brand new person, full of pep and positive energy.

Actually, you'll feel better faster than that. It's a gradual process, but it starts almost right away.

Before beginning any exercise regimen, first check with your doctor. Medication needs may also need adjustment by your doctor.

Speed up your metabolism?

Google the above and you'll got hundreds of thousands of hits. Mostly people trying to sell you something, most not even knowing what the word "metabolism" means.

Your thyroid rules metabolism, and sets the rate at which your muscles – repeat, *muscles* – turn sugar into energy (burn calories). No pill or magic drink can safely "speed up" that Basal Metabolic Rate.

You burn calories faster by having more muscles. And moving them.

Muscles are our machinery. Picture two men working out, hefting the same-weight barbells at the same rate. One is muscular, devoted to exercise, vigorous activity, and working out. The other is skinny and just starting (or his muscles are skinny under lots of fat). They're doing the exact same thing – but who is burning more calories? The muscular one. The muscular one burns more calories just walking down the street!

Our bodies are like cars: the bigger, heavier ones use more fuel. (Our "heaviness" refers only to our muscles.)

Now comes metabolism's bottom line: EVERYTHING breaks down to just one of three things: protein, fat, or sugar. And, "good carbs" break down to sugar just as inevitably as "bad" carbs.

The liver, our metabolism's Houston Control, stores only a certain amount of that sugar, depending on your activities. All excess sugar is converted...into...fat. And that bulge over the belly ("belly fat"), is, again, Poison Central because the fat gets *mainlined* right back into your bloodstream. Round and round. Carbs become sugar which becomes fat which re-enters the bloodstream as sugary-fatty yuck, inflaming and damaging your arteries on the way.

A bit more complicated than that, but within twenty-four hours, that's what it amounts to: Bad, Bad, Belly Fat! So keep it simple. Consider carbs and (unhealthy) fat as the same thing. For health and weight loss you want as little as possible of both in your diet.

Exercise, even moderate exercise, is the only real way to speed up your metabolism. Don't waste your money on frustrating gimmicks.

You won't need to eat carbs *or* saturated fat anymore just to not feel hungry.

Chapter Seven

EXCITING NEW INGREDIENTS

In case you've skipped the first part of the book to get right to the ingredients, recipes, and meal plans, this book's most important information is repeated here.

If you're just starting out or feeling hypoglycemic, have some orange juice or other "fast carbs" to get your glucose levels back up quickly. Simultaneously eat lean protein, which is your longest lasting fuel and will not spike your blood glucose. By the time your carbs have flashed and crashed, your protein will have kicked in and will keep you stabilized for hours. Keep snacking on our protein goodies to keep your blood glucose steady for longer and longer periods.

This chapter will introduce you to some new ingredients, and explain the huge health benefits of using them. For instance:

1. Why does the New Diabetes Diet omit whole grains?
- Because milled flaxseed is healthier than whole grains. One tablespoon (30 calories) contains no absorbable carbs and an astonishing three grams of fiber, which equals the dietary fiber in one slice of whole wheat bread, one-half cup of cooked brown rice, or one-half cup of cooked, chopped broccoli.
- Milled flaxseed also helps to lower blood sugar, and reduces the need for insulin or oral blood sugar lowering drugs. Flaxseed's viscous fibers inhibit the absorption of excess calories, reduce blood sugar reactions after meals, increase cell and tissue sensitivity to insulin, and help to regulate insulin secretion by the pancreas.
- Milled flaxseed contains large amounts of alpha linolenic acid, a plant-derived Omega-3 acid similar to the fatty acids found in salmon and tuna that help to lower blood pressure, blood triglycerides, and cardiovascular risk. It may also keep platelets from becoming sticky, thereby reducing the risk of heart attack, and further boosting heart health.
- Flaxseed's lignans are powerhouse antioxidants that help lower cholesterol, slow the aging process, prevent heart disease and cancer, and also slow complications of type 1 diabetes.

- Milled flaxseed provides *700 times more lignans* than whole grains or legumes.
- Two tablespoons (60 calories, a serving) of this miracle food provides 6,000 lignan antioxidants and 2,600 mg of Omega-3 fatty acids, along with 6 grams of protein, 0 grams of carbs, 6 grams of fiber, and 4.5 grams of heart healthy mono- and poly-unsaturated fat. That's an astonishing amount of health in one little serving.
- A final bonus is milled flaxseed's ability to substitute beautifully for margarine and butter, in a ratio of 3 to 1. That is, 3 tablespoons of flaxseed substitute for 1 tablespoon of butter or margarine. Recipes for pancakes and baked goods come out moist, delicious, and many times more healthy than those made with butter or margarine.

2. These recipes don't use butter or margarine

Butter tastes wonderful, but is hugely high in saturated fat which raises your LDL (bad) cholesterol, causes fatty cholesterol deposits inside your arteries and narrows them, which in turn causes clots, blockage, heart attack and stroke. This news about saturated fat is important for everyone, but for diabetics who are more vulnerable than non-diabetics to cardiovascular disease, it is vital.

What about those margarines aggressively advertised as "healthy?"

They're not.

Do a little experiment. Leave your margarine or buttery spread out for an hour, then look at it. Is it still solid? Probably. Because margarine must contain either saturated or hydrogenated/trans fat in order to be solid at room temperature. It's the old shell game. If the margarine doesn't contain *either* saturated fat or hydrogenated/trans fat (same thing), at room temperature it would be yellow soup.

Read food companies' websites competing for your dollars. If they tell you that their competition uses more trans fats, do they also tell you how much saturated fat they use? Or gleefully say "just 2 grams of saturated fat per tablespoon?" That's a lot, and most folks don't quit at one level tablespoon.

Canola and olive oils are best for sautéing. And milled flaxseed will produce wonderfully moist and tasty baked goods. It will be a surprise when your first batch of muffins or brownies come out. You'll be amazed, and delighted that you used the vastly healthier milled flaxseed.

3. No red meat either

Because of the saturated fat. That goes for trendy "grass fed beef" too (a classier kind of saturated fat?) Incidentally red meat, chicken, and fish all contain cholesterol – about 70 milligrams per 4 oz serving. What chicken and fish don't have is saturated fat. But we'll show you how to get the cholesterol out of them. It's a quick, easy trick.

4. Salt avoided too

These recipes don't need hypertension-causing salt since they include herbs and spices that pack a tasty punch, *and* have powerful antioxidant, anti-inflammatory, anti-cancer, and other health promoting properties. Most of these wonderful herbs and spices are easily found in your supermarket. They are very good medicine. Did you ever imagine that some of the most potent health-boosters might be in your kitchen cabinet instead of the drugstore?

5. Top antioxidant herbs and spices

Surprise: one teaspoon of cinnamon has *5 times* as many antioxidants as ½ cup of blueberries or a full cup (eight ounces) of pomegranate juice. And cinnamon has no calories or sugar.

For the treatment of diabetes, there's mounting evidence that cinnamon helps to regulate and lower blood glucose levels, and to prevent complications of diabetes. It also helps to lower cholesterol and – like milled flaxseed – cinnamon increases the natural production of insulin.

You're likely aware that you should eat dark-skinned fruits and vegetables like blueberries, strawberries, colored peppers, leafy greens, broccoli and eggplant. But recent studies show that certain herbs and spices deliver a much bigger antioxidant boost than those undeniably beneficial foods.

Below to the right is a list of the 10 top health boosting, antioxidant spices and herbs. Look how tiny amounts – *one teaspoon* – of the herbs and spices deliver so much compared to the list on the left of other antioxidant foods, which are measured per half cup. So sprinkle cinnamon on your berries; turmeric on your veggies; and oregano on this eating plan's protein-crust pizza. Now that's healthy!

Note: If you're wondering why garlic, said to have many health benefits, is not on the list it's because it contains only 83 ORAC units (antioxidants) per teaspoon.

ORAC units **per teaspoon**		ORAC units **per ½ cup**	
Cloves	15,720	Cocoa powder	32,000
Cinnamon	13,370	Acai berry	18,500
Oregano	10,005	(high in sugar)	
Turmeric	7,965	Dark chocolate	13,120
Cumin (seed)	3,840	(high in fat and sugar)	
Parsley	3,715	Blueberries	2,400
Basil	3,380	Strawberries	1,540
Sage	1,600	Apple	1,400
Mustard seed	1,465	Spinach, raw	1,260
Ginger	1,365	Raspberries	1,220
		Broccoli florets	900
		Red grapes	739

These top herbs and spices also share another wonderful benefit. Their anti-inflammatory power is commonly described as helping arthritis sufferers and people with other types of pain. But the bigger picture is their ability to reduce inflammation of the inner lining of the arteries (arterial inflammation) and neutralize LDL's ability to deposit fatty, sticky cholesterol, thus preventing atherosclerosis.

Arterial inflammation is both prevented and repaired by antioxidants. Otherwise, arterial inflammation leads to atherosclerosis, caused by fat particles from trans-fats and saturated fats such as red meat and high-fat dairy products; also from excess carbohydrates such as starchy vegetables, *all* kinds of flour, and *all* kinds or sugar – honey, brown sugar, dried fruit etc. These substances all end up as fat deposits.

But those amazing herb and spice antioxidants can hose down arterial inflammation.

6. Astonishing soy protein powder

Imagine a luscious fudge brownie containing 109 calories, 20 grams of protein, 4 grams of carbs, and more nutrients than a glass of fat-free milk *and* a slice of whole wheat bread combined. This amazing brownie and our other baked goods are possible because we've discovered how to completely substitute soy protein powder for flour.

The version of soy protein powder we use is the unflavored kind, since it adapts to the greatest variety of recipes. White, fluffy and flour-like, it is also special because it's the most pure protein, containing no fat, carbohydrates, sugar, or cholesterol. It can be purchased at most supermarkets, Trader Joes, and is also available on Amazon.com.

Soy helps to lower the risk of heart disease, breast cancer and prostate cancer. Recent research also offers hope that soy promotes bone health among post-menopausal women. The Federal Drug Administration (FDA) has enthusiastically endorsed soy, saying that 25 grams of soy protein daily help to lower LDL cholesterol, and to prevent complications of heart disease, cancer, and diabetes.

Another bonus: vitamins B6, B12, Niacin, Riboflavin, and Thiamin—the B vitamins found in whole grains – are present in much higher amounts in soy protein powder. Other soy powder nutrients are: vitamin D, the sunshine vitamin; selenium, an important antioxidant; iodine, which is essential for thyroid hormone manufacture; and iron, which helps to prevent anemia.

The charts below show the nutrition differences between fat-free milk and soy protein powder. Amounts represent all Minimum Daily Requirements:

SPP per 2 scoops serving:	Fat Free milk per 8 oz serving:
110 calories, 23 g protein, 0 carbs	86 calories, 8 g protein, 13 g carbs

Vitamin A.....................35%	Vitamin A......................0%
Vitamin B6...................35%	Vitamin B6 ....0%
Vitamin B12.................35%	Vitamin B12...................0%
Vitamin C....................35%	Vitamin C....................10%
Vitamin D....................35%	Vitamin D....................25%
Vitamin E.....................33%	Vitamin E ..,,,,,,,,,,,,,,,,,,.....0%
Vitamin K....................28%	Vitamin K...................... 0%
Calcium.......................30%	Calcium........................30%
Folic acid....................35%	Folic acid.......................0%
Iodine......................... 35%	Iodine...........................0%
Iron.............................50%	Iron..............................0%
Niacin.........................35%	Niacin...........................2%
Phosphorus.................37%	Phosphorus....................0%
Riboflavin...................35%	Riboflavin......................0%
Selenium....................29%	Selenium........................0%
Thiamin.......................35%	Thiamin........................0%

Soy may also protect men from their own human estrogen.

Males normally produce small amounts of estrogen as well as testosterone. But soy's phytoestrogens (weak estrogen from plants) may help by occupying estrogen receptor sites in the male body and blocking their human male estrogen, which has been associated with prostate cancer and other health issues.

7. Lots of Chocolate recipes...thanks to cocoa

Imagine a miracle substance that could help diabetes; boost your antioxidant levels; diminish the aging process (including of your skin); prevent viruses like flu and the common cold; lower your blood pressure; help prevent cancer, strokes and heart attacks; dilate clogged artery walls – *and* produce that endorphin-y good feeling that helps you stick to a diet, lose the weight that overwhelmingly causes those diseases. Researchers and drug companies have spent decades and billions searching for that magical substance, little suspecting that it was a kitchen staple all along.

Since these findings were announced in December of 2006, physicians are calling cocoa — the unsweetened, non-alkalinized kind — nothing less than a blockbuster drug. (Alkalinization, aka Dutch processed, destroys cocoa's antioxidants. Good brands of this pure cocoa are Hershey's, the little brown box in bakery aisles, and Trader Joes.)

Probably the most multi-tasking of all antioxidants, this superfood carries wellness powers surprisingly more far-reaching than those of other antioxidant foods. It has twice the antioxidants of the much-touted acai berry, which is high in sugar.

Cocoa's antioxidant, a new flavonol called epicatechin, releases a substance called nitric oxide from artery walls. (Epicatechin was only discovered and named in 2008, causing great excitement in scientific circles.)

Why all the excitement about nitric oxide? In a word: **vasodilation.** Nitric oxide dilates arteries in *seconds,* lowering blood pressure and allowing more oxygen and nutrients to reach every organ and tissue, including the heart, brain, kidneys, legs and feet. This helps to heal and prevent the complications of heart disease and strokes, Peripheral Arterial Disease, peripheral neuropathy, and retinal arterial disease.

Research published in the *Journal of the American College of Cardiology* provides substantial evidence that pure cocoa's flavonols greatly improve the health of narrowed blood vessels. "Patients who drank the high-flavonol cocoa for one month had their blood vessel function improve from severely impaired to normal. This research focuses on what's at the heart of the discussion on "healthy" chocolate – it's about cocoa flavonols, the naturally occurring compounds in cocoa in the prevention of cardiovascular complications in diabetic patients."

But – how to turn that pure cocoa into brownies, cookies, cakes, muffins and the rest? First mix it with soy protein powder. Then add a few other ingredients, including milled flaxseed. And then use a whole new technique for cooking and baking which you will find within these pages.

8. No "natural" sugar alternatives (which are really sugar)

We tell the truth about sugar, in all its forms. honey, dried fruit (crammed-with-sugar dates are popular), brown sugar, molasses and agave are all still sugar, just as much as that white stuff in the old sugar bowl. Your body does not know the difference. It converts all these "natural" members of the sugar family into the same blood glucose.

Then there's innocent-sounding fat-free evaporated milk, used in many diet and diabetic recipes. One 12 ounce can contains 45 grams of carbs – which equal over 11 teaspoons of sugar!

On labels, if the amount of sugar is listed below the carbs but is *indented,* that's okay. But if the sugar amount is *not* indented (a common trick), add the grams of carbs and the grams of sugar together, and then divide by 4. Your answer is the equivalent number of teaspoons of sugar you're really eating. (More info on the divide-by-4 rule is in Chapter 3, Common Diabetes Myths, under the heading **Eating too much sugar is what causes diabetes.**)

Below is a list of Sugars in Disguise. Besides nice flavor, they're all just sugar by another name. Your body has no translation for "natural." They all metabolize into blood glucose. Here's the list:

<u>Per Cup</u>:.........................<u>CALORIES</u>........ <u>grams of carbs (÷ 4 = # tsp sugar)</u>
Apple Sauce (unsweetened).......100...........25 grams or 6+ tsp sugar
Banana, mashed.................... 200..............28 grams or 7 tsp sugar
Blueberries, dried.................. 520..............128 grams or 32 tsp sugar
Cranberries, dried.................. 370..............26 grams or 6 ½ tsp sugar
Honey.................................1031..............278 grams carbs or 70 tsp sugar
Molasses.............................977..............252 grams carbs or 63 tsp sugar
Dates (dried, pitted)................503..............128 grams carbs or 32 tsp sugar
Raisins................................500..............98 grams carbs or 24 ½ tsp sugar

It's quite a jolt to realize that one cup of chopped dates contains 128 grams of carbs, which equal 32 teaspoons of sugar – which equals two thirds of a cup of sugar!

Make a healthier, better-tasting cake, brownie or muffin with soy protein powder, milled flaxseed and a good artificial sweetener. Do those ingredients sound not mouth-watering?

Wait, you'll see.

9. The safety of Splenda; info on other sweeteners

We like aspartame and love Splenda (sucralose). Supermarkets now carry their own, cheaper brands of Splenda; they're fine; same molecule. We've used both aspartame and sucralose for many years and have experienced no problems. They have decades-long track records and many, many studies in humans in many countries. Physicians have been calling Splenda a "godsend," but we still had questions, wrote to the government, and received responses from the following organizations: The National Institutes of Health, the National Heart, Lung, and Blood Institutes, the National Cancer Institute, and the National Institute of Child Health and Human Development. All vouch for Splenda. For more information, contact the FDA at 1-888-INFO-FDA.

There are, however, sweeteners that we don't use. They include Stevia, Truvia, agave, and sugar alcohols.

Stevia and Truvia: For many years the FDA refused to approve Stevia, an herb, because of its possible cancer-causing effects. Pro-stevians—and their lobby—argued that it's 1) natural and 2) has been used by South American natives for centuries, although no one knows how long or in what state of health those people lived. We found no years-long studies with control groups done on Stevia. And that, to us, is troublesome. Cancer can take years to develop, as with smoking.

But recently the FDA issued a "letter of no objection" regarding rebaudioside, a processed form of Stevia—but only the rebaudioside—as a Generally Recognized as Safe (or GRAS) substance. In other words, the FDA has not granted approval to Stevia itself, but says it "will not object" to food companies using rebaudioside. One of rebaudioside's brand names is Truvia.

For us, "generally recognized" and "will not object" isn't good enough, and still keeps Stevia and Truvia in a gray zone that does not inspire confidence. There have been hundreds of drugs and medical products given the okay by the FDA—Vioxx, IUDs, Hydroxycut, and Rezulin for example—only to be recalled a few years later amid reports of injury and death.

We only feel safe using products that have been tested and studied for many decades with, as physicians say, "no red flags."

Agave consists of 92% fructose, which is harmful to heart, kidneys, and other vital organs. Compare agave's fructose amount to that of High Fructose Corn Syrup, which contains "only" 55% harmful fructose. Fructose products have been added to hundreds of processed foods, beverages and – more ominously – so-called "diet yummies," telling people they can "cheat and eat" as much as they like. Fructose from any source, including agave, has been linked to insulin resistance, elevated LDL (bad) cholesterol and triglycerides, and central (belly) obesity, which is considered to be the most dangerous kind of obesity.

Sugar Alcohols: Sugar alcohols are one of the main sweeteners in commercial use today. Sugar alcohols are processed from sugar molecules. They are sold under the names sorbitol, mannitol, xylitol, lactitol, maltitol, and others ending in "ol."

Sugar alcohols still have most of the calories of sugar (2 to 3 calories per gram as opposed to 4 calories per gram of standard sugar), and they still affect your blood sugar levels. Their benefit is that they metabolize more slowly than regular sugar, so they hold off for a few minutes more before those need-sweets-again-crashes.

Unfortunately, many products containing sugar alcohols deceptively say they are "sugar free" or are marketed as "no sugar added." That is misleading. Sugar alcohols still break down to sugar, plus they often cause bloating, diarrhea, and gastric upset.

So are you wondering why, if Splenda and aspartame are so great, food manufacturers still use sugar alcohols?

Because only sugar, in one form or another, makes the cookie stiff, the gum bulky, or the candy solid at room temperature. Splenda and aspartame are fine in your coffee or no-fat yogurt or to bake with (Splenda), but they alone can't keep your cakes, muffins, and other baked goodies from falling apart. However, the food manufacturers don't know our secret techniques!

10. The final breakthrough

So far, we've discussed innovations like using soy protein powder to replace flour, milled flaxseed to replace butter and margarine, and Splenda to replace the many forms of sugar. But how do you hold all these ingredients together? Baking's bad boy old glue has always been heated sugar and egg yolks. How can you get around that?

The answer: fat-free white cheese. It's nearly tasteless, and when baked with other ingredients and then allowed to cool – it binds. Holds the muffins, brownies, and the rest together, keeping them just as moist and delicious as unhealthy yolks plus sugar.

This, actually, is the breakthrough we're most excited about. We call it No BEFS cooking: (no **B**utter/margarine, **E**gg yolks, **F**lour, or **S**ugar in *any* form.)

Rushed? This healthy treat takes 90 seconds in the microwave.

Try this recipe for a Chocolate Mighty Muffin – which only needs 90 seconds in the microwave and no cleanup! Each muffin contains 111 calories, 18 g protein, 1 g carb, 2.3 g mono- & polyunsaturated fat, 7,000 antioxidants (4,000 epicatechin and 3,000 lignan antioxidants), and 5 g dietary fiber (3 from the flaxseed, 2 from the cocoa) – more than in a cup of cooked oatmeal (3.7 g), or a slice of whole wheat bread (1.9 g)

Ingredients:
Cooking spray
1 scoop SPP
1 tbsp natural unsweetened cocoa
1 tbsp milled flaxseed
3 tbsp Splenda
½ tsp baking powder
3 tbsp water
2 tbsp liquid egg whites

Directions:
Spray inside of Pyrex measuring cup. In it mix all ingredients. Stir and blend well. Then scrape down the sides, gently pushing mixture down in cup.

Microwave for 90 seconds, cool slightly, and pop out.

That recipe is just a peek into a whole new way, and a whole new life. Good-bye to unnecessary carbs and blood sugar spikes. Good-bye too to worrying about what would be a "safe" snack. Hereafter you won't have to think so hard about what to eat, or work so hard to make "healthful food choices."

They're all here, including your fondest cravings, and they're very, very good for you.

But first, let's go shopping.

Food products this plan's recipes use extensively:

Cocoa: unsweetened and non-alkalinized. Good products are Hershey's (little brown box in bakery aisles) and Trader Joe's. Other choices of pure cocoa are available on Amazon.com, but be careful: some expensive, gourmet brands describe themselves as "unsweetened but Dutch processed," or "mildly Dutch processed." Those have zero or near zero health benefits. You're better off with the much cheaper two brands mentioned, or any others you can find of equal cost and purity. Hershey's is also on Amazon.com.

Milled Flax Seed: available at most supermarkets. Excellent brands are Bob's Red Mill (bobsredmill.com) and Hodgson's Mill (hodgsonmill.com/millled-flax-seed). Milled flaxseed is also available on Amazon.com.

Soy protein powder, unflavored: Pure unflavored soy protein powder is recommended since it is adaptable to all flavors and different kinds of recipes. It is available at most supermarkets, Trader Joes, and on Amazon.com. Sugared or honeyed "soy bars" and commercially flavored Smoothies containing sugar in any form are not recommended.

100% Liquid Egg Whites: Good brands are Papetti Foods, Wilcox and Organic Valley. There are many different brands, available in most supermarkets.

Yogurt, Greek style: Different brands depend on what region or country you live in. In the U.S. and Canada it is available in most supermarkets,

Tofu: extra firm is our favorite. Brands are House Foods, Nasoya, Mori-Nu, Wildwood and Woodstock. There are several consistencies of tofu, such as firm, soft, and "silky" soft. All are available in most supermarkets.

Fat Free Cheddar & American Cheese, both shredded and Singles. In the U. S. Stop & Shop has Fat Free Cheddar Singles, and Kraft has Fat Free Shredded Cheddar Cheese, available in supermarkets.

Fat Free White Cheese, shredded and Singles. The shredded form is used a lot in these recipes. In the U. S., the Stop & Shop brand has excellent Fat Free Singles, and Kraft has Fat Free Shredded white cheese. Other brands are also available in Canada and U.K. supermarkets.

Fat Free Sour Cream: Good brands are Breakstones, Hood, Knudsen, Naturally, and Tillamook. Available in most supermarkets.

Fat Free Cream Cheese: Available in most supermarkets.

Fat Free Ricotta: Good brands are Cremona, Sargento, Sorrento, and Crystal Farms.

Manhattan Clam Chowder, low sodium, excellent for quick and easy Cioppino and other soup-based recipes. Good brands are Progresso and Campbell's, which are in all supermarkets. Note: All commercially prepared soups contain salt; "low sodium" on the label is still pretty vague and not to be trusted. Read the labels.

Jell-O Sugar-Free Fat-Free Pudding & Gelatins: Our most-used pudding flavors are Chocolate and Vanilla. Among the sugar-free gelatins are: Lemon,

Orange, Black Cherry, Lime, Strawberry, Raspberry, Cherry, & more. Available in most supermarts.

Sugar Free Jams & Preserves: Flavors are: Strawberry, Apricot, Peach, Marmalade, Raspberry, Grape, Blackberry, Pineapple, Blueberry, Black Cherry, Peach, & Mint. Available in most supermarts.

Peanut Butter, sugar free and unsalted. Trader Joes Crunchy Unsalted is a great brand made from all natural, unblanched peanuts. Many of the best known commercial brands of peanut butter have salt and sugar added to them. So far, Trader Joes brand is the only one we've found that is both salt and sugar free.

Tang or Crystal Light Orange with Vitamin C: Both are available in supermarkets and on Amazon.com

Splenda: Local supermarkets carry cheaper brands of sucralose which are fine.

Aspartame: (Equal, Natrataste) are fine for sweetening beverages. Neither works for cooking or baking, however, since they respond poorly to heat.

Diet sodas: Okay if made with sucralose or aspartame

Pumpkin Pie filling in 15 ounce cans

For toppings: Fat Free, Sugar Free Reddi-wip. Other brands of frozen whipped topping have saturated fat or trans fats in them.

Dreamfields Low Carb Pasta 1/8 th the carbs of regular pasta and only 5 digestible carbs per serving, Available at most supermarkets or health food stores. Also dreamfieldsfoods.com or Amazon.com.

Shirataki tofu noodles and fettuccini: Comes packaged in a cool liquid and is stored in supermarket refrigerator sections next to the tofu. Rinse off its liquid well and mix with strong spicy flavors like tomato sauce. Available locally or at House-foods.com, Amazon.com, or Trader Joe's.

Log Cabin Sugar Free Maple Syrup: Contains sugar alcohols which affect some people with bloating and slight gastric distress. Use sparingly at first to see if it affects you. We love this product and experience no side affects.

Have on hand either fresh or frozen:

For most fruits and vegetables, frozen is just as nutritious and may even be more so than "fresh" because they're flash-frozen. They don't spend days in a truck or on a shelf, and, to be blunt, haven't been handled by many people before you get to them. There's also the matter of convenience. Most of us are pressed for time, and will be happy to have vegetables in the freezer that just need to be steamed, or tossed directly into soup, casseroles, or stews.

If the season permits, fresh fruit and vegetables are always nice and prettier to look at. But the season doesn't always permit, so feel assured that either way is okay. Another good thing about having fruits and vegetables in the freezer is that you don't have to worry about them spoiling. If you are buying frozen vegetables, look for them already cut or chopped for extra convenience. Here is a list:

Broccoli, fresh or frozen
Carrots, small already-peeled. Frozen or fresh in the fridge for snacks and salads
Carrots, large, frozen and sliced
Cauliflower, frozen
Onions, fresh
Peppers, red, yellow, orange (wash, cut, and store frozen in plastic freezer bags)
Soybeans (Edamame), frozen and shelled
Spinach, fresh or frozen spinach (frozen and chopped is excellent)
Strawberries, blueberries: fresh or frozen

Poultry:
Turkey, deli sliced, low salt, fat-free (refrigerate)
Chicken breasts, skinless & boneless: frozen
Ground turkey, fat free, frozen

Regular staples
Tuna, 5 oz. cans in water, no salt added
Salmon, 6 oz cans Alaskan wild, skinless & boneless, no salt added
Beans, canned: pinto, red, black and kidney
Tomatoes, canned and diced, no salt added
Tomatoes, canned and crushed, no salt added
Tomato paste, 6 oz & 12 oz cans
Tomatoes, sun-dried in olive oil
Chicken broth: powdered, fat-free, no sodium
Soups: Salt-free Minestrone, Manhattan, Lentil

Oils and condiments
Dijon mustard
Red wine vinegar
Balsamic vinegar
Olive oil
Canola oil
Cooking spray, 0 calories from olive or canola oil
Walnuts, chopped baking pieces
Spices: cinnamon, oregano, basil, garlic, tarragon, black pepper, dill, ginger
Diet sodas: okay if made with sucralose, Aspartame

"I shall now attempt to eat a diet lunch consisting of one leaf of lettuce lightly seasoned with… a quart of Mayonnaise." Garfield

Chapter Eight

THE NEW DIABETES DIET 6-WEEK EATING PLAN:

To help people with diabetes and pre-diabetes take control of their lives, and for anyone concerned with eating healthy and/or losing weight
(All recipes listed in Index)

Week One, Day 1

Breakfast
2 Brownies, baked .... 148 calories
1 medium sized orange, sliced into wedges .... 60 calories
Hot cocoa or chocolate drink .... 20 calories

Lunch
Turkey & veggies in all-protein Tortilla Wrap .... 173 calories
Berry Intense Smoothie.. 104 calories

Midafternoon Snack
Medium-sized apple, sliced, sprinkled with cinnamon & 2 tbsp walnut baking
piece.. 125 calories

Dinner
Tuna Niçoise.. 346 calories
Diet Drink (made with sucralose or aspartame)

Dessert
Fruit Chocolate Sundae .... 147 calories
Fudge Sauce .... 20 calories
Cappuccino with Cinnamon .... 10 calories

Evening snack
Homemade Protein Bread slice, cream cheese, & strawberry jam ... 118 calories
Hot cocoa or chocolate drink .... 20 calories
2 Chocolate cookies... 60 calories

Total: 1351

Week One, Day 2

<u>Breakfast</u>
Banana Nut Mighty Muffin .... 226 calories
1 medium orange, sliced into wedges.................................... 60 calories
Hot cocoa or chocolate drink .... 20 calories

<u>Lunch</u>
Inside Out Sandwich .... 325 calories
Mocha Latte .... 120 calories

<u>Midafternoon snack</u>
Chocolate Smoothie .... 80 calories
3 Chocolate cookies .... 90 calories

<u>Dinner</u>
MLA Tex Mex Chicken .... 325 calories
Diet Drink

<u>Dessert</u>
Chocolate Mousse with whipped topping .... 64 calories
Cappuccino with Cinnamon .... 10 calories

<u>Evening snack</u>
Grilled cheese sandwich .... 244 calories

Total: 1564

Week One, Day 3

Breakfast
"TofOats" Cinnamon Flaxseed Cereal .... 160 calories
Banana nut bread, 1 slice .... 110 calories
Green tea and sweetener .... 10 calories

Lunch
Tuna Salad in burger roll .... 222 calories
Strawberry Smoothie .... 195 calories

Midafternoon Snack
Anytime Blondie .... 122 calories
Hot cocoa or chocolate drink .... 20 calories

Dinner
3 Pancakes .... 294 calories
Sauteed apples and almonds .... 152 calories

Dessert
Pumpkin Pie with whipped topping .... 100 calories

Evening snack
Apricot Mighty Muffin .... 121 calories
*Crystal Light Vitamin C Orange drink .... 5 calories
*Has all the C vitamin of o.j. minus o.j.'s 26 g carbs

Total: 1511

Week One, Day 4

Breakfast
Chocolate 'n Nuts Mighty Muffin .... 191 calories
1 medium orange, sliced into wedges.................................. 60 calories
Herbal tea .... 0 calories

Lunch
2 Jam 'n nuts rollups .... 195 calories
1 medium-sized orange sliced into wedges .... 60 calories
Green tea with sugar substitute

Midafternoon snack
2 Baked Cinnamon Muffins .... 202 calories
Chocolate Smoothie .... 80 calories

Dinner
Salmon Dijon .... 232 calories
Crudités .... 155 calories
Vinaigrette .... 60 calories

Dessert
Orange Sherbet with fudge sauce and strawberries .... 60 calories
Cappuccino with cinnamon .... 10 calories

Evening snack
Sweet roll with cream cheese & jam .... 153 calories
Hot cocoa or chocolate drink .... 20 calories

Total: 1478

Week One, Day 5

Breakfast
Egg & Cheese Sandwich .... 259 calories
Hot cocoa or chocolate drink .... 20 calories

Lunch
Tartar Sandwich .... 225 calories
Green tea with sugar substitute

Midafternoon snack
Anytime Blondie .... 122 calories
Crystal Light Vitamin C Orange drink .... 5 calories

Dinner
2 slices Pizza .... 322 calories
Mixed Greens Salad .... 142 calories

Dessert
Vanilla Mighty Muffin with fudge frosting .... 131 calories

Evening snack
Hamburg roll .... 177 calories
2 fat-free cheese slices .... 60 calories
Hot cocoa or chocolate drink .... 20 calories

Total: 1483

Week One, Day 6

<u>Breakfast</u>
Cinnamon 'n Nuts Hotcake ....276 calories
Green tea and sweetener..0 calories

<u>Lunch</u>
4 Quesadillas .... 236 calories
1 medium-sized orange sliced into wedges...60 calories
Green tea with sugar substitute

<u>Midafternoon snack</u>
Strawberry Protein Smoothie ....195 calories
1 Baked Chocolate Mighty Muffin ....111 calories

<u>Dinner</u>
MLA Chicken Stroganoff ....184 calories
Crispy Green Beans .... 107 calories
Diet Drink

<u>Dessert</u>
Anytime Fudge Brownie with walnuts ....135 calories
Cappuccino .... 10 calories

<u>Evening snack</u>
15 whole roasted almonds (unsalted, 7 calories each) ....105 calories
Cocoa drink... 40 calories

Total: **1459**

Week One, Day 7

Breakfast
2-pancake "sandwich" with 4 tbsp ff cream cheese, 3 sliced strawberries & 2 tbsp chopped walnuts...314 calories
Hot cocoa or chocolate drink ....20 calories

Lunch
Grilled cheese sandwich, dressed up...248 calories

Midafternoon snack
Berries, Lime & Chocolate Muffin Parfait ....215 calories

Dinner
Turkey Burger on Roll with sliced onions and tomatoes ....330 calories
Baby Spinach salad .... 110 calories
Coffee with fat free milk and sugar substitute...............................10 calories

Dessert
Key Lime Pie .... 89 calories
Cappuccino with 2 tbsp fat free whipped topping and cinnamon.......15 calories

Evening snack
Banana Nut Bread, slice ....110 calories

Total: **1461**

Week Two, Day 8

Breakfast
"TofOats" Cinnamon Flaxseed Cereal...160 calories
1 small banana, sliced .... 90 calories
Green tea and sweetener .... 0 calories

Lunch
Egg & Cheese Sandwich .... 259 calories
Green tea with sugar substitute

Midafternoon snack
Berry Intense Smoothie ....104 calories
1 slice banana nut bread...110 calories

Dinner
MLA Chili .... 230 calories
Mixed Green Salad .... 142 calories

Dessert
Warm Fudge Nut Cake with whipped topping................................. 201 calories
Cappuccino with fat free milk and cinnamon .... 10 calories

Evening snack
Sweet roll .... 123 calories
Hot cocoa or chocolate drink...20 calories

Total: **1449**

Week Two, Day 9

Breakfast
Banana Nut Mighty Muffin .... 226 calories
Hot cocoa or chocolate drink .... 20 calories

Lunch
Turkey & Veggies in Tortilla .... 173 calories
Berry Intense Smoothie.. 104 calories

Midafternoon snack
Anytime Fudge Brownie with walnuts......................... .... 135 calories
Hot cocoa or chocolate drink..….....20 calories

Dinner
Chicken Tarragon with Sun-dried Tomatoes & walnuts ....…....290 calories

Dessert
Chocolate Berry Parfait ....…...................................…....185 calories
Cappuccino...….....10 calories

Evening snack
Cinnamon 'n Nuts Hotcake .... 276 calories

Total: **1439**

Week Two, Day 10

Breakfast
2 Anytime Fudge Brownies with walnuts ……………….…..…..…. 270 calories
Green tea and sweetener…………………………………………...…0 calories

Lunch
Hotcake Sandwich with jam and fruit …….…………………....…….236 calories
Hot cocoa or chocolate drink …………………………………………..20 calories

Midafternoon snack
Medium-sized apple, sliced, sprinkled with cinnamon & 2 tbsp walnut baking
pieces ……………………………………………………………….. 125 calories
Chocolate Drink………………………………………………………… 20 calories

Dinner
Ratatouille …………………………………………………...….256 calories
Cheddar biscuit ……... ……………………………………………… 153 calories

Dessert
Lemon Sherbet with fudge sauce & strawberries …………………....…60 calories
Cappuccino with Cinnamon …………………………………………… 10 calories

Evening snack
2 Baked Brownies with fudge frosting …………….……………...……178 calories
Hot Cocoa or Chocolate drink…………………………………………… 20 calories

Total: **1348**

Week Two, Day 11

Breakfast
Cinnamon 'n Nuts Hotcake ....276 calories
Herbal tea..0 calories

Lunch
Tuna Salad Wrap with Healthy Mayo substitute...........................160 calories
Strawberry Smoothie...195 calories

Midafternoon snack
Chocolate Mighty Muffin..101 calories
Green tea with sugar substitute

Dinner
Shrimp Scampi and sun-dried tomatoes ....184 calories
Baby Spinach salad ....110 calories

Dessert
Anytime Blondie with chocolate ice cream................................212 calories
Cappuccino ....10 calories

Evening snack
1 medium-sized avocado..165 calories
1 cheddar biscuit..153 calories

Total: **1571**

Week Two, Day 12

<u>Breakfast</u>
Pancake rolled with 4 tbsp ff cream cheese & 2 tbsp chopped walnuts......198 calories
Hot cocoa or chocolate drink ....20 calories

<u>Lunch</u>
4 Quesadillas .... 236 calories
Chocolate Mighty Muffin..111 calories
Diet Drink

<u>Midafternoon snack</u>
Cookie Berry Parfait ....152 calories
Hot or Cold Chocolate Drink...20 calories

<u>Dinner</u>
Quiche, 2 servings ....240 calories
Mixed Greens Salad with toasted almonds ....130 calories

<u>Dessert</u>
Fruit Chocolate Sundae...76 calories

<u>Evening snack</u>
2 Cinnamon Mighty Muffins .... 202 calories
Vanilla Frosting for muffin ....26 calories

Total: **1411**

Week Two, Day 13

Breakfast
Banana Nut Mighty Muffin .... 226 calories
Green tea and sweetener .... 0 calories

Lunch
Tartar salad sandwich ....245 calories
Berry Intense Smoothie ....104 calories

Midafternoon snack
3 Fudge Truffles ....90 calories
Mocha Latte ....120 calories

Dinner
Crispy Omelet..217 calories
Cheesy broccoli .... 43 calories

Dessert
Brownie Ice Cream Sundae . ...177 calories
Cappuccino with Cinnamon ....10 calories

Evening snack
2 slices Banana Nut Bread... 220 calories
Hot cocoa ....20 calories

Total: **1472**

Week Two, Day 14

Breakfast
2 Brownies, baked .... 148 calories
1 small banana, sliced .... 90 calories
Herbal tea... 0 calories

Lunch
Grilled Cheese Sandwich .... 244 calories
Berry Intense Smoothie.. 104 calories

Midafternoon snack
Anytime Fudge Brownie with walnuts...................................... 135 calories
Chocolate smoothie...80 calories

Dinner
MLA Chicken Florentine ....231 calories
Crispy Green Beans .... 107 calories

Dessert
Lime & chocolate chip sherbet ....83 calories
Cappuccino with Cinnamon ....10 calories

Evening snack
15 whole roasted almonds (unsalted, 7 calories each)........................105 calories
3 Chocolate Protein cookies...96 calories
Cocoa drink.. 20 calories

Total: **1453**

Week Three, Day 15

Breakfast
Pancake rolled with 4 tbsp ff cream cheese, 3 sliced strawberries & 2 tbsp chopped walnuts..216 calories
Hot cocoa or chocolate drink ....20 calories

Lunch
Inside Out Sandwich... 325 calories
Diet drink

Midafternoon snack
Chocolate Smoothie .... 80 calories
3 Chocolate cookies .... 96 calories

Dinner
Salmon cake .... 141 calories
Tartar Sauce .... 40 calories
Mixed greens salad with toasted almonds ....130 calories

Dessert
Mighty Vanilla Muffin with fudge frosting .... 131 calories
Cappuccino with Cinnamon ....10 calories

Evening snack
2 slices bread, cream cheese, & strawberry jam ....206 calories
Hot cocoa...20 calories

Total: **1415**

Week Three, Day 16

<u>Breakfast</u>
Cinnamon 'n Nuts Hotcake .... 276 calories
Green tea and sweetener...…..........0 calories

<u>Lunch</u>
Tuna Salad Wrap with Healthy Mayo substitute ....…...….........120 calories
2 Cinnamon Mighty Muffins ....…202 calories
Diet drink

<u>Midafternoon snack</u>
Anytime Blondie ....…..............122 calories
Crystal Light Vitamin C Orange..…...5 calories

<u>Dinner</u>
Cioppino ....…......215 calories
Roll, sliced .... 177 calories

<u>Dessert</u>
Anytime Fudge Brownie with walnuts.. 135 calories
Cappuccino with Cinnamon ....…....10 calories

<u>Evening snack</u>
Marmalade jam 'n nuts rollup ………......….............................…195 calories

Total: **1457**

Week Three, Day 17

Breakfast
Chocolate & Nuts Mighty Muffin ....….................191 calories
Hot cocoa or chocolate drink ....…......20 calories

Lunch
Pancake rolled w 4 tbsp fat-free cream cheese, 3 sliced strawberries & 2 tbsp chopped
walnuts...216 calories
Strawberry Smoothie...195 calories

Midafternoon snack
Lemon Berry Crunch with Fudge Sauce ....184 calories
Green tea with sweetener

Dinner
Tuna Nicoise .... 346 calories

Dessert
Chocolate Berry Parfait .... 185 calories
Cappuccino with fat free milk .... 10 calories

Evening snack
2 Apricot Mighty Muffins .... 121 calories
Crystal Light Orange drink .... 5 calories

Total 1473

Week Three, Day 18

<u>Breakfast</u>
"Tof-Oats" Cinnamon Flaxseed Cereal.............…..............................160 calories
1 small banana, sliced .... 90 calories
Green tea and sweetener .... 0 calories

<u>Lunch</u>
Tuna Salad in burger roll …………..222 calories
Strawberry Smoothie .... 195 calories

<u>Midafternoon snack</u>
Berries, Lime & Chocolate Muffin Parfait ………………....……................... 215 calories

<u>Dinner</u>
Tex Mex Chicken .... 325 calories

<u>Dessert</u>
2 Chocolate Crepes ....……..............140 calories
Fudge Sauce filling, 4 tbsp ....…...........40 calories
Cappuccino with Cinnamon .... 10 calories

<u>Evening snack</u>
15 whole roasted almonds (unsalted, 7 calories each).........................105 calories
Cocoa drink…………………………………………………...……..............…....20 calories

Total: **1522**

Week Three, Day 19

Breakfast
2 Chocolate Mighty Muffins .... 222 calories
1 orange sliced into wedges.. 60 calories
Herbal tea... 0 calories

Lunch
Turkey & veggies Tortilla .... 173 calories
Chocolate & Nuts Mighty Muffin,.. 191 calories
Diet drink

Midafternoon snack
Berry Intense Smoothie... 75 calories
Small banana.. 90 calories

Dinner
Salmon Risotto .... 328 calories
Diet Drink

Dessert
Anytime Blondie topped with vanilla ice cream .... 200 calories
Cappuccino with Cinnamon .... 10 calories

Evening snack
Vanilla Mighty Muffin with fudge frosting .... 131 calories

Total: **1480**

Week Three, Day 20

Breakfast
Eggs & cheese in Tortilla Wrap ……………………………….……133 calories
Hot cocoa or chocolate drink …………………………………..……..20 calories

Lunch
Jam 'n nuts rollup………………………………….……...........195 calories
Green tea with sugar substitute

Midafternoon snack
Cinnamon 'n Nuts Hotcake ……………..……………………....….. 276 calories
Diet drink

Dinner
3 Pancakes………………………………………………...…....294 calories
Sauteed Apples and Almonds …………………………………….…152 calories

Dessert
Fruit Chocolate Sundae ……………………………………….....147 calories
Cappuccino with Cinnamon………………………………...……...10 calories

Evening snack
1 medium-sized avocado……………………………………….......170 calories
1 cheddar biscuit ……………………………………………....153 calories
Crystal Light Vitamin C Orange drink……………………………..5 calories

Total: **1555**

Week Three, Day 21

Breakfast
2 Chocolate Mighty Muffins .... 222 calories
Herbal tea .... 0 calories

Lunch
4 Quesadillas ....236 calories
Berry Intense Smoothie .... 104 calories

Midafternoon snack
Sweet roll with cream cheese & jam .... 153 calories
Diet drink

Dinner
2 slices Pizza... 322 calories
Mixed Greens Salad ....142 calories

Dessert
Lemon Sherbet with fudge sauce & strawberries ....60 calories
Cappuccino .... 10 calories

Evening snack
Cinnamon 'n Nuts Hotcake ....276 calories

Total: **1525**

Week Four, Day 22

<u>Breakfast</u>
"Tof-Oats" Cinnamon Flaxseed Cereal..160 calories
1 small banana...90 calories
Green tea and sweetener...0 calories

<u>Lunch</u>
Inside Out Sandwich ....325 calories
Mocha Latte ....120 calories

<u>Midafternoon Snack</u>
Anytime Fudge Brownie with walnuts ....135 calories
Crystal Light Vitamin C Orange drink..5 calories

<u>Dinner</u>
Turkey Burger on a roll with sliced onion and tomatoes ....330 calories

<u>Dessert</u>
Vanilla Mighty Muffin with fudge frosting ....131 calories
Cappuccino with Cinnamon ....10 calories

<u>Evening snack</u>
Grilled cheese sandwich ....244 cal

Total: 1550

Week Four, Day 23

Breakfast
Chocolate & Nuts Mighty Muffin.. 191 calories
Hot cocoa or chocolate drink .... 20 calories

Lunch
Tuna Salad in burger roll .... 222 calories
Strawberry Smoothie .... 195 calories

Midafternoon Snack
2 Anytime Blondies .... 244 calories
Diet drink

Dinner
MLA Chili .... 230 calories
Baby Spinach Salad .... 110 calories

Dessert
Orange Sherbet with fudge sauce & strawberries .... 60 calories
Cappuccino .... 10 calories

Evening snack
Sweet roll with cream cheese & jam .... 153 calories
Hot cocoa .... 20 calories

Total: **1455**

Week Four, Day 24

<u>Breakfast</u>
Cinnamon 'n Nuts Hotcake...276 calories
Hot cocoa or chocolate drink ....20 calories

<u>Lunch....</u>
Tartar Sandwich ....225 calories
Green tea with sugar substitute

<u>Midafternoon Snack</u>
Medium-sized apple, sliced, sprinkled with cinnamon & 4 tbsp walnut baking pieces..205 calories

<u>Dinner</u>
Salmon Dijon ....232 calories
Crudités ....155 calories
Vinaigrette sauce .... .60 calories

<u>Dessert</u>
Chocolate Berry Parfait ....152 calories
Cappuccino...10 calories

<u>Evening snack</u>
Eggs & cheese in Tortilla Wrap ....133 calories
Hot cocoa or chocolate drink..20 calories

Total: **1488**

Week Four, Day 25

Breakfast
2 Chocolate Mighty Muffins .... 222 calories
1 orange cut into wedges .... 60 calories
Green tea and sweetener .... 0 calories

Lunch
Turkey & veggies in Tortilla Wrap .... 173 calories
Cinnamon Mighty Muffin .... 101 calories
Green tea with sugar substitute

Midafternoon snack
Strawberry Protein Smoothie .... 195 calories
1 small banana .... 90 calories

Dinner
MLA Chicken Stroganoff .... 184 calories
Crispy Green Beans .... 107 calories

Dessert
Key Lime Pie .... 89 calories
Cappuccino .... 10 calories

Evening snack
Plain hotcake .... 98 calories
Hot Cocoa or Chocolate drink .... 20 calories

Total: **1349**

Week Four, Day 26

Breakfast
2 Anytime Blondies... 244 calories
Hot cocoa or chocolate drink .... 20 calories

Lunch
Grilled cheese sandwich .... 258 calories
Berry Intense Smoothie..104 calories

Midafternoon snack
Lemon Berry Crunch with Fudge Sauce .... 184 calories
Green tea with sweetener

Dinner
Cioppino..215 calories
Mixed Greens salad ....142 calories

Dessert
Fruit Chocolate Sundae .... 76 calories
Cappuccino with Cinnamon .... 10 calories

Evening snack
Apricot Mighty Muffin .... 121 calories
Hot cocoa or chocolate drink..20 calories

Total: **1394**

Week Four, Day 27

<u>Breakfast</u>
Banana Nut Mighty Muffin ....226 calories
Herbal tea.. 0 calories

<u>Lunch</u>
Tuna Salad in burger roll ....222 calories
Berry Intense Smoothie,...104 calories

<u>Midafternoon snack</u>
Cookie Berry Parfait ....152 calories
Hot or Cold Chocolate Drink..20 calories

<u>Dinner</u>
Chicken Tarragon with Sun-dried Tomatoes & walnuts ....290 calories
Mixed greens salad .... 142 calories

<u>Dessert</u>
Lemon Sherbet with fudge sauce & strawberries ....60 calories
Cappuccino ....10 calories

<u>Evening snack</u>
2 Anytime Blondies ....244 calories

Total: **1470**

Week Four, Day 28

Breakfast
1 Chocolate & Nuts Mighty Muffin.. 191 calories
1 Clementine... 60 calories
Green tea and sweetener .... 0 calories

Lunch
Egg & Cheese Sandwich .... 259 calories
Berry Intense Smoothie.. 75 calories

Midafternoon snack
Cinnamon 'n Nuts Hotcake .... 276 calories
Green tea with sugar substitute

Dinner
Ratatouille .... 256 calories
Sweet roll .... 123 calories

Dessert
Mighty Vanilla Muffin with fudge frosting ....…....131 calories
Cappuccino with Cinnamon ….......................................…...10 calories

Evening snack
5 walnuts and 5 almonds (unsalted)...…....100 calories
Hot Cocoa or Chocolate drink.. 20 calories

Total: **1501**

Week Five, Day 29

Breakfast
"TofOats" Cinnamon Flaxseed Cereal…………....………………......…160 calories
1 small banana, sliced ....…… 90 calories
Herbal tea..…… 0 calories

Lunch
Inside Out Sandwich ....…… 228 calories
Diet drink

Midafternoon snack
Orange Berry Crunch with Fudge Sauce ....…… 184 calories

Dinner
Quiche, 2 servings ....…… 240 calories
Mixed Greens Salad with toasted almonds ....…… 130 calories

Dessert
Warm Fudge Cake with whipped topping ....…… 201 calories
Cappuccino with fat free milk...…… 10 calories

Evening snack
Grilled cheese sandwich ....…… 244 calories
Hot cocoa or chocolate drink ....…… 20 calories

Total: **1507**

Week Five, Day 30

Breakfast
Mighty Banana 'n Nuts Muffin…………………………………….....226 calories
Green tea and sweetener……………………………………………0 calories

Lunch
Tartar salad sandwich……………………………………………… 245 calories
Strawberry Protein Smoothie ……………………………………… 205 calories

Midafternoon snack
3 Fudge Truffles ………………………………………………… 90 calories
Mocha Latte ……………………………………………………… 100 calories

Dinner
Avocado Salad …………………………………………………… 380 calories

Dessert
Lime & chocolate chip sherbet ………………………………… 115 calories

Evening snack
Anytime Fudge Brownie w walnuts ……………………………… 135 calories
Hot Cocoa or Chocolate drink……………………………………… 20 calories

Total: **1516 calories**

Week Five, Day 31

Breakfast
"TofOats" Cinnamon Flaxseed Cereal..160 calories
1 small banana, sliced..90 calories
Hot cocoa or chocolate drink .... 20 calories

Lunch
Grilled Cheese Sandwich, dressed up..........................…......248 calories
Berry Intense Smoothie .... 75 calories

Midafternoon snack
Anytime Fudge Brownie ....…..135 calories
Hot cocoa or chocolate drink...40 calories

Dinner
MLA Chicken Florentine .... 231 calories
Crispy Green Beans .... 107 calories

Dessert
Chocolate Berry Parfait .... 185 calories
Cappuccino with fat free milk... 10 calories

Evening snack
Cinnamon Mighty Muffin.. 101 calories
Vanilla Frosting ....…....26 calories

Total: **1428**

Week Five, Day 32

<u>Breakfast</u>
2-pancake "sandwich" with 4 tbsp ff cream cheese, 3 sliced strawberries & 2 tbsp chopped walnuts..314 calories
Hot cocoa or chocolate drink .... 20 calories

<u>Lunch</u>
Inside Out Sandwich ....228 calories
Mocha Latte ....100 calories

<u>Midafternoon snack</u>
Chocolate Smoothie .... 90 calories
4 Chocolate protein cookies.. 136 calories

<u>Dinner</u>
Salmon Risotto ....328 calories

<u>Dessert</u>
Orange Sherbet with fudge sauce & strawberries ....60 calories

<u>Evening snack</u>
Vanilla Mighty Muffin with fudge frosting ....131 calories
Hot Cocoa or Chocolate drink...20 calories

Total: **1427**

Week Five, Day 33

Breakfast
Cinnamon 'n Nuts Hotcake ....276 calories
Hot cocoa or chocolate drink .... 20 calories

Lunch
4 Quesadillas...236 calories
Mocha Latte ....100 calories

Midafternoon snack
2 Baked Chocolate Mighty Muffins .... 222 calories
Crystal Light Vitamin C Orange drink...................................5 calories

Dinner
MLA Chili .... 230 calories
Mixed Greens salad.. 142 calories

Dessert
Key Lime Pie .... 89 calories

Evening snack
Slice Banana Nut Bread ....110 calories
Hot Cocoa or Chocolate drink.. 20 calories

Total: **1450**

Week Five, Day 34

Breakfast
Banana Nut Mighty Muffin .... 226 calories
Green tea and sweetener.. 0 calories

Lunch
Tuna Salad Wrap with Healthy Mayo substitute .... 120 calories
Berry Intense Smoothie... 104 calories

Midafternoon snack
Anytime Blondie .... 122 calories
Chocolate Smoothie ....80 calories

Dinner
Cioppino .... 215 calories
Roll, sliced .... 177 calories

Dessert
Warm Fudge Cake with whipped topping .... 201 calories
Cappuccino with fat free milk.. 10 calories

Evening snack
Strawberry jam 'n nuts rollup .... 195 calories

Total: **1450**

Week Five, Day 35

<u>Breakfast</u>
2 Apricot Mighty Muffins ....242 calories
Hot cocoa or chocolate drink .... 20 calories

<u>Lunch</u>
Grilled cheese sandwich ....258 calories
Berry Intense Smoothie .... 75 calories

<u>Midafternoon snack</u>
Berries, Lime & Chocolate Muffin Parfait .... 215 calories
Green tea with sweetener

<u>Dinner</u>
Tex Mex Chicken..325 calories
Diet Drink

<u>Dessert</u>
Fruit Chocolate Sundae... 147 calories
Cappuccino with Cinnamon ....10 calories

<u>Evening snack</u>
Sweet roll with cream cheese & jam ....153 calories

Total: **1445**

Week Six, Day 36

<u>Breakfast</u>
2 Chocolate Mighty Muffins .... 222 calories
1 orange cut into wedges.. 60 calories
Decaff coffee with fat free milk and artificial sweetener .... 10 calories

<u>Lunch</u>
Turkey & veggies in Tortilla Wrap .... 179 calories
Berry Intense Smoothie.. 75 calories

<u>Midafternoon snack</u>
Lemon Berry Crunch with Fudge Sauce .... 184 calories
Green tea and sweetener

<u>Dinner</u>
2 slices Pizza... 322 calories
Mixed Greens salad .... 142 calories

<u>Dessert</u>
Lemon Sherbet with fudge sauce & strawberries................................ 60 calories
Cappuccino .... 10 calories

<u>Evening snack</u>
Mighty Vanilla Muffin .... 116 calories
Black Cherry Frosting for muffin .... 26 calories

Total: **1406**

Week Six, Day 37

Breakfast
Egg & Cheese Sandwich .... 259 calories
Herbal tea.. 0 calories

Lunch
Tuna Salad in burger roll .... 222 calories
Berry Intense Smoothie,.. 104 calories

Midafternoon snack
Medium-sized apple, sliced, sprinkled with cinnamon & 2 tbsp walnut baking
pieces .... 125 calories

Dinner
Ratatouille .... 256 calories

Dessert
2 Anytime Fudge Brownies with walnuts .... 270 calories

Evening snack
Hamburg roll .... 177 calories
2 fat-free cheese slices.. 60 calories
Cocoa drink... 20 calories

Total: **1493**

Week Six, Day 38

Breakfast
Banana Nut Mighty Muffin ....226 calories
Hot cocoa or chocolate drink .... 20 calories

Lunch
Inside Out Sandwich ....228 calories
Diet drink

Midafternoon snack
Berry Intense Smoothie..…....75 calories
3 Chocolate protein cookies ....…..94 calories

Dinner
Chicken Tarragon with Sun-dried Tomatoes & walnuts....................…....290 calories
Baby Spinach salad .... 110 calories

Dessert
Mighty Vanilla Muffin with fudge frosting ....…........….....131 calories
Cappuccino with whipped topping and cinnamon..........,,...............10 calories

Evening snack
Grilled cheese sandwich ....…..244 calories
Hot cocoa or chocolate drink .... 20 calories

Total: **1448**

Week Six, Day 39

Breakfast
Cinnamon 'n Nuts Hotcake ....276 calories
Green tea and sweetener...0 calories

Lunch
Egg & Cheese Sandwich,...259 calories
Green tea with sugar substitute

Midafternoon snack
Strawberry Protein Smoothie .... 205 calories
1 small banana..90 calories

Dinner
Turkey Burger on a roll with sliced onion and tomatoes ....330 calories

Dessert
Lime & chocolate chip sherbet ....83 calories
Cappuccino ....10 calories

Evening snack
2 Apricot Mighty Muffins .... 242 calories
Crystal Light Vitamin C Orange drink.......................................5 calories

Total: **1500**

Week Six, Day 40

Breakfast
"Tof-Oats Cinnamon Flaxseed Cereal.. 160 calories
Hot cocoa or chocolate drink .... 20 calories

Lunch
Tuna Salad in burger roll .... 222 calories
Strawberry Smoothie .... 90 calories

Midafternoon snack
Lemon Berry Crunch with Fudge Sauce .... 184 calories
Green tea and sweetener

Dinner
Salmon Dijon .... 232 calories
Crudités ....155 calories
Vinaigrette sauce ....60 calories

Dessert
Warm Fudge Cake with whipped topping .... 201 calories
Cappuccino with fat free milk.. 10 calories

Evening snack
1 sweet roll.. 123 calories

Total: 1457

Week Six, Day 41

Breakfast
Banana Nut Mighty Muffin..226 calories
1 medium-sized orange cut into wedges...60 calories
Hot cocoa or chocolate drink ....20 calories

Lunch
Turkey & veggies in Tortilla Wrap ....179 calories
Berry Intense Smoothie..75 calories

Midafternoon snack
Medium-sized apple, sliced, sprinkled with 3 sliced strawberries, cinnamon, & 4
tbsp walnut baking pieces.. 226 calories

Dinner
Quiche, 2 servings ....240 calories
Mixed Greens Salad with toasted almonds ....130 calories

Dessert
Orange Sherbet with fudge sauce & strawberries .... 60 calories
Cappuccino with fat free milk..10 calories

Evening snack
Strawberry jam 'n nuts rollup ....195 calories

Total: **1421**

Week Six, Day 42

<u>Breakfast</u>
Chocolate & Nuts Mighty Muffin ....191 calories
1 medium orange...60 calories
Green tea and sweetener...0 calories

<u>Lunch</u>
Tartar Sandwich .... 265 calories
1 small Clementine .... 60 calories
Strawberry Smoothie .... 195 calories

<u>Midafternoon Snack</u>
Anytime Blondie .... 122 calories
Hot cocoa or chocolate drink .... 40 calories

<u>Dinner</u>
3 Pancakes .... 294 calories
Apples & Almonds, Sauteed.. 152 calories

<u>Dessert</u>
Pumpkin Pie with whipped topping..................................... 100 calories
Cappuccino with Cinnamon .... 10 calories

<u>Evening snack</u>
Apricot Mighty Muffin .... 121 calories
Crystal Light Orange drink...5 calories

Total: **1615**

Chapter Nine

THE RECIPES

First... quick cooking tips

- MLA means Make Lots Ahead. So you can cook just 2-3 times a week, freeze leftovers, then thaw and heat for quick, healthy meals next time
- Have Pyrex cups on hand in the 1 and 2 cup sizes. They are great for fast, microwavable meals and snacks. Plus no cleanup!
- All baked treats, pancakes & tortillas can be made in quantity, frozen, then thawed or microwaved for readymade portable meals and snacks.
- Cinnamon, milled flaxseed, spices, and cocoa are used *a lot* for their spectacular antioxidants and – in the case of cinnamon and flaxseed – their ability to lower blood sugar and cholesterol, and increase the natural production of insulin.
- Soy protein powder cooks at slightly lower temperatures than flour. Medium-high heat is best for cooking pancakes, salmon cakes etc.

Chocolate Mighty Muffin

A health powerhouse made with cocoa, milled flaxseed, and the purest protein. Plus it takes only 90 seconds in the microwave - and no cleanup!

Serves One
Cooking spray & one 1-cup size Pyrex cup
1 scoop Soy Protein Powder
1 tbsp natural unsweetened cocoa
1 tbsp milled flaxseed
3 tbsp Splenda
1/2 tsp baking powder
3 tbsp water
2 tbsp liquid egg whites

Spray interior of measuring cup.

Compare to:
* One cup of cooked oatmeal contains 150 calories, 25 g carbs & 2 g fiber.
* A slice of whole wheat bread contains 128 calories, 24 g carbs & 2 g of fiber.

In it mix all ingredients, using soup spoon to stir and blend well.
Scrape batter back down the cup's sides, gently pushing mixture down in cup.
Raise cup and gently slam down to get out any air bubbles.
Microwave for 90 seconds, cool slightly, and pop out.

Per Serving
111 calories, 1 g carb, 18 g protein, 5 g fiber, 2 g monounsaturated fat, & 20,000 antioxidants (8,000 epicatechin + 12,000 Omega-3 lignan antioxidants)

Turkey & veggies in all-protein Tortilla Wrap

If you have tortillas already made, this grab 'n run lunch or snack takes seconds to make.
Recipe makes one serving

all protein tortilla (recipe follows)
2 teaspoons mustard
¼ cup fat free shredded cheddar cheese
2 slices low sodium deli turkey
fresh baby spinach, diced tomato & onion

Spread mustard on tortilla.
Sprinkle shredded cheese over mustard, stopping 1" from edge.
Microwave for 20 seconds or till cheese melts.
Remove & quickly lay on turkey slices and veggies.
Roll up like a jellyroll. Place with fold side down; cooling cheese will seal wrap.

Per Serving
173 calories, 30 g protein, 2 g carbs, 3 g monounsaturated fat, and 5,143 lignan antioxidants (from the tortilla's flaxseed, one of the richest sources of Omega-3 fatty acids for cardiovascular health).

All-protein Tortillas
Most "healthy" store-bought tortillas still pack carbohydrates. These tortillas are mega healthy with no carbs!
Recipe makes seven servings.

Cooking spray
2/3 cup Soy Protein Powder
3 Tbsp milled flaxseed
3 Tbsp Splenda
1 cup liquid egg whites
2/3 cup water (batter should come to 2 cups)

In a small bowl combine all ingredients, stirring to get lumps out.
Mist a wide skillet and the tip of a spatula with cooking spray.
Heat misted skillet on medium heat for just under a minute.
Use large serving spoon (equals about ¼ cup) to pour in first tortilla's batter.

Tilt the pan with one hand and with the other use the back of the spoon to quickly spread the batter into a wider circle.

Cook for 60-90 seconds. Loosen edges with the spatula, flip the tortilla, and cook the second side for 45-60 seconds.

Remove skillet from heat and re-spray between tortillas.

To speed the process you can have 2 skillets going at once.

Per Serving
61 calories, 11 grams protein, 0 g carbs, 3 g monounsaturated fat, and 5,143 lignan antioxidants

Berry Intense Smoothie

This frothy delight contains calcium, more than half your Vitamin C and one quarter of your Vitamin A daily requirements.
Makes one serving

1/2 cup canned mandarin oranges, well drained
4 strawberries
1/2 teaspoon powder of Orange sugar-free Jello gelatin
4 oz fat-free Greek yogurt
1/2 cup diet orange soda, or ½ cup Orange Crystal Light

Combine first four ingredients in blender. Add diet drink and blend until smooth.

Per Serving
104 calories, 11 g protein, 15 g carbs

Banana Nut Mighty Muffins

90 seconds in the microwave, healthier than most meals, and no clean up.
Walnuts, like flaxseed, are high in fiber, antioxidants and Omega-3 fatty acids.
Cinnamon contains 13,370 antioxidants per teaspoon.
Recipe makes one serving

cooking spray and one 1-cup size Pyrex cup
1 scoop Soy Protein Powder
1 tbsp milled flaxseed
1 ½ tsp cinnamon
1 pinch each nutmeg & ginger
½ tsp baking powder
1 tbsp + 1 tsp Splenda
½ small, ripened banana
1 tbsp water
2 tbsp liquid egg whites
2 tbsp walnut baking pieces

Spray inside of measuring cup. Into it put the soy protein powder, milled flaxseed,
spices, baking powder, and Splenda. Combine well.
Mash banana right in the cup, blending with dry ingredients.
Add water, egg whites, and walnuts. Mix all.
Scrape and spoon batter back down in cup.
Microwave for 90 seconds, cool slightly, and pop out.

Per serving
**226 calories, 11 g carbs, 19 g protein, 5 g fiber, 2 g monounsaturated fat, 1 g
saturated fat, and 32,545 antioxidants**

Inside Out Sandwich

Surprise, the protein's on the outside! Make your own Homemade Protein Bread (it's easy, no yeast or waiting), pile salad on the inside and enjoy a tasty, filling meal.
Makes one serving

2 slices protein bread (recipe follows)
1 1/2 tbsp mustard
1 1/2 tbsp vinaigrette
Arugula and baby spinach
1/4 cup shredded coleslaw
sliced onion
sliced tomato

Spread mustard on both bread slices. Set aside, mustard side up.
Toss salad with vinaigrette and place on one bread slice.
Cover with second bread slice, mustard side down.
Cut in half and serve.

Per Serving
325 calories, 37 grams protein, 3 grams carbs, 7 g fiber, and 6, 405 antioxidants

Homemade Protein Bread
"Healthy! Natural!" read many bread labels. But besides tons of carbs, their ingredients can include High Fructose Corn Syrup, calcium dioxide, ethoxylated mono and diglycerides, sodium steroyl lactylate, ammonium phosphate, ammonium sulfate, ammonium chloride, calcium proprionate, preservatives/chemicals "to maintain freshness/retard spoilage" and natamycin, a mold inhibitor.
This bread is pure health, can serve for any meal or snack, and *contains no* *carbs.*
Makes one 8" loaf (16 slices) Recipe makes 16 servings

Cooking spray
3 cups Soy Protein Powder
1/4 cup milled flaxseed
1 1/3 cups Splenda
1 Tbsp baking powder

2 ½ cups egg whites
1 cup water

Preheat oven to 400 °F. Mist 8"x4" baking loaf pan with cooking spray.
Mix protein powder, milled flaxseed, Splenda and baking powder.
Separately mix egg whites and water. Add to dry ingredients and blend well.
Ease batter into loaf pan, using moistened fingers to neaten top. Raise loaf pan
and let it slam back down to remove any air bubbles.
Mist top of loaf with cooking spray.
Cover loosely with an aluminum foil tent and bake for 35 minutes. Remove foil
and bake uncovered for another 9-10 minutes, or until top turns golden. Cool
before slicing. Keep refrigerated for maximum freshness.

Per Serving
**Each slice contains 88 calories, 18 g protein, 0 g carbs, 2 g fiber, & 3,000 lignan
antioxidants**
Optional fillers:
- 2 tbsp fat-free cream cheese: 10 calories, 2 g carbs, 0 g total fat, 4 g protein.
- 2 tbsp sugar-free preserves: 20 calories, 10 g carbs, 0 g total fat, 0 g protein
- 2 tbsp peanut butter (sugar & salt free): 190 calories, 7 g carbs, 3 g fiber,
  14 g monounsaturated fat, 2 g saturated fat, 7 g protein

Parmesan Herb Bread

A savory variation of the regular protein bread, for any sandwich, meal or snack.

Makes one 8" loaf (16 slices)

Cooking spray
3 cups Soy Protein Powder
1/4 cup milled flaxseed
1 1/3 cups Splenda
1/4 cup grated parmesan cheese
1/2 tsp black pepper
1 Tbsp + 1 tsp powdered oregano
1 Tbsp powdered garlic
1 Tbsp baking powder
2 ½ cups egg whites
1 ¼ cup water

Preheat oven to 400 °F. Mist 8"x4" baking loaf pan with cooking spray.
Combine protein powder, milled flaxseed, Splenda, cheese, spices and baking powder.
Mix egg whites and water separately, then add to dry ingredients and blend well. Ease mixture into pan, using moistened fingertips to neaten top.
Mist top of loaf with cooking spray. Cover loosely with aluminum foil tent and bake for 35 minutes.
Remove foil and bake uncovered for another 9-10 minutes, or until top turns golden. Cool before cutting. Keep refrigerated for maximum freshness.

Per serving (1 slice): 97 calories, 19 g protein, 0 g carbs, 3 g fiber, & 4,017 antioxidants

Mocha Latte

Save calories and money with this healthier alternative.
Recipe makes one serving

1 cup heated fat-free milk
1 Tbsp unsweetened cocoa
1 Tbsp Splenda
1 tsp instant coffee, regular or decaf
1 tbsp fat-free Reddi-Wip*
1/2 teaspoon ground cinnamon

Place milk, cocoa, Splenda and coffee in a blender and blend. Or, put the mixture in a clean, empty container and shake it. Top with whipped topping and sprinkled cinnamon.

Per Serving
120 calories, 8 grams protein, 18 grams carbs, 1 g fiber, and 8,000 antioxidants**
* Frozen whipped topping contains trans fats. Reddi-Wip is recommended
** from the cocoa

Chocolate Smoothie

Luscious, low cal and so healthy.
Makes one serving

1/2 cup fat-free Greek yogurt
2 tbsp unsweetened cocoa
2 tbsp Splenda or Equal
1 cup Diet Coke

In a measuring cup, mix first 3 ingredients.
Pour in half of Diet Coke. Mix, watch it froth.
Add remaining Diet Coke; mix until smooth.

Per Serving
80 calories, 12 g protein, 5 g carbs, 2 g fiber, and 16,000 antioxidants

Chocolate cookies: delicious, filling snacks with 5 g protein and only 1/3 g carb each!

Recipe makes 12

Cooking spray
1/2 cup SPP
1/4 cup (4 tbsp) natural unsweetened cocoa
1/4 cup (4 tbsp) milled flaxseed
3/4 cup Splenda
1/2 cup + 1 tbsp water
1/4 cup liquid egg whites

Preheat oven to 350 degrees. Cover cookie sheet with parchment paper & mist with cooking spray.
Mix together protein powder, cocoa, milled flaxseed, & Splenda.
Separately mix water and egg whites, then add to dry ingredients and blend well.
Drop 12 cookies by soupspoon onto parchment paper. Use moistened fingertips to even out and flatten slightly.
Bake for 9 minutes. Cool slightly; remove from cookie sheet onto wire rack to cool completely.

Per Serving
Each cookie 30 calories, 5 g protein, less than 1 g carb (1/3 g), 1.6 g fiber, 1/2 g polyunsaturated fat, 6,667 antioxidants (both epicatechin and Omega-3 lignan)

"TofOats" Cinnamon Flaxseed Cereal

A small amount of Cheerios for crunchiness, combined with cinnamon and tofu.
(1/4 cup of Cheerios has 5 grams of carbs.)
Recipe makes one serving

1/5 pkg (about 1" slice) extra firm tofu
1/4 cup Cheerios
2 teaspoons cinnamon
1 tbsp milled flaxseed
Splenda or aspartame to taste
1/4 cup fat free skim milk

Chop up tofu in cereal bowl. Mix with Cheerios. Sprinkle with cinnamon, flaxseed, and sweetener Add milk.

Per Serving
160 calories, 14 g protein, 7 g carbs, 5 g fiber, 70 mg sodium, and 38,740 antioxidants from the cinnamon and flaxseed.

Tuna Salad in All-Protein Burger Roll

First, tuna salad
Made with Healthy Mayo Substitute (first 3 ingredients), this recipe gives you half the calories and no saturated fat.
Makes two servings

1/4 cup non-fat Greek yogurt
1/4 tsp powder of Sugar-Free Jell-o Vanilla pudding
1/8 tsp powder of Sugar-Free Jell-o Lemon gelatin
1 5 oz can Solid White Albacore Tuna (in water, salt free, well drained)
1/4 cup chopped onions
1/4 cup chopped celery
Baby spinach
1 tomato, sliced
2 All Protein Burger Rolls, sliced (recipe follows)

Mix together the yogurt, vanilla and lemon powder.
Drain tuna liquid completely. Combine tuna, onions, and celery with yogurt mixture.
Place tuna mixture on bottom halves of each roll. Top with spinach and sliced tomato.
Place remaining half of each roll on top and serve.

Per serving
222 calories, 40 g protein, 4 g carbs, and 10,502 antioxidants

Hamburg Rolls
Fill these with salad, peanut butter and sugar-free preserves, fat free cream cheese, anything – the protein's on the outside!
Makes 4 rolls

Cooking spray
1 1/2 cups Soy Protein Powder
2/3 cup Splenda
2 tbsp milled flaxseed
1 tsp baking powder
1 tsp garlic
1 tsp oregano
1/4 tsp black pepper
1 1/4 cup liquid egg whites
1/2 cup water

Preheat oven to 400. Mist parchment-covered baking tray with cooking spray.
Combine the soy, Splenda, milled flaxseed, baking powder, and spices.
Add egg whites and water; mix well.
With moistened hands form batter into 4 balls, place on cookie sheet, and flatten slightly.
Spray tops with cooking spray and bake for 12-13 minutes, or until tops turn golden. Remove from oven, cool, and slice.

Per Serving
177 calories, 36 g protein, 0 g carbs, and 9,502 antioxidants.

Strawberry Smoothie

Filling, tasty, and more nutritious than most meals (a hamburger has 12 g protein),
Makes one serving

1/2 cup fat-free milk
1/2 cup fat free yogurt
1 scoop soy protein powder
1/2 cup strawberries (frozen is ok)
1 Tbsp Splenda or aspartame, or to taste
1/2 cup diet Sprite

Blend milk, yogurt, protein powder, strawberries and sweetener in blender.
Stir in diet soda and serve.

Per Serving
195 calories, 27 g protein, 13 g carbs & 1,540 antioxidants

Anytime Blondies uses the No BEFS technique: no **B**utter/margarine, **E**gg yolks, **F**lour, or **S**ugar in any form (honey, dried fruit, brown sugar, etc.) This multi-breakthrough recipe is an example of three new baking techniques: 1) substitute milled flaxseed for butter and margarine; 2) use soy protein powder to replace flour; 3) replace baking's old glue – sugar and egg yolks – with fat-free, nearly tasteless white cheese to *bind* the ingredients. The result brings zero guilt, mega health goodies. A win win!

Anytime Blondies, great for snacks or portable meal replacement bars

Makes twenty servings.

Cooking spray, pastry brush
3 cups Soy Protein Powder
1/4 cup milled flaxseed
1 3/4 cups Splenda
3 tbsp cinnamon
2 tsp ginger, or to taste
2 tsp nutmeg, or to taste
3 cups cold water
1 oz pkg Jell-o Sugar-Free Vanilla Pudding
1 3/4 cup liquid egg whites
2 Tbsp vanilla extract
1 cup chopped walnuts
1 cup shredded fat-free mozzarella (white) cheese
3 tbsp Apricot sugar-free preserves
1 more tbsp cinnamon

Preheat oven to 350°F. Spray *both* 9x13 inch baking pan and a high-sided skillet.
In the skillet combine the Soy Protein Powder, flaxseed, Splenda, and spices. Start to gently heat these dry ingredients on low heat.
In a large bowl, add cold water slowly to the Jell-o powder, stirring most lumps out. Add liquid egg whites and vanilla extract to the pudding. Stir, and then add whole pudding mixture to dry ingredients in skillet.
Raise heat to medium, mixing all ingredients together.
Add nuts and cheese. Stir until cheese is melted and completely blended in.
Microwave sugar-free apricot preserves in small bowl for one minute or until melted.

Working next to sink with a thin stream of lukewarm water running, spoon batter from skillet into baking pan. Moisten palms to spread and "neaten" batter in pan.

Use pastry brush to "paint" melted fruit preserves over top of batter.

Sprinkle on more cinnamon (and nuts, if desired. Press nuts down into surface.)

Bake for 26 minutes. Cool before cutting, which allows the cheese to re-bind.

Per Serving : 122 calories, 16 g protein, less than 3 g carbs, less than 1 g saturated fat, and 2,674 antioxidants

Chocolate & Nuts Mighty Muffin

Another delight of just 90 seconds in the microwave - and no cleanup!
Makes one serving

Cooking spray
1 scoop Soy Protein Powder
1 tbsp unsweetened cocoa
1 tbsp milled flaxseed
3 tbsp + 2 tsp Splenda
1/2 tsp baking powder
3 tbsp + 1/4 tsp water
2 tbsp liquid egg whites
2 tbsp walnut baking pieces

Spray inside of Pyrex measuring cup. Mix all ingredients in it and stir well.
Spoon-scrape down the sides, gently pushing batter back down in cup.
Microwave for 90 seconds, cool slightly, and pop out.

Per Serving
191 calories, 20 g protein, 2 g carb, 2.3 g monounsaturated fat, 1 g saturated fat, 7,500 antioxidants, and 6 g fiber.

Jam 'n Nuts Rollup

If you have pancakes already made in the fridge, this treat will take just seconds to make. Crunchy delicious!

1 World's Healthiest Pancake (recipe next page)
2 tbsp shredded fat-free mozzarella (white) cheese
2 tbsp sugar-free apricot preserves
2 tbsp chopped walnut pieces
1/2 tsp cinnamon or to taste

Sprinkle one pancake with shredded cheese, stopping at about 1" from the edge.
Dot and spread fruit preserve over the cheese.
Sprinkle walnuts over pancake's center
Sprinkle all with cinnamon
Microwave on regular setting for 1 minute, then remove and roll pancake tightly like a jellyroll.
Place with seam side down. Cheese cools fast and will bind the rollup.

Per Serving
195 calories, 18 g protein, 13 g carbs, 1 g saturated fat & 3 g monounsaturated fat
* Other sugar-free preserves include strawberry, marmalade, cherry, grape, and blueberry.

World's Healthiest Pancakes

Make stacks of these, freeze extras, and heat them for anytime. They can be meals or rolled or folded into all kinds of snacks.
Makes six servings.

Cooking spray
1 cup Soy Protein Powder
1 teaspoon baking powder
4 Tbsp Splenda
2 egg whites (1/3 cup)
1 1/4 cups fat-free milk
1/4 cup water
2 Tbsp canola oil
Optional: For more delicate, crepe-like pancakes add a bit more water to batter.

Combine the protein powder, baking powder and Splenda. Add egg whites, milk, water, and *one* tablespoon of the oil. Mix batter well.
Mist tip of a spatula and the back of a large serving spoon with cooking spray.
Pour second teaspoon canola oil into pan and swirl around.
With the skillet on medium heat, pour in about 1/4 cup of batter.
Tilt the pan and use the back of the spoon to quickly spread batter into a wider circle, 6-7 inches in diameter.
Cook about 1 minute, loosen edges with the spatula, and flip. The second side cooks more quickly.
To speed the process you can have two skillets going at once.
Remove the skillet(s) and re-mist with cooking spray between pancakes.

Per Serving
98 calories, 15 g protein, 3 g carbs and 2 g monounsaturated fat

Sauteed Apples and Almonds

Almonds contain almost no carbs and are very heart healthy. They also contain more calcium than any other nut, and are a great source of vitamin E: one small handful provides 70 percent of E's recommended daily allowance.
Makes four servings.

Cooking spray
1/2 cup slivered almonds
3 medium-sized apples, unpeeled
2 tbsp cinnamon

Wash and cut apples into wedges, leaving skin on (that's where the antioxidants are).
In ungreased skillet, toast almonds on medium heat, stirring occasionally, until they turn golden. Set aside.
Mist skillet with cooking spray.
On medium-high heat, fry the apples, sprinkling them with cinnamon as you stir and turn them.
When the apples look golden, lower heat, add toasted almonds, and serve.

Per Serving
152 calories, 17 g carbs, 4 g protein and 19,605 antioxidants

Anytime Fudge Brownies (walnuts optional)

Fudgey and luscious for snacks or portable meal bars.
Recipe serves 20.

Cooking spray
3 cups Soy Protein Powder
1 3/4 cups Splenda
1/4 cup unsweetened cocoa
1/4 cup milled flaxseed
3 1/4 cups cold water
2 one oz pkg Jell-o Sugar Free Chocolate Pudding
1 3/4 cup liquid egg whites
1 tbsp vanilla extract
1 cup fat-free shredded mozzarella (white) cheese
*Optional: ½ cup chopped walnuts

Preheat oven to 350°F. Spray *both* 9x13 inch baking pan and a high-sided skillet (for easier cleanup).
In the skillet combine the Soy Protein Powder, Splenda, cocoa, and flaxseed. Start to heat gently on low heat.
In a bowl add water gradually to the chocolate pudding powder, stirring most lumps out.
Add egg whites and vanilla, stir again, then add whole pudding mixture to dry ingredients in skillet.
Raise heat to medium.
As batter heats add cheese and stir until it melts and blends in completely. Add walnuts too if desired.
Working by sink with thin stream of water running, push heated batter into baking pan. Use wet hands to push and smooth batter down in pan. Ok if surface "puddles."
Bake for 26 minutes.
Cool before cutting, which allows the cheese to re-bind.

Per Serving
Without walnuts each brownie contains: 109 calories, 20 grams protein, 4 g carbs, 3 g fiber, 1 g monounsaturated fat, and 1,866 antioxidants.
With walnuts each contains: 135 calories, 21 g protein, 5 g carbs, 5 g fiber, 2,140 antioxidants, less than 1 g saturated fat, .3 g monounsaturated fat, and 2 g polyunsaturated fat

Eggs & Cheese Sandwich

Fast and easy if you've already got the bread made.
Makes one serving.

Cooking spray
1/4 cup liquid egg whites
1/4 cup shredded fat-free cheese
garlic & pepper to taste
1 tsp dried oregano
2 slices Homemade Protein Bread

Spray skillet with cooking spray and preheat to medium-high heat.
Pour eggs and cheese together into pan, sprinkle with spices, and scramble until cheese is melted and egg looks done.
Spoon scrambled egg mixture onto one bread slice, close the sandwich, and cut in half.
Serve warm, or carry and re-heat.

Per Serving
259 calories, 53 g protein, 2 carbs, and 13,007 antioxidants (from the oregano and the milled flaxseed in the bread).

Hotcake Sandwich with jam and fruit: Three minutes in the microwave, your favorite jam with berries, and no cleanup! Makes one serving.

Cooking spray
1/4 cup Soy Protein Powder
1/2 tsp baking powder
1 tbsp + 1 tsp Splenda
1 tsp cinnamon
2 tbsp egg whites
1/3 cup fat-free milk
1 tsp canola oil
2 tbsp sugar-free preserves*
4 tbsp blueberries and sliced strawberries

Spray inside of one 4-cup Pyrex measuring cup. In it spoon all ingredients together except preserves and fruit.
Spoon batter back down the sides. Raise cup and slam it gently down to get any air bubbles out. Microwave 3 minutes. Pop out onto absorbent paper towel for a moment to take up any extra steam. Cut in half like an English muffin. On one half spread preserves and arrange fruit. Close and serve.
*Sugar-free preserves per 2 tbsp serving: 20 calories, 10 g carbs, 0 g total fat, 0 g protein

Per Serving: 236 calories, 31 g protein, 21 g carbs, 2 g monounsaturated fat, and 1,350 antioxidants

Hot Cocoa or cold Chocolate Drink

This is tops for your health. See Ch 7, #7 and find the word, "vasodilation." Pure cocoa's antioxidant, epicatechin, is a drug. Probably, like all drugs, its amazing effects last for hours.

2 tbsp unsweetened, non-alkalinized cocoa
2 tbsp Splenda
1 cup water, more or less, depending on desired consistency*
Optional: 2 tbsp whipped topping (Fat-free Reddi-wip**, per 2 tbsp, has 5 calories, 2 g carbs, 0g total fat, and 0g protein.)

Mix together the unsweetened cocoa and Splenda. Stir with hot or cold water. Same formula for any quantity: Equal amounts of unsweetened cocoa and Splenda, plus water to the desired consistency.
Idea: keep a container full in fridge, ready to just shake and pour.

*There is evidence that milk inhibits the absorption of antioxidants.
** Frozen whipped topping not recommended since it contains trans fats.

Per serving: 20 calories, 1 g protein, 2 g carbs, 4 g fiber, and 16,000 epicatechin antioxidants

Cinnamon 'n Nuts Hotcake

An any-meal powerhouse, this provides over half your daily requirement of heart-healthy Omega-3 fatty acids from both the flaxseed and the walnuts.
Makes one serving.

Cooking spray
1/4 cup Soy Protein Powder
1 tbsp milled flaxseed
1/2 tsp baking powder
1 tsp cinnamon
2 tbsp chopped walnut baking pieces
1/4 cup Splenda
2 tbsp egg whites
1/3 cup fat-free milk

Spray inside of 4-cup Pyrex measuring cup. In it spoon together and mix all ingredients.
Spoon down the sides of cup to "neaten."
Microwave 3 minutes. Pop out and lay on absorbent paper towel to take up extra steam. Serve warm or freeze for ready snacks.

Per Serving
276 calories, 32 g protein, 7 g carbs, 5 g fiber, 1 g saturated fat, 4 g monounsaturated fat, & 14,507 antioxidants

Tuna Salad Wrap with healthy mayo substitute

This combines three recipes: flourless all-protein tortillas, tuna salad, and healthy mayonnaise substitute.
Makes one serving.

1 Protein Tortilla
1 tbsp Healthy Mayonnaise Substitute (recipe next page)
2 pieces lettuce
¼ cup tuna salad

Spread Healthy Mayonnaise Substitute across tortilla.
Place lettuce on the tortilla and tuna salad down the center, stopping 2" from each end.
Fold bottom of tortilla up over the salad. Then fold the sides over like closing a book, and tuck the top in.

Per Serving
160 calories, 20 grams protein and 4 grams carbs

Healthy Mayonnaise Substitute

This is pretty close to mayonnaise and so worth it. Mayo labels saying "80% Less Fat Than Real Mayonnaise" mean that 20% saturated fat is still there.
Makes two servings of 1/4 cup each

1/2 cup fat-free Greek yogurt
1/2 tsp powder of Jell-O Sugar-Free Vanilla pudding
1/4 tsp powder of Jell-O Sugar-Free Lemon gelatin

In a small bowl mix all the ingredients.

Per Serving
30 calories, 5.5 grams protein, 1.5 grams carbs, 0 g of saturated fat.

Tuna Salad

A healthier new take on an old favorite with zero saturated fat.
Makes four servings.

1/2 cup plain non-fat yogurt
1/2 tsp powder of Sugar-Free Jell-o Vanilla pudding
1/4 tsp powder of Sugar-Free Jell-o Lemon gelatin
2 5 oz cans Solid White Albacore Tuna (in water, salt-free)
1/2 cup chopped onions and celery
1/2 cup cherry tomatoes, cut in half
Boston lettuce leaves

Mix the first three ingredients together.
Mix in the tuna, onions, and celery.
Add tomatoes last, gently folding in.
Divide salad and serve on bed of lettuce

Per Serving
88 calories, 17 grams protein and 1 gram carb

Quesadillas

Gooey cheesy classic in carb-free tortillas. The whole quesadilla contains 352 cal, 59 g protein, 10 g carbs, 0 g total fat, and 10,286 lignan antioxidants.
Makes six servings.

Cooking spray
2 protein tortillas
1/2 cup diced scallions
1/2 cup diced onions
1/4 cup cherry tomatoes, halved
1 cup fat-free shredded cheddar cheese.

Preheat oven to 450 degrees F.
Mist one side of both tortillas with cooking spray. Set one aside.
Place the other tortilla, sprayed side down, on an ungreased baking sheet.
Top it with the vegetables and cheese mixed together.
Cover with second tortilla, sprayed side down. Mist top too with cooking spray.
Bake for 10 minutes or until golden brown. Cool slightly, then cut into six wedges.

Per Serving
59 calories, 10 grams protein, 2 grams carbs, 1 g mono unsaturated fat and 1,714 lignan antioxidants

Cookie Berry Parfait

Makes one serving

2 tbsp blueberries
3 strawberries, sliced
1/2 tsp powder of sugar-free Black Cherry Jello gelatin
4 oz non-fat sugar-free yogurt
2 chocolate protein cookies

Line dessert cup with fruit; microwave 40 seconds.
Mix black cherry powder with yogurt.
Pour yogurt mixture onto warmed fruit and top with crumbled chocolate cookies

Per Serving
152 calories, 19 g protein, 13 carbs, and 8,150 antioxidants

Tartar Sandwich

The protein's on the outside in your own homemade bread. And for something different fill your sandwich with veggies made tangy with pickles.
Makes one serving

1/4 cup non-fat plain or Greek yogurt
1/4 tsp powder Sugar-Free Jello Vanilla pudding
1/8 tsp powder Sugar-Free Jello Lemon gelatin
1 tbsp pickle relish
1/4 cup cherry tomatoes, halved
2 tbsp diced onion
1/4 cup shredded carrots
1/4 cup shredded coleslaw
2 slices Homemade Protein Bread

Mix the yogurt with the vanilla and lemon powder, then mix in the relish.
Add all veggies to the yogurt mixture and toss to blend.
Spread salad on one bread slice, top with the second slice, and serve.

Per serving
225 calories, 41 g protein, 5 g carbs, 7 g fiber & 12,000 antioxidants

Fudge Truffles

An incredibly luscious treat packed with health. Keep them around for craving moments.
Makes six servings.

1/2 cup unsweetened, non-alkalinized cocoa
1/2 cup Splenda
1/3 cup + 1 tbsp water
2 tbsp walnut baking pieces
2 tbsp extra cocoa
2 tbsp extra Splenda

Dry mix unsweetened cocoa & Splenda. Add water, just enough to make thick, fudgey mixture. Add walnuts and blend in.
Separately combine the extra cocoa and Splenda, and sprinkle onto wide, flat plate. Set aside.
Use soupspoon to divide fudge mixture into 1" balls. One at a time, roll them around on plate sprinkled with cocoa/Splenda mixture. As they take up the extra cocoa/Splenda powder, you can roll them into nice round shapes in the palms of your hands.

Per Serving
30 calories, 2 g protein, 2 g carbs, 4 g fiber, less than 1 g total fat, and 22,283 epicatechin antioxidants.

Grilled cheese sandwich

Warm cheesy comfort without the bread carbs. Makes one serving

Cooking spray
2 slices Homemade Protein Bread
2 slices fat-free cheese slices

Spray skillet and one slice of bread with cooking spray.
Put bread, sprayed slide down, in skillet over low-medium heat.
Spray the second bread slice and set aside.
When the cooking bread turns golden (2-3 minutes), top with cheese and the second bread slice, sprayed side up.
Spray spatula tip and turn the sandwich. Cook until the second side turns golden, and serve.

Per Serving
244 cal, 38 g protein, 6 g carbs, 4 g fiber, and 3,000 lignan antioxidants

Lemon Berry Crunch with Fudge Sauce

Tangy, crunchy, topped with fudge sauce *and* healthy? Yes!
Makes one serving

1/4 teaspoon powder of sugar-free Jello Lemon gelatin
4 oz fat-free Greek yogurt
2 tbsp walnut baking pieces
2 tbsp blueberries
3 strawberries, sliced
2 tbsp fudge sauce

Mix the lemon powder with the yogurt. Mix in the walnuts.
Gently fold in the berries, and top with fudge sauce.

Per Serving
184 calories, 15 g protein, 7 g carbs, and 16,000 epicatechin antioxidants

Berries, Lime and Chocolate Muffin Parfait

Looks decadent but is healthier than most meals.
Makes one serving

1 chocolate Mighty Muffin
1/2 teaspoon powder of sugar-free Lime gelatin
4 oz non-fat Greek yogurt
2 tbsp blueberries
3 strawberries, sliced
2 tbsp Fudge Sauce

Break muffin in half. Crumble one half and put into dessert cup.
Mix lime powder with yogurt and spoon over the muffin.
Combine berries and spoon over the yogurt.
Top with crumbled second half of muffin, and top that with Fudge Sauce.

Per Serving
215 calories, 31 g protein, 7 g carbs, 5 g fiber, & 7,006 antioxidants

Eggs and Cheese in Tortilla Wrap

Great for breakfast or anytime portable meal
Makes one serving

Cooking spray
1 protein tortilla
1 tbsp mustard
1/4 cup liquid egg whites
1/4 cup shredded fat-free cheese
1 tsp dried oregano
garlic & pepper to taste

Spread mustard over tortilla and set aside.
Spray skillet with cooking spray and preheat to medium-high heat.
Pour eggs first and then and cheese into pan, sprinkle with spices, and scramble until cheese is melted & egg looks done. Lower heat.
Warm tortilla in microwave for 20 seconds. Quickly spoon egg mixture into tortilla.
Roll tortilla like a jellyroll and. place with fold side down. The cooling cheese will bind it closed.

Per Serving
133 calories, 24 g protein, 3 g carbs, and 10,007 antioxidants

All Protein Sweet Rolls

Great for dunking, or fill with fat free cream cheese or sugar-free jam.
Makes six servings.

Cooking spray
1 1/2 cups Soy Protein Powder
2/3 cup Splenda
2 tbsp milled flaxseed
1 tsp baking powder
2 tsp cinnamon
1 1/2 cup liquid egg whites
1/4 cup water
1 tbsp more cinnamon mixed with 1 tbsp Splenda

Prehat oven to 400. Cover cookie sheet with parchment paper and mist with spray. Combine the soy, Splenda, milled flaxseed, baking powder, and cinnamon.
Mix egg whites and water separately, then add to dry ingredients; blend well.
Drop batter onto cookie sheet in 6 equal mounds. With moistened hands neaten into roll shapes.
Spray tops with cooking spray, and sprinkle lightly with cinnamon/Splenda mixture.
Bake for 11 minutes. Remove from oven and cool.

Per Serving:
123 calories, 30 g protein, 0 g carbs, and 16,457 antioxidants

Cinnamon Mighty Muffin Super healthy and 90 minutes in the microwave

Makes one serving

Cooking spray
1 scoop SPP
1 tbsp milled flaxseed
1 tbsp Splenda
1 1/2 tsp cinnamon, or to taste
1/2 tsp baking powder
2 tbsp + 1 tsp water
2 tbsp liquid egg whites

Spray inside of Pyrex measuring cup. In it mix all ingredients. Stir well, spoon sides back down, and gently press batter down in cup.
Microwave 90 seconds, cool slightly, and pop out.

Per Serving
101 calories, 17 g protein, 0 g carbs and 20,055 antioxidants

Orange Berry Crunch with Fudge Sauce

Makes one serving

1/4 teaspoon powder of sugar-free Jello Orange gelatin
4 oz sugar-free Greek yogurt
2 tbsp walnut baking pieces
2 tbsp blueberries
3 strawberries, sliced
2 tbsp fudge sauce

Mix the orange Jello powder with the yogurt. Mix in the walnuts.
Gently fold in the berries, and top with fudge sauce.

Per Serving
184 calories, 15 g protein, 7 g carbs, and 16,540 epicatechin antioxidants

Chocolate Mighty Muffins, Baked

Makes six servings

6 cupcake liners
Cooking spray
1 cup soy protein powder
1/2 cup natural unsweetened cocoa
1/2 cup milled flaxseed
1 1/4 cup Splenda
1 tbsp baking powder
1 cup + 2 tbsp water
3/4 cup liquid egg whites

Preheat oven to 350 degrees.
Place cupcake liners into 6-muffin pan and mist each with cooking spray.
Separately mix the protein powder, cocoa, flaxseed, Splenda, and baking powder.
Add water and egg whites, mix thoroughly, and spoon batter into the prepared
liners. With moistened fingertips, press and neaten muffin tops.
Bake for 18 minutes or until toothpick inserted in the middle comes out clean.

Per Serving
**111 calories, 18 g protein, 1 g carb, 2.3 g monounsaturated fat, and 7,000
antioxidants (4,000 epicatechin and 3,000 lignan antioxidants)**

Apricot Mighty Muffins

Fruity delicious, 90 seconds in the microwave and no clean up.
Makes one serving

Cooking spray
1 scoop Soy Protein Powder
1 tbsp milled flaxseed
1 1/2 tsp cinnamon
1/2 tsp baking powder
1 tbsp + 1 tsp Splenda
2 tbsp sugar free apricot preserves
2 tsp water
2 tbsp liquid egg whites

Spray inside of Pyrex measuring cup. In it mix all ingredients. Stir well, blending in the sugar free preserves. Scrape down the sides, pushing mixture down in cup.
Microwave for 90 seconds, cool slightly, and pop out.

Per Serving:
121 calories, 17 g protein, 10 g carbs, 2.3 g mono- & polyunsaturated fat, and 23,055 antioxidants
*Other sugar free preserves are: marmalade, peach, strawberry, blueberry, grape, blackberry & raspberry

Vanilla Mighty Muffin with fudge frosting

Makes one serving

Cooking spray
1 scoop SPP
1 tbsp milled flaxseed
1 tbsp Splenda
1 tbsp powder of Jello sugar-free Vanilla Pudding
1/2 tsp baking powder
1 tbsp vanilla extract
2 1/2 tbsp water
2 tbsp liquid egg whites
fudge frosting, 1 tbsp (recipe follows)

Spray Pyrex measuring cup. In it mix all ingredients. Stir well, spoon sides down, and push mixture back down in cup.
Microwave 90 seconds, cool slightly, and pop out.
Spread on frosting and serve.

Per Serving
Without frosting: 116 calories, 34 g protein, 3 g carbs, 3 g fiber, and 12,000 antioxidants
With frosting: 131 calories, 34.5 g protein, 4 g carbs, 4 g fiber, and 20,000 antioxidants

<u>**Fudge Frosting**</u> Makes one serving.

1 tablespoon unsweetened non-alkalinized cocoa
1 tablespoon Splenda
1 tsp powder of Jello Vanilla pudding
1 tbsp + 2 tsp water

Mix all together and spread on muffin or cupcake.
Per Serving
15 calories, less than 1 g protein, 1 g carb, 2 g fiber, and 8,000 epicatechin antioxidants

<u>Vanilla Frosting</u> Makes one serving.

1 tbsp powder of sugar free Vanilla Jello pudding
1 tbsp water
1 1/2 tsp fat free Greek yogurt

Mix all together and spread on muffin or cupcake.
Per Serving
26 calories, 0 g protein, 6 carbs

<u>Black Cherry Frosting</u> Makes one serving.
1 tbsp powder of sugar free Black Cherry Jello gelatin
1 tbsp water
1 1/2 tsp fat free Greek yogurt

Mix all together and spread on muffin or cupcake.
Per Serving
26 calories, 0 g protein, 6 carbs

Hotcake Two minutes in the microwave and no cleanup!

Makes one serving

Cooking spray
2 tbsp Soy Protein Powder
1/2 tsp cinnamon
1/4 teaspoon baking powder
2 tsp Splenda
1 tbsp egg whites
3 tbsp fat-free milk
1/2 tsp canola oil

Spray inside of 4-cup Pyrex measuring cup. In it mix all ingredients. Scrape down the sides to "neaten." Raise the cup and slam it down gently down to get any air bubbles out.
Microwave 2 minutes. Loosen edges, then pop out onto absorbent paper towel to take up any extra steam. Serve hot or cold. These freeze well for ready snacks.

Each contains 98 calories, 15 g protein, 3 g carbs, 2 g monounsaturated fat, & 6,535 antioxidants
- Optional: Spread with sugar-free preserves (per 2 tbsp serving: 20 calories, 10 g carbs, 0 g total fat, 0 g protein)
- fat free cream cheese (per 2 tbsp 10 calories, 2 g carbs, 0 total fat, 0 g protein)
- Other spices can be substituted for the cinnamon.

Tuna Nicoise

A year-round fast, easy favorite. Serve hot or cold, makes an elegant salad. Makes two servings.

1/2 cup Vinaigrette (recipe follows)
1/4 16-oz bag broccoli florets
1 5 oz can of tuna, no salt added, well drained
1 15 oz can red kidney beans, well drained
1 small onion, diced
1 cup cherry tomatoes, cut in half

Pour the vinaigrette into skillet.
Add broccoli and cook on medium heat for 3-4 minutes if fresh, 5 minutes if frozen.
Add tuna and kidney beans, stirring until evenly warmed.
Add onions and tomatoes last; stir briefly to warm but leave onions crunchy

Per Serving
346 calories, 32 g protein, 24 carbs, 5 g monounsaturated fat, and 1,512 antioxidants

Lo-cal Vinaigrette
This is an indispensable, classic recipe, watered down for fewer calories.
Makes four servings of 2 tbsp. each

4 tablespoons extra virgin olive oil
2 tablespoons red wine vinegar
2 teaspoons Dijon mustard
1/2 cup water
garlic powder to taste
tarragon, dried to taste

Combine olive oil, red wine vinegar, mustard and water.
Add garlic & tarragon, and whisk with a fork. Or if you have a covered jar, replace top and shake vigorously.
Keep a container of vinaigrette in the refrigerator for future, readymade use in salads and other recipes.
If you wish even fewer calories per serving, add more water, garlic and tarragon.
The spices are what give vinaigrette its strong, aromatic taste.

Per Serving
60 calories, less than 1 g carb, 0 g protein & 5 g monounsaturated fat

MLA Tex Mex chicken

Pretty colors and comes out tasting like Tex Mex brisket. Make lots, as in recipe below. It's nutrient-packed and freezes well. Divide leftovers into plastic bags for freezer.
Makes eight servings.

Cooking spray
2 pounds skinless, boneless chicken breasts
2 tbsp olive oil
2 tsp black pepper
1/2 bottle low sugar, low salt barbecue sauce
1/2 cup water
Frozen broccoli florets, 1 lb bag
1 cup yellow squash, sliced
2 cups red and orange peppers, cut

Optional first step: Cholesterol melts at 325 degrees Fahrenheit (162 degrees Centigrade). To get it out — fish & chicken do have cholesterol; what they don't have is saturated fat – first parboil the chicken in about two inches of water for 3-4 minutes. Then carefully carry the skillet to the sink. Under lukewarm water from the tap, pour off all the pink-gloppy drippings (the cholesterol); even rinse and clean chicken under the water, with the chicken still in the skillet.

Return skillet with chicken in it to stove and add olive oil.
Toss chicken in the oil, sprinkle with pepper, and cook over medium-high heat until golden, pulling chunks apart and sautéing the now smaller pieces until they too turn golden.
Lower heat. Add barbecue sauce and water; mix with chicken.
Then add broccoli, squash and peppers. Heat all, stirring occasionally, and serve.

Per Serving
325 calories, 28 g protein, 11 g carbs, & 6,000 antioxidants

Tip: Keep a plastic bag of pre-washed & cut squash and peppers in the freezer. This makes it faster and more convenient to just toss them into the next Tex Mex you're making or re-heating.

Salmon Dijon

Cooking spray
Heavy duty aluminum foil
4 oz salmon per person
1 tablespoon Dijon mustard per person
Garlic powder, to taste
Dill, dried, to taste

Line broiling platter with aluminum foil, spray with cooking spray, and place salmon fillets on foil, skin side down.
"Finger paint" Dijon over each fillet. Then balance platter over sink and sprinkle on lots of garlic powder and dill.
Broil (2nd shelf down) until Dijon topping starts to brown.
Close oven door and switch to bake for another 4-5 minutes, or until fillets are delicately browned and easily "flaked." Dijon mixture prevents them from drying. Serve hot or cold.

Per Serving
232 calories, 28 g protein, 0 g carbs, 9 g Total Fat (1 g saturated fat, 8 g polyunsaturated fat.)

Crudités

Pronounced crudi*tay*; means any raw veggies appetizer or side dish.
Makes two servings.

1/4 cup Broccoli florets, raw & cut small
1/4 cup Carrots, cut small
1/4 cup cherry tomatoes, halved
1/2 cup diced onion
6 tbsp vinaigrette sauce

Arrange all on main plate or side dish. Drizzle each serving with 1 1/2 tbsp vinaigrette

Per Serving
155 calories, 1 g protein, 9 g carbs, and 1,330 antioxidants

Pizza

Spicy and nutrient-packed on a healthy crust
Makes six servings.

1 tbsp olive oil
1/2 cup sliced mushrooms
6 garlic cloves, minced
1 cup sliced onions
2 tsp oregano
1 1/4 cup Soy Protein Powder
3 tbsp Splenda
2 tbsp milled flaxseed
1 tsp powdered garlic
1/2 tsp powdered black pepper
1 1/4 cups liquid egg whites
Cooking spray
1/2 cup commercial tomato sauce
1/2 cup shredded fat-free cheddar cheese

Preheat oven to 350 degrees.
Add oil to 12" sauté pan and cook mushrooms, garlic, oregano and onions until onions are golden.
Remove veggies from pan and set aside.
In a bowl combine protein powder, Splenda, flaxseed and spices. Add egg whites and blend.
Spray original pan with cooking spray.
With moistened fingertips, push dough into skillet and press out to reach edges.
Spread tomato sauce evenly over top of dough.
Sprinkle cheese onto sauce. Then top the cheese with cooked veggies.
Sprinkle toppings with more powdered garlic and oregano, if desired.
With pizza still in its skillet bake for 10 minutes, or until cheese melts and crust has puffed and turned golden.
Cool slightly and serve.

Per Serving
161 calories, 26 g protein, 3 g carbs, 5 g fiber, 1.5 g monounsaturated fat and 8,370 antioxidants

Mixed Greens Salad

Makes four servings

2 cups arugula and baby spinach
1/2 cup broccoli, fresh
1/4 cup red onions, chopped
5 tbsp fresh oregano leaves, or 2 tbsp dried oregano
6 tbsp vinaigrette sauce

Wash greens and tear into smaller pieces. Cut broccoli into bite-size pieces.
Combine with onions and oregano.
Add vinaigrette, toss, and serve.

Per Serving
142 calories, 1 g protein, 2 g carbs, and 5,136 antioxidants

MLA (Make Lots Ahead) Chicken Stroganoff

Luscious and creamy with no cholesterol or saturated fat as with beef stroganoff. Double or triple this recipe. Freeze leftovers and just thaw for quick re-heat next time.
Makes four servings.

4 boneless, skinless chicken breasts
1 tbsp olive oil
black pepper to taste
1 medium onion, chopped
1/2 pound fresh mushrooms, sliced
1 tbsp garlic powder, or to taste
3/4 cup chicken bouillon, salt-free
3 tbsp dried tarragon, or to taste
4 oz fat free sour cream

*If you want to get the cholesterol out – fish & chicken have cholesterol which melts at 325 degrees; what they don't have is saturated fat – first parboil the chicken breasts in 2" of water for 3 – 4 minutes. Then carefully carry skillet to sink and, under lukewarm tap water, pour off all the pink-gloppy drippings (the cholesterol); even rinse & clean chicken under the water, with the chicken still in the skillet.
Return skillet and chicken to stove & add olive oil.
Toss chicken in the oil, sprinkle with pepper, and cook over medium-high heat. Turn, sautéing and cutting into smaller pieces. As those pieces turn golden, push to far side of skillet.
Add onions, garlic, and mushrooms; cook until onions are golden.
Lower heat. Add chicken broth and tarragon; stir.
Add sour cream last. Stir chicken back into rest of mixture, combining all ingredients. Simmer for 5 minutes, stirring occasionally, and serve.

Per Serving
184 calories, 27 g protein, 5 g carbs, 8 g mono-and polyunsaturated fat

Crispy Green Beans

A crunchy, delicious accompaniment to creamy casseroles.
Makes two servings.

1 1/2 tbsp olive oil
1 1/2 cups green beans, raw or frozen, salt free
2 tbsp garlic powder, or to taste

Pour oil into wide skillet with heat off.
Toss beans in the oil, sprinkle with garlic powder, and toss again.
Arrange beans so they're all mostly lining the skillet bottom.
Turn heat up to high.
Sautee beans until they turn golden and toasted on one side.
Use two forks to turn them.
Continue sautéing on nearly high heat until beans look toasted and crispy on both sides.

Per Serving
107 calories, 1 g protein, 4 g carbs, 10 g monounsaturated fat

Turkey Burgers on Rolls with sliced onions and tomatoes.

Milled flaxseed is in both the burgers and the rolls; oregano has huge amounts of antioxidants (10,005 per tsp). The burgers also freeze well. Make lots, freeze, and thaw for quick, easy dinners..
Makes five servings including the rolls.

5 hamburger rolls
1 20 oz (1.25 lbs) pkg of Fat-Free Ground Turkey
1 med-sized onion, finely chopped
1 tbsp garlic powder, or to taste
1 tsp black pepper, or to taste
1 tsp dried oregano, or to taste
1/4 cup liquid egg whites
4 tbsp milled flax seed
5 slices onion
5 slices tomato

These can be grilled, roasted, or pan-fried. If you choose to roast, preheat oven to 400 degrees. Line a broiler pan with heavy foil, spray with cooking spray and set aside.
In a large bowl, combine the turkey, onion, spices, egg whites, and flaxseed.
Shape into 5 burgers and arrange on sprayed skillet or broiler pan.
If frying, cook 4-5-minutees each side on medium-high.
If roasting, roast until tops brown, about 30 minutes.
Place in rolls, top with sliced onions and tomato, and serve.

Per Serving
330 calories, 65 g protein, 4 g carbs, 2 g polyunsaturated fat, and 17,302 antioxidants

- Ketchup per 2 tbsp: 30 calories, 0 g protein, and 6 g carbs
- Mustard per 2 tbsp: 22 calories, 1 g protein, and 2.5 g carbs

Baby Spinach Salad

Makes four servings

6 cups fresh baby spinach
1/2 cup fresh chopped red onion
1 cup fresh mushroom slices
2 tbsp balsamic vinegar
2 tbsp olive oil
1/2 tsp black pepper, or to taste
1 tsp garlic powder, or to taste
freshly ground black pepper

Combine spinach, onions and mushrooms
Separately mix vinegar, olive oil, pepper and garlic
Add to salad mixture and toss
Top with freshly ground black pepper

Per Serving
110 calories, 2 g protein, 4 g carbs, and 10 g mono-and polyunsaturated fat

MLA Chili

An anytime crowd pleaser. Make it by the truckload, freeze leftovers and thaw for quick healthy meals.
Makes fifteen 4 oz servings.

Cooking spray
3 skillets
3 20 oz (1.25 lbs) pkgs Fat-Free Ground Turkey
2 28 oz cans Crushed Tomatoes, salt free
3 large onions, diced
6 packets Taco Seasoning Mix
3 cans Dark Kidney Beans, well drained

Spray each skillet with cooking spray.
On medium high heat sautee the turkey throroughly. (More effort is required to stir and separate ground-turkey "crumbles" than with high-fat, slippery ground beef.)
Lower heat. Pour off drippings, which are liquid cholesterol.
Add the crushed tomatoes, onions, and Taco Seasoning. Stir and combine.
Drain all liquid from kidney beans (that's where they hide the salt).
Add beans, stir, and let chili simmer for 5-10 minutes.
If desired garnish with diced tomatoes, shredded lettuce, & fat-free cheese (30 calories per slice). Or fat free sour cream (30 calories, 5 g carbs, 1 g protein per 2 tbsp).

Per Serving
230 calories, 6 g carbs, 26 g protein, 800 antioxidants

Avocado Salad

Besides being delicious and filling, avocados contain heart-healthy monounsaturated fat, vitamins A and E, B vitamins, protein, and potassium (a necessary electrolyte for cell metabolism).
Makes two servings.

2 medium-sized avocadoes, peeled, pitted, and diced
1/2 onion, fresh, chopped
1/2 cup cherry tomatoes, halved
1/2 cup baby spinach
2 tbsp fresh cilantro, chopped
1/4 cup vinaigrette

Combine all ingredients. Gently toss with vinaigrette and serve.

Per Serving
380 calories, 5 g protein, 9 g carbs, 2 g saturated fat, 15 g monounsaturated fat, and 900 antioxidants

MLA Chicken Tarragon with Sun-dried Tomatoes and Walnuts

Make Lots Ahead, freeze leftovers, and just heat and serve next time.
Makes four servings.

4 skinless, boneless, chicken breasts
1 tbsp olive oil
2 tsp black pepper, or to taste
3 oz sun-dried tomatoes, drained of oil
3 tbsp powdered garlic, or to taste
3 tbsp dried tarragon, or to taste
1/2 cup Lo-cal Vinaigrette
1/2 cup chopped walnuts

First get the cholesterol out – fish & chicken have cholesterol, which melts at 325 degrees; what they don't have is saturated fat. Parboil the chicken in 2" of water. Then pour off the pink-gloppy foam (the cholesterol); even rinse and clean under warm water, with the chicken still in the skillet.
Return skillet and chicken to stove and add olive oil.
Toss chicken in the oil and sprinkle with pepper. Cook over medium-high heat, cutting and sauteing into smaller pieces, until the chicken turns golden.
Push chicken pieces to far side of skillet.
Add tomatoes, garlic and tarragon. Lower heat.
Add the vinaigrette and stir, combining the pan scrapings with chicken and tomatoes. Add walnuts, stir, and simmer for another 3-4 minutes.

Per serving
290 calories, 28 g protein, 5 g carbs, 5 g monounsaturated fat and 890 antioxidants

Ratatouille

This Mediterranean vegetable stew can also be served as a cold salad. It's quick, easy, antioxidant-packed, and as pretty as a magazine cover.
Makes four servings

3 Tbsp olive oil
1 large onion, chopped
6 minced garlic cloves
1 1/2 cups green and red peppers, coarsely chopped
Large eggplant, cubed, skin on
2 medium zucchini, sliced
1 tsp black pepper
2 Tbsp dried basil
2 Tbsp dried oregano
1/2 cup sun-dried tomatoes

In a large skillet heat oil over medium-high heat. Add the onion and garlic and sauté.
Add peppers, eggplant and zucchini. Blend all together, stirring.
Add spices and sun-dried tomatoes; stir for another 10 minutes.
Lower heat. Simmer the ratatouille down to the consistency you like, and serve.

Per Serving
256 calories, 4 g protein, 15 grams carbs, 9 grams monounsaturated fat and over 7,158 antioxidants.

Shrimp Scampi and sun-dried tomatoes: Spicy and filling. In the tomatoes' concentrated form are high amounts of lutein, important for eye health.
Makes four servings

1 lb pre-cooked shrimp
black pepper to taste
1 cup sun-dried tomatoes, drained of their olive oil
4 garlic cloves, minced
3 tbsp freshly squeezed lemon juice
2 tbsp dried oregano
4 tbsp freshly chopped parsley

Season shrimp with pepper. Set aside.
Place skillet on medium-high heat. Fork tomatoes, and with your free hand use scissors to cut them into smaller pieces; add these to skillet.
Add garlic and cook with tomatoes until garlic is golden.
Raise heat to high and add shrimp. Stir for 3 – 4 minutes.
Reduce heat. Add lemon juice and dried oregano.
Stir, scraping in any browned bits from bottom of pan.
Add parsley, toss to combine, and serve.

Per Serving
184 calories, 25 g protein, 7 g carbs, 3 g monounsaturated fat and 6,606 antioxidants

Quiche

Makes six servings, including the crust.

Make healthy pie crust first (recipe next page)
Filling:
Cooking spray
1/2 cup sliced onions
1/2 cup sliced mushrooms
3/4 cup broccoli, cut bite-sized
1/4 tsp black pepper
1 tsp ground nutmeg, or to taste
2 tsp cinnamon
1 cup shredded fat-free cheddar cheese
1 1/2 cups liquid egg whites

Preheat oven to 400°F. Mist a large skillet with cooking spray.
On medium-high heat sauté onions and mushrooms. Add broccoli and stir briefly.
Lower heat and add pepper, nutmeg and cinnamon.
Add the cheese, stirring with a rubber spatula until it starts to melt.
Add egg whites slowly, stirring until cheese is completely melted and mixture looks soupy.
Pour into crust and bake for 20 minutes. Serve hot or cold.

Per Serving, crust included
120 calories, 14 g protein, 5 g carbs, 1 g fiber, 2 g monounsaturated fat and 10,784 antioxidants (including milled flaxseed in crust)

Healthy Pie Crust

Use this recipe and you will never think of crust the same way.
Makes one 9" inch pie, six servings

Cooking spray
1/2 cup quick oats
2 scoops Soy Protein Powder
1/2 cup Splenda
3 tbsp milled flaxseed
3/4 cup water

Spray pie plate with cooking spray.
Mix the oats, soy protein powder, Splenda, and flaxseed.
Add the water and mix well.
From a spoon drop dollops of batter across the pie plate. Then press across bottom and up sides, moistening fingertips as you go.

Per Serving (crust alone)
44 calories, 5 grams protein, 3 g carbs, 1 g fiber, 2 g monounsaturated fat, and 6,000 lignan antioxidants

Mixed Greens Salad with toasted almonds

Makes four servings

1/2 cup slivered almonds
2 cups mixed arugula, Boston lettuce and baby spinach
1/2 cup sliced onions
2 tbsp fresh oregano leaves, or 1 tsp dried oregano
4 tbsp vinaigrette

Heat almonds in a dry skillet on medium heat.
After a few minutes they'll start to turn golden. Stir and heat them until they look toasted.
Remove from heat, cool slightly, and combine with other salad ingredients.
Pour on vinaigrette, toss, and serve.

Per Serving
130 calories, 17 g protein, 3 g carbs, and 5,500 antioxidants

Crispy Omelet

Cheesy and crunchy with no saturated fat. The secret happens when cheese hits hot oil.
Makes two servings.

2 tbsp canola oil
1 1/4 cups liquid egg whites
1/4 cup fat-free shredded mozzarella
4 garlic cloves, minced
2 tsp dried oregano

In a large skillet, heat the oil on high heat.
Add eggs and wait till they begin to solidify on the bottom (2-3 minutes, depending on your stove).
Sprinkle cheese over the eggs. Add garlic and oregano on top of the cheese.
Reduce heat, and cover eggs with a lid or aluminum foil for about 2 minutes to allow cheese to melt.
Remove the cover and raise heat to high again. Using two flexible spatulas, fold one quarter of the egg over the middle, then continue to roll like a jellyroll, ending with the fold underneath, still cooking.
Check frequently until desired degree of crunchiness is obtained, turning and rolling again if desired.
Remove from heat, cool for about a minute, then cut in half.

Per Serving
217 calories, 25 grams protein, 1 g carb, 14 grams monounsaturated fat, and 10,148 antioxidants

Cheesy Broccoli

Makes four servings.

1/2 cup water
2 cups Broccoli, fresh or frozen, salt free
1 tbsp powdered garlic, or to taste
3 slices fat-free cheese

Heat broccoli in water on medium heat, cutting pieces smaller if desired.
Raise heat to medium-high, sprinkle on garlic, and mix.
Tear cheese into smaller pieces and add to the broccoli.
Stir and mix as the cheese melts. Simmer 3-5 minutes, and serve.

Per Serving
43 calories, 6 g protein, 3 g carbs, 960 antioxidants

MLA Chicken Florentine

Creamy and elegant. Make lots to reheat for future, quick easy meals.
Makes 4 servings

4 boneless, skinless chicken breasts
1 tbsp olive oil
black pepper to taste
1 medium onion, chopped
1/2 pound fresh mushrooms, sliced
1 cup chicken bouillon, salt-free
2 tsp garlic powder
3 tbsp tarragon, dried
1 cup spinach, frozen, salt free
3/4 cup fat free shredded mozzarella (white) cheese
4 oz fat free sour cream

First get the cholesterol out – fish & chicken have cholesterol which melts at 325 degrees; what they don't have is saturated fat – first parboil the chicken in 2" of water, then pour off the pink-gloppy drippings (the cholesterol); even rinse & clean under warm water, with the cleaned chicken still in the skillet.
Return skillet and chicken to stove & add olive oil.
Toss chicken in the oil, sprinkle with pepper, and cook over medium-high heat until golden. Push chicken to one side of skillet.
Add onions and mushrooms; cook until onions are golden. Stir in chicken broth, garlic, tarragon, and spinach.
Lower heat and add cheese, stirring till it melts and blends.
Add sour cream last and stir entire mixture.
Simmer for 5 more minutes, stirring occasionally, and serve.

Per Serving
231 calories, 35 g protein, 7 g carbs, 610 antioxidants, and 2 g monounsaturated fat

Salmon Cakes

Double Omega-3s from the salmon and the milled flaxseed. Crunchy delicious too.
Makes four servings.

Cooking spray
1/4 cup sliced scallions
1/4 cup fresh red pepper, minced
1/4 cup minced chopped onions
2 tsp powdered garlic, or to taste
1 tsp black pepper, or to taste
12 oz canned wild salmon, skinless, boneless, no salt added
2/3 cup liquid egg whites
4 tbsp milled flaxseed

Mist skillet and tip of spatula with cooking spray.
In a bowl mix together all ingredients.
Form 4 cakes with hands, flatten slightly, and place in skillet.
Cook on medium heat for about 4 minutes on each side.

Per Serving
131 calories, 24 g protein, 3 g carbs, 3 g fiber, and 12,000 antioxidants

Tartar Sauce

Creamy like its fat-crammed cousin but so much healthier.
Makes two 1/4 cup servings.

1/2 cup non-fat plain or Greek yogurt
1/2 tsp powder Sugar-Free Jello Vanilla pudding
1/4 tsp powder Sugar-Free Jello Lemon pudding
1 Tbsp pickle relish
Lemon juice to taste

Combine all ingredients. Toss with salad, use for sandwiches, or serve as a dip.

Per Serving
40 calories, 5.5 grams protein and 3 g carbs

Cioppino

A fast and easy version of San Francisco-style Italian fish stew.
Makes four servings.

1 19 oz can Manhattan Clam Chowder
1 28 oz can Crushed Tomatoes, No Salt Added
2 5oz cans Solid White Tuna, No Salt Added
1 cup frozen cut carrots
2 tsp powdered garlic, or to taste
2 tsp dried oregano, or to taste
1/2 tsp black pepper, or to taste
1 medium onion, sliced

Heat clam chowder and crushed tomatoes combined over medium high heat.
Add both cans of tuna, being sure to squeeze out the liquid first.
Add carrots and spices; stir till carrots start to soften.
Add onions last, stir just briefly so onions will stay crunchy.
Serve hot.

Per Serving
215 cal, 19 g protein, 20 g carbs, 480 mg sodium, 23 mg cholesterol, 1 g monounsaturated fat, & 6,245 antioxidants

Salmon Risotto: White and brown rice are both loaded with carbs, no getting away from it. This recipe offers a tasty alternative to rice – spicy, diced, sautéed tofu – with just 1 gram of carbs per serving.
Makes two servings

2 one inch wide slices tofu, extra firm
2 tbsp olive oil
1/2 cup minced onions
1/2 cup cut scallions
1/2 cup diced red bell pepper
1 tsp powdered garlic, or to taste
1 tsp dried oregano, or to taste
1 tsp black pepper, or to taste
6 oz canned wild salmon, skinless, boneless, no salt added
1 fresh lemon

Place tofu slices on double layer of paper towels to soak up moisture.
Heat olive oil in a skillet over medium-high heat. Sautee the onions, scallions and peppers for about 4 minutes.
Add tofu to skillet and mash.
Add spices to mixture, stir for 4-5 minutes longer, or until tofu starts to turn golden.
Blend all and lower heat.
Add salmon chunks on top, cover with foil, and heat for another 4-5 minutes.
Uncover and drizzle with juice of one half the lemon.
Cut second half of lemon into wedges, arrange on plates, and serve.

Per Serving
328 calories, 30 g protein, 10 g carbs, 5 g fiber, 3 mg. monounsaturated fat, and 10,196 antioxidants

More Recipes for Luscious, Zero-Guilt Desserts

Pumpkin pie, Key Lime pie, chocolate mousse, orange sherbet with fudge sauce, warm fudge nut cake with whipped topping... More follows, adding to the snack-all-day brownies, blondies, muffins, etc. you've already seen. Does this eating plan seem almost like one continuous dessert? It well might. But with ingredients so healthy they're right up there with medicine, without the side effects.

Have *lots* of chocolate sauce always ready in the fridge. Pyrex cups with their ready pour spouts make good containers; you can mix the ingredients right in the cup. Each 2 teaspoon serving of chocolate sauce contains huge amounts of cocoa's healthy antioxidants.

The quickest, easiest dessert is chocolate sauce poured over blueberries, strawberries, sliced bananas, and chopped walnuts for their heart-healthy Omega 3 acids. Pour it on, it's good for you!

Fruit Chocolate Sundae

Luscious, crammed with antioxidants and easy to make. Fruits can be fresh or frozen. You'll be heating them in the microwave, which creates a sophisticated-looking sauce from the fruit.

Makes one serving.
2 tbsp blueberries
3 strawberries, sliced
1/4 small banana, sliced
*2 tbsp fudge sauce (recipe next page)
2 tbsp walnut baking pieces

Place fruit in dessert cups. Microwave for 2 minutes if fruit is frozen, 90 seconds if fruit is fresh.
Top with fudge sauce.
Sprinkle walnuts over fudge sauce and serve.

Per Serving
147 calories, 3 grams protein, 6 grams carbs, 7 g fiber, 1 g monounsaturated fat, more than 16,000 antioxidants, & walnuts' heart-healthy Omega-3 acids

Fudge Sauce

The luscious taste of chocolate with health benefits beyond measure.*
Makes one 2 tbsp serving.

2 Tbsp unsweetened, non-alkalinized cocoa**
2 Tbsp Splenda
1 tsp powder of Jell-O sugar-free Vanilla pudding

Mix together the cocoa, Splenda, and vanilla powder.
(Formula is always equal amounts of cocoa & Splenda, a little vanilla powder, plus water.)
Add fresh, cold water a bit at a time, stirring, until sauce reaches desired consistency.
Microwave if you like for hot fudge sauce.

Per 2 tbsp:
20 calories, 2 g protein, 2 g carbs, 4 g fiber, 1 gram monounsaturated fat, and 16,000 epicatechin antioxidants
* If you skipped the first part of this book, see Ch. 7, #7, for the spectacular health benefits of pure cocoa
**Good brands are Hershey's (little brown box in bakery aisles), and Trader Joes. Alkalinization, also called Dutch process, destroys cocoa's antioxidants.

Cappuccino

Make your regular coffee or decaff, pour into mugs and add artificial sweetener if desired.

Keep about 4" inches of fat free milk in a separate fridge container, with several inches of empty space above it.

Shake it vigorously, watch it foam. Pour about 2 tbsp of the milky froth onto your coffee as a topping.

Sprinkle the topping with 1/2 tsp of cinnamon. Cocoa too, if desired

Per Serving
10 calories, 0 g carbs, 0 g protein & 6,503 antioxidants if cinnamon used.

Chocolate Mousse

Decadent-tasting and a guilt-free joy.
Makes four servings.

1 oz. pkg Jell-O Sugar-Free Instant Chocolate Pudding
2 cups cold fat free milk
4 tbsp unsweetened cocoa
4 tbsp Splenda
3/4 cup fat free milk
3/4 cup shredded fat-free mozzarella cheese
2 tbsp Fat Free Reddi-wip (per 2 tbsp: 5 calories, 2 g carbs, 0g total fat, and 0g protein.)

Preheat oven to 350°F.
In a small bowl, add the pudding mix to the cold milk. Whisk for 2 minutes or until pudding thickens. Set aside.
In a microwaveable mixer bowl, combine the cocoa, Splenda, 3/4 cup of milk and cheese. Microwave for 2 minutes, and stir.
Add the pudding to the microwaved mixture.
Beat at medium speed until well combined.
Pour into 4 individual dessert cups. Bake for 17-18 minutes, or until mousse starts to rise around interior rims.
Cool or refrigerate. Add whipped topping and serve.
(Frozen whipped topping not recommended since it contains trans fats.)

Per Serving without whipped topping: 59 calories, 13 grams protein, 12 grams carbs, and 13,370 epicatechin antioxidants.
The whipped topping brings the calorie total to 64 calories.

Pumpkin Pie

The usual pumpkin pie recipe calls for 3/4 cup sugar, 2 –3 eggs (yolks alone = 900 mg cholesterol), and an innocent-sounding 12-oz can of fat free evaporated milk, which contains 45 g carbs, which in turn quickly metabolize into over 11 teaspoons of sugar (divide by 4).
This version tastes just as delicious and is much healthier.
Makes eight servings, including crust.
Serves 8

Make unbaked healthy crust first.
Filling:
1 15 oz can pumpkin pie filling
3/4 cup Splenda
2 tsp cinnamon
1 tsp nutmeg, or to taste
1 tsp ginger, or to taste
3/4 cup fat free shredded mozzarella (white) cheese
3/4 cup liquid egg whites
cooking spray

Preheat oven to 400 degrees.
Spoon pumpkin filling into skillet and start to heat on low-medium heat.
Add Splenda and spices. Mixture stirs best with a flexible spatula.
Raise heat to medium and add cheese, stirring until it melts and blends in.
Add the egg whites bit by bit, stirring. (If eggs start to cook, remove from heat, still stirring, for 30 seconds.)
When all is heated and blended, use spatula to push filling into crust.
Bake at 400 degrees for 10 minutes. Reduce temperature to 350; bake 20 minutes more or until filling along the crust rim puffs up.
Remove from oven. Cool slightly and serve with topping.

Per Serving
90 calories, 12 grams protein, 6 grams carbs, 2 g monounsaturated fat, and 3,624 antioxidants

Orange Sherbet with fudge sauce & strawberries

Makes two half cup servings.

1 cup (8 oz) fat-free Greek yogurt
1 tsp powder of sugar-free Orange Jello gelatin
3 strawberries, sliced
4 tbsp fudge sauce

Mix together the yogurt and gelatin powder. Place in freezer for 40-45 minutes. Remove, stir to aereate. Replace in freezer for another 15 minutes. Top with strawberries and fudge sauce.

Tip: If in a hurry, use any bake plate with a wide surface. Stir to aereate at shorter intervals or it will become too solid.

Per Serving
60 calories, 7 g protein, 4 g carbs, & 32,000 epicatechin antioxidnts
Sherbet alone per half cup serving: 33 calories, 5 g protein, 1.5 g carbs.

Key Lime Pie

Intense, refreshing flavor of the tropics.
Makes one 9" inch pie including crust. Serves six.

Bake pie crust first and set aside to cool.
Filling:
3 oz pkg. sugar-free Lime flavor Jell-O gelatin
3/4 cup boiling water
4 ice cubes
8 oz plain fat-free yogurt

Dissolve gelatin thoroughly in boiling water.
Turn off heat, remove pot from stove, add ice cubes, and stir to quick-cool.
When gelatin begins to firm, remove remaining ice.
Stir in yogurt and mix. No need to get last little lumps out.
Chill until thickened but not set, about 45 -50 minutes.
Beat at highest speed until doubled in volume.
Spoon into prepared pie crust. Lift pie and slam down gently to get air bubbles out.
Smooth top with the side of a knife and chill until firm. Garnish as desired and serve.

Per Serving
89 calories, 6 g carbs, 9 g protein and 2 g monounsaturated fat

Warm Fudge Nut Cake with whipped topping

Swoony delicious. Walnuts and flaxseed are both high in Omega 3 acids.
Makes one serving.

Cooking spray
1 scoop Soy Protein Powder
1 tbsp unsweetened non-alkalinized cocoa
1 tbsp milled flaxseed
3 tbsp + 2 tsp Splenda
1/2 tsp baking powder
3 tbsp + 2 tsp water
2 tbsp liquid egg whites
2 tbsp walnut baking pieces*
Fat free whipped topping (not frozen kind; it contains trans fats)
*(If you prefer this without nuts, subtract 80 cal, 2 g protein, 1 g carbs, 1 g sat. fat)

Spray inside of small bowl. In it mix all ingredients. Scrape down the sides, gently pushing mixture back down.
Microwave for 90 seconds. Remove and cool for 30 seconds.
Place dessert dish on top of bowl, invert, and ease out the cake. Garnish with whipped topping and serve.

Per Serving
201 calories, 20 g protein, 4 g carbs, 6 g fiber, 4.6 g mono- and polyunsaturated fat, 2 g saturated fat, & 20,000 antioxidants
Top with 4 tablespoons Reddi-wip (per 2 tbsp: 5 calories, 2 g carbs, 0 g fat, 0 g protein)

Chocolate Berry Parfait

Makes one serving

1/4 small banana, sliced
3 sliced strawberries
1/4 cup blueberries, fresh or frozen
1/2 cup non-fat Greek yogurt
1/4 tsp powder of Jell-O sugar-free gelatin flavor: Orange, Lime, Black Cherry etc.
2 tbsp fudge sauce
2 tbsp walnut baking pieces

Arrange fruits in dessert cup; if fresh heat 90 seconds in microwave, 2 minutes if frozen.
Mix yogurt with powder of sugar-free gelatin
Remove warmed fruit from microwave.
Top with yogurt mixture, and top that with fudge sauce.
Sprinkle with walnuts and serve.

Per Serving
185 calories, 17 g protein, 7 g carbs, 5 g fiber, 1 g saturated fat, and 16,000 epicatechin antioxidants

Lemon Sherbet with fudge sauce and strawberries

Makes two half cup servings.

1 cup (8 oz) fat-free Greek yogurt
1 tsp powder sugar-free Lemon flavor Jell-O gelatin
6 strawberries, sliced
4 tbsp fudge sauce

Mix together the yogurt and gelatin powder.
Place in freezer for 45 minutes.
Remove and stir to aereate. Replace in freezer another 15 minutes.
Remove to dessert dishes. Top with strawberries and fudge sauce.
Tip: If in a hurry, use a wide bake plate. Stir to aereate at slightly shorter intervals or ice cream will become too solid.

Per Serving
60 calories, 7 g protein, 4 g carbs, & 32,000 epicatechin antioxidants

Lime and Chocolate Chip Sherbet

Tangy sherbet with chocolate chips made in a whole new way.
Makes two servings.

wax paper
4 tbsp fudge sauce
8 oz fat-free Greek yogurt
1 tsp powder of sugar-free Lime Jell-O gelatin

Cover a separate, flat plate with wax paper and drizzle fudge sauce on it.
Place fudge on its wax paper in freezer for 45-50 minutes.
In a bowl mix the yogurt and gelatin powder.
Place lime yogurt mixture in freezer for 45 minutes.
Remove and stir to aereate. Then remove frozen fudge "squiggles."
Hold them over the freezing yogurt, and bunch the wax paper so they fall in small pieces into the yogurt.
Fold chocolate bits into the lime sherbet, freeze another 20 minutes, and serve.
Note: Recipe can be changed to any gelatin flavor.

Per Serving
83 calories, 13 g protein, 10 g carbs, 8 g fiber & 32,000 epicatechin antioxidnts

Chocolate Crepes

Makes nine servings.

Cooking spray
1 cup Soy Protein Powder
1 teaspoon baking powder
1/3 cup Splenda
1/4 cup unsweetened, non alkalinized cocoa
2 egg whites (1/3 cup)
1 tablespoon canola oil
1 1/4 cup fat free milk
1 tsp vanilla extract
1/4 cup water

Combine the SPP, baking powder, Splenda and cocoa.
Separately mix egg whites, canola, milk, vanilla, & water, then add to dry ingredients. Mix and blend all.
Mist pan, tip of spatula, & back of large spoon with cooking spray.
Heat oil in pan on medium heat, then pour in large spoonful of batter (about 1/4 cup).
Tilt pan & use back of spoon to quickly spread top of batter into wider circle, 6-7 inches in diameter.
When bubbles start to appear, loosen edges with spatula. Flip after about 1 minute. Second side cooks more quickly.
When crepe looks done, use spatula to slide from pan to paper towel-covered plate.
Re-spray pan between crepes.
Crepes can be garnished as desired, or filled and rolled up.
Some fillings are fudge sauce, sugar free preserves, fruit, or chopped walnuts.

Per Serving
70 calories, 13 g protein, 3 g carbs, 8 g fiber and 4,571 epicatechin antioxidants

Baked Cinnamon Muffins

Cinnamon's high antioxidants and flaxseed's Omega-3 for an anytime health boost
Makes six servings.

6 paper cupcake liners
Cooking spray
1 cup Soy Protein Powder
3 tbsp cinnamon, or to taste
1/2 cup milled flaxseed
1 1/4 cups Splenda
1 tbsp baking powder
1 cup + 3 tbsp water
3/4 cup liquid egg whites

Preheat oven to 350 degrees. Place cupcake liners into 6-muffin pan and mist with cooking spray.
Separately mix the soy powder, cinnamon, flaxseed, Splenda, and baking powder. Add the water and egg whites, mix, and spoon batter into the prepared liners. Bake for 18 minutes or until toothpick in the middle comes out clean.

Per serving
101 calories, 17 g protein, 0 g carb, 2.3 g mono- and polyunsaturated fat, and 27,055 antioxidants

Banana Nut Bread

A delicious, healthy breakfast or anytime snack
Makes 8 one inch slices.

cooking spray
1 cup Soy Protein Powder
1/2 cup milled flaxseed
3 tbsp cinnamon
1 1/2 tsp nutmeg
1 tsp ginger
1 tbsp baking powder
1 cup Splenda
3 small bananas, mashed
1/2 cup water
2 tsp vanilla
3/4 cup liquid egg whites
3/4 cup walnut baking pieces

Preheat oven to 350 degrees F. Line 8 ½ x 4" loaf pan with foil, pressing creases flat, and mist foil with cooking spray.
In a bowl, mix together the soy protein powder, milled flaxseed, cinnamon, nutmeg, ginger, baking powder and Splenda.
On a flat plate mash bananas separately. Then add to dry ingredients, blending as much as possible. Mixture will be crumbly.
Separately mix water, vanilla, and egg whites together, then combine with other ingredients.
Add walnuts and mix again.
Push batter into loaf pan. Raise loaf pan and let it drop back down to remove any air bubbles.
Spray top of batter with cooking spray.
Bake for 50 minutes, or until bread top looks crunchy and toothpick inserted in center comes out clean.
Cool 10 minutes in pan on wire rack, a step which releases steam and potential sogginess from bottom. If you don't have a wire rack, place on cool stove top rings.
Grasp foil at both ends and remove bread from pan.
Cool completely. Remove foil and slice.

Per Serving
110 calories, 11 g protein, 7 g carbs, 1.7 g mono- & polyunsaturated fat, 7,138 antioxidants, and 1,075 Omega-3 acids

Chocolate Ice Cream This treat requires timing and aeration. Ice cream machines churn constantly. If Carvel's were to use the best ingredients without that constant churning (aeration), the result would be tasty ice.
Makes 1 serving.

1/2 cup fat free Greek yogurt
1 tbsp powder of sugar-free Jell-O chocolate pudding

In a small bowl mix yogurt and chocolate powder.
Place in freezer for 40 minutes. Remove from freezer, stir and churn to aerate.
Return to freezer for another 15 minutes, or until texture seems right.
Remove and transfer to dessert dish.
*Note: Experiment with the timing in your freezer, since different freezers may vary.

Per Serving
90 calories, 9 carbs, 11 g protein

To make 4 servings:
2 cups fat free Greek yogurt
3 tbsp + 1 tsp powder of sugar-free Jell-O chocolate pudding

Blend yogurt and chocolate powder together in wide bowl.
Freeze for 40 minutes, and check to see how solid it has become.
Stir and churn to aerate, including scraping down the sides.
Return to freezer for another 15 minutes.
Remove again, scoop onto dessert dishes, and serve.

Per Serving
90 calories, 9 carbs, 11 g protein

Vanilla Ice Cream Makes one serving

1/2 cup non-fat Greek yogurt
1 1/2 tsp powder of sugar-free Jell-O Vanilla pudding

Blend yogurt and vanilla powder in a bowl. Place in freezer for 35-40 minutes.
Remove from freezer, stir and churn to aerate.
Return to freezer for another 15 minutes, or until texture seems right.
Remove and transfer to dessert dish.

Per Serving
78 calories, 7 carbs, 11 g protein

To make **4** servings:
2 cups fat free Greek yogurt
2 Tbsp powder of sugar-free Jello Vanilla pudding

Blend yogurt and vanilla powder together in wide bowl. Freeze for about 35 minutes, and check to see how solid it has become. Stir and churn to aerate, including scraping down the sides. Pat back down and return to freezer for another 15 minutes.
Remove again, scoop onto dessert dishes, and serve.

Brownie Ice Cream Sundae

Top a brownie with vanilla ice cream, then top that with two tablespoons of fudge sauce and two tablespoons of fat free Reddi-wip. Can you believe *this* is super healthy? Rapture.

Per serving
177 calories, 25 g protein, 9 g carbs, 5 g fiber, 1.5 g mono- & polyunsaturated fat, & 4,666 antioxidants.
Here's the breakdown of each:
- One baked brownie: 74 calories, 12 g protein, less than 1 g carb, 1.5 g mono-unsaturated fat, and 4,666 antioxidants
- Vanilla Ice Cream: per serving: 78 calories, 7 carbs, 11 g protein
- Fudge Sauce: Each 2 tbsp serving contains 20 calories, 2 g protein, 2 g carbs, 4 g fiber, 1 gram monounsaturated fat, and 16,000 epicatechin antioxidants
- FF Reddi-wip: per 2 tbsp: 5 calories, 2 g carbs, 0g total fat, and 0g protein

Note: Frozen whipped topping is not recommended since it contains trans fats.

Brownies, Baked

Makes nine servings.

Cooking spray
1 cup SPP
1/2 cup unsweetened cocoa
1/2 cup milled flaxseed
1 1/2 cup Splenda
1 tbsp baking powder
1 cup + 2 tbsp water
3/4 cup liquid egg whites

Preheat oven to 350 degrees. Mist 8 x 8" bake pan with cooking spray.
Mix together the soy powder, cocoa, flaxseed, Splenda, and baking powder.
Separately combine the water and egg whites. Add to dry ingredients, blend
well, and spoon batter into bake pan. Use moistened fingertips to spread batter
in pan.
Bake for 24 minutes or until toothpick inserted in the middle comes out clean.
Cool, then cut into 9 brownies.

Per Serving
74 calories, 12 g protein, less than 1 g carb, 1.5 g monounsaturated fat, & 4,666
antioxidants (2,666 epicatechin & 2,000 Omega-3 lignan antioxidants)

Zucchini and Broccoli Sautee

A tasty accompaniment to any meal.
Makes two servings.

1 1/2 tbsp olive oil
1 cup fresh zucchini cut into round discs
1 cup broccoli florets, raw or frozen, salt free
2 tbsp garlic powder, or to taste
1 tbsp oregano, dried

Pour oil into wide skillet with heat off.
Toss zucchini in the oil and sprinkle with garlic powder.
Arrange zucchini one side down in the skillet.
Turn heat up to nearly high. Sautee zucchini until golden on one side.
Sprinkle tops with more garlic if desired, and use 2 forks or small spatula to flip them. Continue sautéing on nearly high until zucchini looks golden on both sides.
Lower heat. Add sprinkled oregano and broccoli on top of zucchini.
Heat for 4 -5 minutes more, then fold broccoli and oregano into zucchini.
Continue cooking on medium heat until broccoli is softened and heated.

Per Serving
110 calories, 2 g protein, 4 g carbs, 5,240 antioxidants

Carrots with Orange Glaze

Sweet carrots with cinnamon, nutmeg and orange.
Makes two servings.

1 tbsp lemon juice
1 tbsp water
2 tbsp Sugar-Free Orange Marmalade
1 cup cut carrots, raw or frozen, salt free
1 tsp cinnamon
1/2 tsp nutmeg
2 tbsp cold water
1 tsp cornstarch

Mix together lemon juice, water, and marmalade in skillet.
Raise heat to medium, add carrots, and simmer till semi-crunchy.
Sprinkle on cinnamon and nutmeg. Toss, then push carrots to one side of skillet.
Separately mix cornstarch and water. Tilt skillet so liquid collects on side away from carrots.
Add cornstarch mixture to liquid, stir 20 seconds, right skillet again and combine all.
Spoon orange glaze over carrots and serve.

Per Serving
35 calories, 2 g protein, 3 g carbs, 2 g fiber, and 6,750 antioxidants

Garlic Parmesan Flaxseed Crackers

Crunchy and super healthy. The whole recipe before cutting is 10 grams of carbs and 48 grams of fiber.
Makes 50 crackers

Cooking spray
1 cup flaxseed meal
1/3 cup Parmesan cheese, grated
1/4 cup quick oats
1 tsp garlic powder
1 tsp dried oregano
1/2 tsp black pepper
2/3 cup water

Pre-heat oven to 350 F.
Lay parchment paper over two cookie sheets and mist with cooking spray
Mix all ingredients together.
Divide mixture in half. Spoon each halved mixture onto a cookie sheet.
Cover both mixtures with wax paper, and press out to about 1/8 inch thick. Use a rolling pin or the shorter-length can of cooking spray like a rolling pin.
Avoid letting mixtures get too thin around the edges or that part will bake unevenly.
Remove wax paper. Push any thin edges with your fingers to even mixture thickness.
Use a pizza cutter to cut crackers into squares.
For circle crackers you can use cookie cutters.
Bake crackers about 23-25 minutes, or until centers are no longer soft.
Cool completely on cookie sheets. Crackers will continue to crisp up.

Per serving (1 cracker)
14 cal, 1.3 g protein, 0 g carbs, 0 g saturated fat, 1 g fiber, & 3,840 lignan antioxidants

Guacamole

Avocados are like olives, high in heart-healthy monounsaturated fat, vitamins, minerals, and dietary fiber.
Makes 16 servings

2 medium-ripe avocados
3 tbsp fresh lemon juice
1 medium tomato, diced
1/4 cup onion, minced
1 tsp garlic powder, or to taste
Fresh celery, green beans, red and yellow peppers seeded and cut into strips

Halve both avocados, discard pits, and scoop out soft part into a medium bowl. Mash with lemon juice. Fold in tomato, onion and garlic powder. Serve in small bowl placed in center of large plate surrounded by celery and other veggies.

Per Serving:
38 calories, 0 g carbs, 0 g protein

Cheese 'n Crackers Canapes

Crispy delicious with no fat, no carbs, and lots of fiber.

24 Garlic Parmesan Flaxseed crackers
1/4 cup fat-free shredded cheddar cheese

Place 1/2 teaspoon cheese on each cracker. Heat under broiler until melted and golden.

Per serving (one cracker plus cheese):
16 calories, 0 g carbs, 1.5 g protein. 0 g saturated fat, 1 g fiber, and 3,840 lignan antioxidants

Barbecue Grilled Chicken Breasts

Makes eight 1/4 pound servings

1/4 cup olive oil
1/4 cup water
2 tablespoons red wine vinegar
3 tbsp Dijon mustard
1 tbsp garlic powder, or to taste
1 tbsp dried tarragon, or to taste
2 lbs chicken breasts, boneless and skinless

Mix first six ingredients in wide, non-metallic bowl. Add chicken, turning to coat. Cover and chill 1-2 hours.
Drain chicken, reserving marinade. Grill on an uncovered grill over medium coals for 20 minutes.
Turn chicken and grill for 15 minutes more or until chicken is tender and no longer pink when cut.
Brush with remaining marinade for last 5 minutes of grilling. Serve hot or cold.

Per serving:
310 calories, 1 g carb, 38 g protein, 2 g monounsaturated fat

Grilled Zucchini and Yellow Squash

Makes 4 servings

1/4 cup sugar-free Apricot preserves
2 tbsp olive oil
1 tbsp red wine vinegar
1 tsp garlic
1/2 tsp fresh cracked black pepper
1/2 pound fresh large zucchini
1/2 pound fresh large yellow squash

In a wide shallow dish whisk first five ingredients.
Slice zucchini and squash into long, 1/2 inch thick slices. Toss in dish with the apricot dressing.
Place on a hot grill and cook for 4-5 minutes, or until grill marks appear and vegetables look done.

Per serving:
55 calories, 6 g carbs, 0 g protein, 1 g monounsaturated fat

Barbecue Turkey Cheeseburgers

Moist, delicious, and in rolls containing milled flaxseed & no carbs. Hugely more healthful than high-fat beef patties in carby rolls.
Makes four servings.

Cooking spray
1 20 oz (1.25 lbs) pkg of Fat-Free Ground Turkey
1 medium-sized onion, finely chopped
1/4 cup sugar free ketchup or barbecue sauce
2 tbsp liquid egg whites
2 tsp garlic powder, or to taste
1/2 tsp black pepper, or to taste
1 tsp dried oregano, or to taste
4 tbsp milled flax seed
4 slices fat-free cheese
4 crisp lettuce leaves
4 slices tomato
4 all-protein hamburg rolls

In a bowl, combine the turkey, onion, ketchup or barbecue sauce, egg whites, spices, and flax seed.
Divide turkey mixture into 4 equal portions, shaping each into a patty.
Spray grill with cooking spray.
Place patties on grill; cook 5 minutes on each side or until done.
Place each patty topped with cheese, lettuce, & tomato on the bottom half of each bun.
Cover with top halves of buns.

Per serving:
370 calories, 64 g protein, 0 g carbs, 2 g polyunsaturated fat, and 17,302 antioxidants

Pistachios: Skinny super-nuts

Besides being a delicious snack, pistachios have the highest content of phytosterols, a plant substance that reduces cholesterol absorption from other foods. In a new study published by the American Journal of Clinical Nutrition, researchers found that eating two handfuls of pistachios a day reduced LDL cholesterol (L for lousy) cholesterol by 12 per cent.

Pistachios are also full of filling protein and fiber, and tie with almonds for having the most antioxidants of nuts. They are also an excellent source of vitamin B6, are the lowest in fat & calories of all nuts, and also have the most lutein of all nuts. Lutein, a carotenoid antioxidant, is most commonly found in tomatoes, spinach and kale.
Snacking on pistachios is good for you. Keep a bunch on hand on a regular basis. They're great help in avoiding junk food and hunger pangs.

Almonds, also tops for health
Unsalted almonds are a close second to pistachios for a top health snack. Besides being delicious, they're high in protein, contain almost no carbs, and help to prevent heart disease.

They also contain more calcium than any other nut, are a great source of vitamin E – one small handful provides 70% of E's recommended daily allowance – and, like pistachios, they contain phytochemicals which help to lower LDL cholesterol.

They also help with weight loss. Again, one small handful has enough protein and fiber to promote a feeling of fullness, making that and all of almonds' other benefits perfect for snacking and overall health.

Roast Turkey: Traditional holiday favorite, moist and healthy.

Makes twenty 4-oz servings

Aluminum foil
Meat thermometer
Turkey baster
One 12 to 14 pound turkey
1/2 cup fresh sage, chopped
1 teaspoon ground black pepper
2 tablespoons olive oil

Preheat oven to 425 degrees F. Cover shallow roasting pan with aluminum foil.
Remove neck bone and giblets from turkey, then rinse inside of turkey and pat dry with paper towels.
In a small bowl, stir together sage, pepper and olive oil.
Season inside of turkey with half of the herb mixture.
Fasten neck skin with a skewer. Tuck drumsticks ends under the band of skin across the tail.
Place turkey, breast side up, on the foil-covered roasting pan. Brush turkey with remaining oil and herb mixture. Insert meat thermometer into the center of turkey thigh, not touching bone. Cover turkey loosely with foil tent.
Roast for 30 minutes, then reduce oven temperature to 325 degrees F.
Roast for 2-1/2 to 3 hours more or until the thermometer reads 180°F.
About 45 minutes before end of roasting, remove foil.
Use turkey baster to take up drippings in pan and baste turkey. You may want to do this more than once.
When turkey is done the juices should run clear, not pink, and the drumsticks should move easily.

Per Serving:
230 calories, 0 g carbs, 34 g protein

Turkey Stuffing, Just as yummy as commercial stuffing and slightly less than 2 carbs per serving.
Makes 10 servings.

Cooking spray
3/4 cup fresh chopped celery, with leaves
1 small onion, chopped
4 cups cubed all-protein Herb Parmesan Bread
1/2 tsp black pepper
1/2 tsp ground sage
1/2 tsp ground thyme
1 cup reduced salt chicken broth

Mist wide skillet with cooking spray. On medium-high heat sauté onion until softened but not brown. Add celery and stir.
Lower heat and add bread cubes, spices and chicken broth. Stir to combine thoroughly.
If too dry, add more chicken broth.

Tip: Stuff turkey cavity loosely. Tie drumstick tips together with mini-skewers and white cotton string, leaving room for expansion as stuffing roasts.

Per Serving:
55 calories, 18 g protein, 2 g carbs, 4 g fiber, & 1,500 antioxidants

Green Beans and Almonds:

Elegant, crunchy delicious, and filling
Makes 8 servings

1 1/2 tbsp olive oil
2 cups green beans, raw or frozen salt free
1 1/2 tbsp garlic powder, or to taste
½ cup slivered almonds

Pour oil into wide skillet with heat off.
Toss beans in the oil and sprinkle with garlic powder
Arrange beans so they're mostly touching the skillet bottom.
Turn heat up to high. Sautee beans until they turn dark golden on one side. Use spatula to stir and turn them over.
Continue sautéing on nearly high heat until beans look almost overdone and crispy.
Lower heat to medium. Add almonds and stir until almonds turn golden.
Stir again and serve hot.

Per Serving:
148 calories, 3 g protein, 5 g carbs, 2 g monounsaturated fat

Latkes

Crispy on the outside, latkes are typically served with sour cream or applesauce.
Makes twelve servings

Cooking spray
1 medium-sized onion
1 cup milled flaxseed
1/3 cup instant mashed potatoes
1 tsp powdered garlic
½ tsp black pepper
1 cup liquid egg whites

Mist wide skillet with cooking spray.
Use a food processor or grater to coarsely chop the onions.
Mix onions and remaining ingredients together.
Heat skillet to medium-high heat.
Drop 2 tablespoons of the latke mixture into the pan. Shape and flatten the mound.
Fry for 2-3 minutes, then flip over and brown the other side.
Remove to paper towels to drain.
Serve hot or keep warm in a 250 degree oven.

Per Serving (1 latke):
56 cal, 3 g carbs, 4 g protein, 4 g fiber, 16,000 antioxidants

Cheese Blintzes

Makes 12 blintzes

<u>Basic Crepe Batter</u>:
Cooking spray
1 cup Soy Protein Powder
1 teaspoon baking powder
4 Tbsp Splenda
2 egg whites (1/3 cup)
1 ¼ cups fat-free milk
1 tbsp canola oil

In a bowl combine the protein powder, baking powder and Splenda.
Add egg whites, milk, and oil to dry ingredients and mix well.
Mist an 8" crepe pan or nonstick skillet. Over medium heat pour in 2 tablespoons of batter, swirling around to make a circle.
Pour in more batter circles, cooking each about 1 minute on the first side. Flip, and lightly fry other side for just a few seconds. When done turn blintz shells onto plate.
Re-spray pan as needed.

<u>Cheese filling</u>
1 cup fat free ricotta cheese
1/4 cup liquid egg whites
1/2 tsp vanilla
2 tsp cinnamon
1 tsp Splenda or to taste

Mix all filling ingredients together. Place a mounded tablespoon of filling in center of each blintz shell. Fold over from both sides and roll up from bottom. Before serving, mist prepared blintzes with cooking spray and heat in 325 oven for 10 minutes or until golden.

Per Serving:
62 calories, 3 g carbs, 10 g protein, 1 g monounsaturated fat, 2 mg cholesterol, 2,217 antioxidants

Serve with sour cream, applesauce, or fruit preserves.

Roast Chicken: Makes 8 servings.

1 whole chicken (6-8 lbs)
1 tbsp olive oil
1 tsp pepper
1 tbsp dried thyme
½ tsp dried sage
Stuffing, 3 cups

Preheat oven to 400 degrees. Cover roasting platter with aluminum foil.
Mix together olive oil, pepper, thyme and sage; set aside.
Remove and discard chicken skin, giblets, and lumps of fat. Rinse bird well inside and out. Pat dry with paper towels.
Rub chicken with oil and spices. Lay breast up on roasting platter.
Fill cavity loosely with stuffing and truss drumsticks. Cover with aluminum foil tent.
Roast 1 1/2 to 1 3/4 hours, or until meat thermometer reads 180 degrees.
During last 45 minutes, remove foil and baste with pan drippings. This will turn chicken golden as roasting finishes.
When done, discard extra pan juices. Let chicken cool slightly for 10 minutes.
Slice chicken and arrange on clean, different serving platter.

Per Serving:
80 calories, 0 g carbs, 3 g protein

Carrot Casserole

Mashed carrots and onions in a delicate creamy sauce
Makes eight servings

Cooking spray
3/4 cup fat-free shredded cheddar cheese
1/3 cup fat free milk
1 tsp garlic or to taste
1/2 tsp black pepper
2 1/2 cups sliced carrots, cooked, mashed
1 1/2 cups onions, sliced

Preheat oven to 325 degrees F. Coat 2-quart casserole dish with cooking spray.
Combine cheese, milk, garlic, and black pepper in small bowl. Microwave for 2 minutes, and stir to mix.
Pour cheese mixture into casserole dish, add carrots and onions, and stir to combine.
Bake for 40 minutes, or until heated thoroughly.
Then broil for 5 minutes, or until top turns golden.

Per serving
52 calories, 6 g carbs, 4 g protein

Rugelach

Any sugar-free preserve works with this recipe. Slice into transverse sections like pinwheel cookies. Makes 8 servings.

Cooking spray
2 World's Healthiest Pancakes
1/4 cup shredded fat free mozzarella (white) cheese
2 tbsp sugar-free apricot or strawberry preserves
4 tbsp walnut baking pieces
1/2 cup raisins
2 tsp cinnamon or to taste

Preheat oven to 325 F. Spread parchment or aluminum foil over cookie sheet.
Place pancakes on a plate or paper towel. Sprinkle with shredded cheese, coming close to the edges.
Starting 1" from the edge, spread fruit preserves over cheese.
Sprinkle walnuts, cinnamon, and raisins over the fruit preserves.
Microwave on regular setting for 1 minute, then remove.
Starting on one side, roll up pancakes tightly like jellyrolls.
Place with seam side down. Let cool for 5 minutes.
Cut each rollup into 4 pieces. Spray each rugelach with cooking spray and place on cookie sheet.
Bake for 8-10 minutes, or until rugelach turn golden. Let cool again to re-firm.

Per Serving
80 calories, 11 g carbs, 4.5 g protein, 0 g saturated fat, 0 g monounsaturated fat, and 3,251 antioxidants

Christmas Dip

Blended cheeses and holiday colors brighten this festive dip.
Serves 8.

1/2 cup fat-free cream cheese, softened
2 tbsp fat-free milk
1/4 cup fat-free shredded cheddar cheese
1 fresh scallion, finely chopped
1/4 cup red bell peppers, diced
1 tsp garlic powder, or to taste
1/4 tsp black pepper, or to taste
3 tbsp salt-free green pistachios, chopped

In a small bowl, mix the cream cheese, milk, and shredded cheese together.
Mix in the scallion, red pepper, garlic and black pepper.
Chill for 45 minutes.
Press pistachios pieces into surface of dip and serve.

Per serving (with one Garlic Parmesan Flaxseed cracker):
44 cal, 1 g carbs, 3 g protein, 0 g saturated fat, 1 g fiber, 3,840 lignan antioxidants

Baked Acorn Squash with Cinnamon

These say comfort and joy any time.
Makes eight servings.

Aluminum foil
2 medium-sized acorn squash
1/2 tbsp canola oil
2 tsp cinnamon
1/4 cup raisins

Preheat oven to 350 F.
Cut squash into halves, then quarters, and clean out the seeds.
Pour 1/4 inch water into a glass baking dish. Place squash pieces upside down in it and cover with wax paper. Microwave for 8 minutes, rotating the dish once. Remove carefully (hot!). Transfer squash right side up to foil-covered oven platter.
Brush each piece with 1/2 teaspoon oil.
Sprinkle with cinnamon, & place 1/2 tablespoon raisins in each squash center.
Bake for 25 minutes, or until the squash looks soft and golden.

Per serving:
50 calories, 11g carbs, 1 g protein, 1 g polyunsaturated fat, and 2,502 antioxidants

Chocolate Layer Cake_ Easy to make. Swoony delicious with fudge frosting.

Recipe serves 8
*Fudge frosting recipe for 2-layer cake follows

Cooking spray
2 cups SPP
1 cup natural unsweetened cocoa
1 cup milled flaxseed
3 cups Splenda
2 tbsp baking powder
2 and 1/4 cups water
1 1/2 cup liquid egg whites

Preheat oven to 350 degrees. Mist two 8" cake pans with cooking spray. Note: If using 9" cake pans, bake for 2-3 minutes less than you would for 8" pans.
Mix together the soy powder, cocoa, flaxseed, Splenda, and baking powder.
Separately combine the water and egg whites. Add to dry ingredients, blend well, and divide batter into the 2 cake pans.
Use moistened fingertips to spread batter in pans.
Bake 24 minutes for 8" cake pans, or 22 minutes for 9" pans.
Cake is done when toothpick inserted in center comes out clean.
Cool for 10 minutes, then move both layers to cookie rack.

Per 2 layer serving (unfrosted): 185 calories, 30 g protein, 2 g carbs, 10 g fiber, 1 g monounsaturated fat & 40,000 antioxidants (24,000 lignan and 16,000 epicatechin antioxidants)

Per 2 layer serving (frosted): 230 calories, 32.5 g protein, 5 g carbs, 16 g fiber, 1 g monounsaturated fat & 51,700 antioxidants

Fudge frosting for 2-layer cake:

Makes 1 1/2 cups frosting for 8 serving cake

1 1/2 cups unsweetened cocoa
1 1/2 cups Splenda
1/2 cup powder of Jello Vanilla pudding
2 1/2 cups water

Combine cocoa, Splenda, and vanilla pudding powder.
Add water and mix until smooth.

Per Serving:
45 calories, 2.5 g protein, 3 g carbs, 6 g fiber, and 11,700 antioxidants

How to Frost a Layer Cake:
Bake cake, remove layers from pans, and cool completely.
Place four strips of waxed paper in a square on a serving platter, leaving an open space almost the size of the cake in the middle.
Place one cake layer on the wax paper, flat side up. Spread frosting over the top of that layer.
Carefully place the second layer on top of the frosting, lining up the edges.
Next frost the sides of the cake, using your knife or spatula to make peaks and swirls. Build up a bit extra at the top edge of the cake.
Frost the top of the cake, swirling frosting to the edges to combine with the frosting on the sides.
Carefully slide out the waxed paper strips. Your platter is clean of smudges and ready to serve.

Cranberry Sauce

Thanksgiving favorite with far fewer carbs
Recipe serves eight

1 1/2 cup cranberries (fresh or frozen)
2 tbsp Splenda, or to taste
1 cup cold water

Combine cranberries and water in a saucepan. Heat to boiling; reduce heat to low, add Splenda, and simmer for 20 minutes.
Refrigerate until serving time.

Per Serving:
9 calories, 1.5 g carbs, less than 1 g protein

Cheddar Biscuits: For dunking, or cutting into cheese omelets, or filled with salad, fat free cream cheese, sugar-free jam and peanut butter, anything – the protein's on the outside!
Recipe serves six

Cooking spray
1 1/2 cups Soy Protein Powder
1/2 cup Splenda
2 tbsp milled flaxseed
1 Tbsp baking powder
1 tsp garlic powder
2 tsp dried parsley
1 cup fat-free shredded cheddar cheese
1 1/2 cup liquid egg whites
1/4 cup water

Preheat oven to 400. Cover cookie sheet with foil and mist with spray.
Combine the soy powder, Splenda, milled flaxseed, baking powder, garlic and parsley.
Add cheese, egg whites and water; mix well.
Drop batter onto cookie sheet in 6 equal mounds. Using two large spoons helps with this. "Mark" six places with a little batter first, then come back and add more batter to even their size.
With moistened fingers neaten into biscuit shapes.
Spray tops with cooking spray and bake for 11 minutes. Remove from oven and cool.

Per Biscuit:
153 calories, 36 g protein, 1 g carb, 2 g fiber, and 5,238 antioxidants from the parsley and flaxseed.

Grilled cheese sandwich, Dressed Up: The same comforting favorite, a little fancier. Makes one serving

Cooking spray
2 slices Parmesan Herb Protein Bread
2 slices fat-free cheese
tomato slice
onion slice
arugula leaves

Spray skillet, tip of spatula, and one slice of bread.
Put bread in skillet, sprayed side down, over low-medium heat.
Spray the second slice of bread and set aside.
When the cooking bread turns golden (2-3 minutes), top with one slice of cheese and the tomato, onion, and arugula.
Top all with second slice of cheese and the second bread slice, sprayed side up.
Use spatula to turn the sandwich. Cook until the second side turns golden, and serve.

Per Serving
248 cal, 38 g protein, 6 g carbs, 5 g fiber, and 3,000 lignan antioxidants

Salmon Dip A delicious spread mixed with sour cream and lemon juice.
Makes eight servings
1 tsp unflavored gelatin (from a 1/4 ounce envelope)
4 ounces smoked salmon, coarsely chopped
1 cup fat-free sour cream
2 tablespoons fresh lemon juice
1 tsp garlic, powdered
1 tsp dill, powdered
fresh dill for garnish, if desired

Sprinkle gelatin onto 3 tablespoons of cold water in a small saucepan. Let soften for five minutes, stirring once. Heat gently over low heat, stirring, until gelatin dissolves. Set aside and cool slightly.
In a food processor, combine salmon, sour cream, lemon juice, garlic, and dill. Puree until smooth. Add slightly cooled gelatin mixture, and blend until combined.
Transfer to serving bowl. Cover and refrigerate until firm but spreadable, about 2 hours. Garnish mousse with fresh dill, if desired.

Per serving:
35 calories, 5 g carbs, 3.5 g protein

Fruit and Almond Compote

Combine toasted almonds with beautiful fruit, and you have a perfect side dish, snack, or even dessert.
Recipe serves eight.
Cooking spray
1 cup slivered almonds
4 medium-sized apples, with skin
1 cup canned mandarin oranges, well drained
3 tbsp cinnamon

Wash and cut apples into wedges, leaving skin on.
In ungreased dry skillet, toast almonds on medium-high heat, stirring occasionally, until they turn golden. Move to a bowl and set aside.
Mist skillet with cooking spray. On medium-high heat, sautee the apples, sprinkling them with cinnamon as you stir and turn the slices.
Use two forks to sautee first one side of slices, then the other.
When the apples look golden, lower heat and add toasted almonds.
Stir gently, then fold in the well-drained mandarin oranges.
Heat just long enough to warm the oranges, and serve.

Per Serving:
163 cal, 20 g carbs, 4 g prot and 19,605 antioxidants

Holiday Recipes

Summer Barbecue

Appetizers:
Guacamole Dip
Garlic Parmesan Flaxseed Crackers
Low-salt Bruschetta on toasted Sweet Roll slices

Main Course:
Grilled Chicken Breasts
Grilled Turkey Cheeseburgers
Grilled Zucchini and Yellow Squash
Mixed Greens salad with almonds
Diet soda (made with sucralose, aspartame)

Dessert:
Key Lime Pie
Lemon Sherbet with fudge sauce and strawberries
Reddi-wip

Thanksgiving Recipes

Appetizers:
Salt-free Almonds
Salt-free pistachios
Salmon Dip
Flaxseed Crackers
Cheese Canapes

Main Course:
Roast Turkey
Stuffing
Cranberry Sauce
Carrot Casserole
Green beans and almonds

Dessert:
Pumpkin Pie
Bowl of Fruit Chocolate Sundae
Reddi-wip, Fat-Free

Chanukah Recipes

Appetizers:
Latkes
Cheese blintzes
Cheese 'n Crackers Canapes

Main Course:
Roast Chicken
Stuffing
Fruit & Almond Compote
Orange-glazed carrots
Sauteed Broccoli and Zucchini

Dessert:
Rugelah
Pumpkin Pie
Chocolate Layer Cake
Fudge Truffles

Christmas Recipes

Appetizers:
Christmas Dip
Flaxseed Crackers
Cheese Canapes
Unsalted almonds and pistachios

Main Course:
Roast Turkey
Stuffing
Cranberry Sauce
Cheddar Biscuits
Baked Acorn Squash with Cinnamon
Green Beans with Almonds

Dessert:
Pumpkin Pie
Chocolate Layer Cake
Fudge Truffles

Appendix 1

DIABETES AND CARDIOVASCULAR DISEASE (CVD): AN OVERVIEW

Classification of CVD: Both large and small arteries
  Macrovascular Disease (large artery disease):
      1. Heart Disease (heart attack): coronary arteries
      2. Stroke: carotid and cerebral arteries
      3. Peripheral Artery Disease (leg amputations): leg arteries

  Microvascular Disease (small artery disease):
      4. Retinal Disease (blindness):.retinal arteries
      5. Nerve Disease (loss of sensation in limbs): small arteries to nerves
      6. Chronic Kidney Disease: small arteries within kidney filtering

A. Diabetes and Cardiovascular Disease:
Some grim statistics: CVD is a major complication of diabetes and the leading cause of early death among people with diabetes. A staggering *five out of six people with diabetes die with diagnosed heart disease (68%) and stroke (16%).* Adults with diabetes are two to four more times likely to have heart disease or stroke than people without diabetes. Higher blood glucose in adults with diabetes increases the risk for heart attack, stroke, angina, and coronary artery disease. People with type 2 diabetes also have high rates of high blood pressure, lipid [cholesterol] problems, and obesity, which contribute to their high rates of CVD. [19]

In 2004–2005 [NIH Report 2008], Seventy-five percent of diabetics ages 20-74 had high blood pressure. Diabetes was the leading cause of blindness in that age range. Sixty-seven percent had neurological symptoms, 30% had loss of sensation in their feet. More than 60% of non-traumatic amputations occurred in diabetics. [19, 20]

Grim statistics indeed. But the good news is that improved glycemic control (improving your day in day out blood sugar) works:
Every percentage point drop in your A1c blood test—for example, from 8 to 7 percent—can reduce the risk of microvascular [small artery] complications— eye, kidney, and nerve diseases—by 40 percent. [A1c is a measure of average blood glucose during the preceding 2-3 months.] From: National Diabetes Statistics, 2007. (June, 2008.)

Progression to diabetes among those with pre-diabetes *is not inevitable*. Studies have shown that people with pre-diabetes who lose weight and increase their physical activity can prevent or delay diabetes and even return their blood glucose levels to normal.
In the Diabetes Prevention Program, a large prevention study of people at high risk for diabetes, lifestyle intervention reduced the development of diabetes by 58 percent over 3 years. The reduction was even greater, 71 percent, among adults ages 60 years or older. [19, 20]

Question from The National Diabetes Education Program [NDEP] publication *The Link Between Diabetes and Cardiovascular Disease* (Feb 2007), published by the NIH and CDC, and 200 associated organizations:

Question: What is the link between diabetes and cardiovascular disease (CVD)? [20]
Answer: *High blood sugar ends up as belly fat, fat particles re-enter the blood and inflame the arterial inner wall, provoking cholesterol deposits and clots which block circulation.*

NDEP's Control Your Diabetes For Life Education campaign strives to help health care professionals and their patients control the multiple risk factors associated with CVD and diabetes. It also helps people with diabetes learn how to reduce their risk of diabetic kidney, eye, and nerve disease. The campaign focuses on comprehensive control of diabetes and urges optimal management of A1c, Blood pressure, and Cholesterol. [20]

The ABC treatment goals for most people with diabetes are:
A A1c (blood glucose) less than 7 percent
B Blood Pressure less than 130/80
C Cholesterol – LDL less than 100 mg/dl
   (Less than 70 mg/dl if multiple risk factors for CVD) [20]
   • Normal A1c is about 5.0-6.0.
   • As A1c increases, especially over 8.0, the hazard of cardiovascular disease increases.

Different studies (the ACCORD [5] and the ADVANCE [6] studies, for example) differed on how far down to push blood sugar, how intensively to treat. But it is generally agreed the above goals, when achieved, *substantially* lower risk for cardiovascular disease: reduce risk of heart attack, stroke, or death from CVD by 57%. BP control in diabetics reduces risk of vascular disease by 33-50%. Cholesterol control reduces CVD by 20-50%.

About Tobacco: To reduce your risk of CVD: "Smoking doubles the risk of heart disease and stroke in people with diabetes." [20]

About Aspirin: One or two baby aspirin daily [81-162 mg/day] reduces CVD risk in diabetics. Get your doctor's OK. Aspirin can cause bleeding in a very small percent of people. [27]

About Salt: Sodium in excess of 1500 mg. per day [about 2/3 of a teaspoon of salt] increases risk for high blood pressure and congestive heart failure: a bad combination with cardiovascular disease due to diabetes. The risk lies less in your salt shaker than in canned, frozen, and processed foods.

B. Diabetes and Chronic Kidney Disease: A very small percentage of Diabetics have Chronic Kidney Disease or Kidney Failure.

National Institutes of Health (NIH) data [19] shows that over 99% of diabetics *do not* have kidney failure. The American Diabetes Association (ADA) [18] and the NIH [17] state in their publications that *it is prolonged high blood sugar levels that do the damage to the filtering units (nephrons) in the kidneys.* The NIH [17] reports [exact quote]:

"If glucose stays in the blood instead of breaking down, it can act like a poison. Damage to the nephrons from unused glucose in the blood is called diabetic kidney disease."

Most people with diabetes do not develop chronic kidney disease (CKD) that is severe enough to progress to kidney failure (Stage 5 CKD). In the small percent of diabetics who eventually get CKD, it takes at least 15-25 years to develop. If CKD hasn't occurred in 25 years it is unlikely to do so at all.

The NIH reported for 2005 that 99.8% of diabetics did not develop kidney failure that year, and *of all diabetics in the US, 99.2% did not have kidney failure* [19]. Medicare (US Renal Data System 2007) reported that in the 65 and older age group, a total of 7.8 % had chronic kidney disease *from all causes* [21]. The NIH reported in 2009 that diabetes accounts for a little over one third of people over 65 with CKD (Stage 5). [22]

Other causes such as high blood pressure, kidney infection, kidney stones, kidney blockage, tumors, etc. account for the rest. Similar data was also reported by the American Diabetes Association, 2008 [23].

Of the entire Medicare population, about 2.6% (1/3 of 7.8%) had CKD due to diabetes, which means that diabetics were free of CKD in 97.4 % of cases in the age group that had diabetes the longest. A cheering statistic! But the long term trend shows slow, gradual increase in these numbers, and is likely to continue to do so, as long as the incidence of diabetes in adults over age 20 increases [24, 25].

For anyone with chronic kidney disease from any cause, consultation with their physician is necessary to keep protein intake in the right range for them, since the kidneys excrete the leftover products from protein metabolism. This might be done by using the recipes in this book for only part of their food intake, as determined by their doctor.

Kidney function is very easy to test with two simple tests, one on a urine specimen for (micro)albumin in the urine, and the other a blood test (Creatinine) from which blood flow rate through the kidneys is calculated.

Appendix 2

YOUR DAILY PROTEIN INTAKE RANGE

Protein: As noted in the text earlier but worth repeating here: For *the 97% of diabetes patients who do not have chronic kidney disease* it's easy to figure your own protein daily intake range. Multiply your weight in pounds by 0.9. That's all. (For example: 180 pounds times 0.9 = up to 162 grams of protein per day.) That's less than one gram of protein per pound of body weight. In metric units, this gives you about 2.0 grams of protein per kilogram (2.2 lbs) of body weight. Usually 2.0-2.8 grams of protein per kilogram of body weight is given as the daily *maximum* limit.

Normally the *minimum* daily requirement for an adult is about 50 grams. Most adults in the U.S. normally consume much higher amounts of protein without any problem. [See Table Below.] A typical American diet of bacon and eggs for breakfast, a cheeseburger or turkey sandwich for lunch, a mid-afternoon snack of a bag of peanuts or a hot dog, a chicken or meat dish at dinner [plus appetizer and dessert], and a raid on the refrigerator at night contains more than 125-150 grams of protein per day (plus saturated fat, sugar, carbs and calories in unhealthy doses). This is well within normal kidney capacity to process, especially so in a predominately plant-based protein diet. [1,28,29]

Our recipe plan can provide up to 125-150 grams of protein per day and 1400-1500 calories per day without all the animal protein baggage, and can be varied up or down to suit your needs. The Atkins Diet, for comparison, was a high protein diet and also contained about 125-150 grams of protein per day (but from animal sources, and burdened by saturated fat and cholesterol).

A slightly lower range of 1.6-1.8 grams per kilogram will provide roughly 25% of your typical daily caloric intake as protein. Multiply your weight in pounds by 0.8 to figure your protein limit for a 1.8 grams per kilogram intake.

Appendix 3

CAN YOU SAVE MONEY ON DIABETIC MEDS AND SUPPLIES?

"My Novolog costs $118 a bottle!"
"My health plan won't pay for my Byetta"
"Can you get test strips on eBay?"

The new numbers: Now one out of three Americans are diabetic or pre-diabetic. In Canada it's one out of four. In the U.K. it's one out of seven.

If these trends continue, one in three Americans will have the full-blown disease by 2050. Diabetes, chronic and often crippling, already costs the country's health care system an astonishing $174 billion a year. Many other countries, including impoverished and Third World, are experiencing epidemics almost as serious.

Would it be going too far to call it the plague of this century? Maybe not.

"Diabetes is the noninfectious epidemic of our time," said Dr. Ronald Loeppke, vice chairman of U.S. Preventive Medicine, a company that offers wellness and prevention programs to employers and individuals.

Lost beneath these statistics, however, are individual patients struggling to pay for their illness. Those with insurance are near depleting their savings on co-pays for doctor visits and the medications and supplies that Medicare doesn't cover. Those without insurance do not get the care they need, and wind up sooner and sicker in emergency wards with the complications of diabetes such as heart disease, strokes, blindness, and limb amputations.

The CDC estimates that diabetic patients pay more than twice as much for health care as those without the illness. So the expense makes the problem worse, both for the country and for individuals who only manage to obtain care by making steep financial sacrifices.

Can anything be done to help? Here are some money-saving tips culled from emails, online diabetes forums, and word of mouth:

Try older generic drugs first. These are often just as effective as new drugs, plus they have established safety records. Sometimes newer diabetes drugs, like Avandia, have been found to increase health risks. "Newer drugs are not necessarily better," said Dr. Marvin Lipman, chief medical adviser for Consumer Reports Health and a practicing endocrinologist. "The expensive drugs are third- and fourth-line drugs. If you don't get results with the less expensive drugs, you go to those. But you shouldn't start there. The vast majority of cases can be treated with the less expensive drugs."

For example, a 500 mg dose of metformin, well esteemed by physicians and available generically, costs on average only $18 a month, and even less than that at stores like WalMart and Target, which offer big generic drug discounts.

Another thought is to search the internet for sites like BlueSkyDrugs.com. Novolog, for example, is a new, expensive, fast-acting insulin. If your doctor approves, you might be able to try a different fast-acting insulin that is available as a generic. Be sure to talk to your doctor first though, because s/he may feel that Novolog, or whatever new drug s/he has prescribed, has some special advantage in your case.

You can also ask your doctor if s/he has any free samples.

For further help check out Partnership for Prescription Assistance at PPARX. org/en/prescription_assistance_programs They have information on free clinics, and many people get help with their medications from them. Another link that should help is HealthFinder.gov at healthfinder.gov/findservices/

Call the company that makes your meter and strips. They often send free supplies to people with no insurance.

Contact the American Diabetes Association too, and ask if they know of any programs. Their "Contact Us" link is at the bottom of their web site home page.

Another place to contact is the pharmaceutical company that made the drug you need, and ask for free samples. They often do give them out for free, or a modest cost if you are having economic problems.

Every hospital has a diabetes unit, and they too may be able to help or to offer ideas on where to find help in your area.

All states have some form of assistance that helps patients buy their meds at low cost. You need to call your town clerk to find out what agency of the town or state to contact. Or you can google your state's name and then the words "financial help to buy medicines." Or you can call your state Department of Health to ask for this help. Most states also have an 800 number to call with questions about anything, including help with medications and medical supplies.

The important thing is to make that first call, even if it isn't exactly the right office or agency. They will help you from there and tell you who to call.

Geographically, you're in luck if you're in Ohio, Pennsylvania or West Virginia, Giant Eagle Grocery stores are offering Free Diabetes Medications. The list is on their website which is GiantEagle.com/pharmacy/diabetes-care

Next are the big chains Sams Club (samsclub.com) and Walmart (walmart.com). They have their own pharmacies that offer free or low cost items, and there is talk that they, too, will soon be offering diabetes drugs and supplies at big savings.

In Canada there are government sponsored programs and free programs offered by the hospitals. In the U.S., the approach is to individually approach each manufacturer of the drugs and supplies that you need: we hear increasingly that they can give you free or lower cost items, and all have programs for people who cannot afford their medications.

These are all good steps that diabetes patients and their loved ones can take to lower their costs of treatment. The trick is to take an active role, make those calls, initiate those contacts. Once you're in "the pipeline" you'll find friendly people who are happy to help. Between them, listening to your doctor, eating healthy and exercising, you'll lower your expenses and still achieve top quality care for yourself.

SOURCES AND REFERENCES

. . .

1. *Arch Intern Med.* 2009 Jun 8;169(11):1046-54. Jenkins DJ, et al
The effect of a plant-based low-carbohydrate ("eco-atkins") diet on body weight
and blood lipid concentrations in hyperlipidemic subjects. *Arch Intern Med.* 2009
Jun 8;169(11):1046-54.

2. *Standards of Medical Care in Diabetes.* Diabetes Care 2010; Vol 33 Suppl 1: S4-
S10. doi:10.2337/dc10-S004.

3. *BMJ* 2007;335:132 (21 July), doi:10.1136/bmj.39247.447431.BE (published
25 June 2007) Farmer, A et al
Impact of self monitoring of blood glucose in the management of patients with
non-insulin treated diabetes: open parallel group randomised trial.

4. *BMJ* 2008;336:1174-1177 (24 May), doi:10.1136/bmj.39534.571644.BE
(published 17 April 2008) O'Kane, MJ, et al
Efficacy of self monitoring of blood glucose in patients with newly diagnosed
type 2 diabetes (ESMON study): randomised controlled trial

5. *N Engl J Med.* 2008 Jun 12;358(24):2545-59. Epub 2008 Jun 6.
Effects of intensive glucose lowering in type 2 diabetes.
Action to Control Cardiovascular Risk in Diabetes Study Group, Gerstein HC, et
al [ACCORD Trial]

6. *Lancet.* 2007 Sep 8;370(9590):829-40.
Effects of a fixed combination of perindopril and indapamide on macrovascular
and microvascular outcomes in patients with type 2 diabetes mellitus (the
ADVANCE trial): a randomised controlled trial.
Patel A, et al [ADVANCE Collaborative Group]

7. *Arch Intern Med.* 2010 Jan 25; Vol. 170 (No. 2): 126-135.
Effects of the DASH Diet.....with Exercise and Weight Loss on Blood Pressure and Cardiovascular Biomarkers.....The ENCORE STUDY. Blumenthal, JA, et al

8. *Arch Intern Med.* 2010 Apr 26; Vol. 170 (No. 8): 732-734.
Research Letter: Sodium Content of Lunchtime Fast Food Purchases at Major US Chains. Johnson, CM et al.

9. Clinical Practice Guidelines for Chronic Kidney Disease in Adults: Part I. Definition, Disease Stages, Evaluation, Treatment, and Risk Factors
Cynda Ann Johnson, M.D., et al M.B.A., et al. Brody School of Medicine at East Carolina University, Greenville, North Carolina
Am Fam Physician. 2004 Sep 1;70(5):869-876.

10. Detection and Evaluation of Chronic Kidney Disease
Susan Snyder, M.D., and Bernadette Pendergraph, M.D., Harbor-University of California, Los Angeles Medical Center, Torrance, California
Am Fam Physician. 2005 Nov 1;72(9):1723-1732.

11. A Review of Issues of Dietary Protein Intake in Humans.
Bilsborough, S and Mann, N
IJSNEM, 16(2), April 2006

12-15. *Kidney and Urologic Diseases Statistics for the United States (2006 - 2009)* NIH
16. Beyond the Zone: Protein Needs of Active Individuals. Lemon, Peter. *Journal of the American College of Nutrition* 2000: 19 (5): 513–521.

17. *NIH Publication No. 09-3195 February 2009*
The Kidneys and How They Work
Sections: Why Do Kidneys Fail? & Diabetic Kidney Disease. NIH [NIDDK/ NKUDIC]
http://kidney.niddk.nih.gov/Kudiseases/pubs/yourkidneys/#why

18. *American Diabetes Association*
Living With Diabetes
Kidney Disease (Nephropathy)
http://www.diabetes.org/living-with-diabetes/complications/kidney-disease-nephropathy.html

19. *NIH publication #08-3892 June 2008* NIDDK (NDIC): National Diabetes Statistics 2007.
http://diabetes.niddk.nih.gov/DM/PUBS/statistics/

20. *The National Diabetes Education Program [NDEP]:* The Link Between Diabetes and Cardiovascular Disease (Feb 2007) from the NIH and CDC.
http://ndep.nih.gov/media/CVD_FactSheet.pdf

21. *Renal Business Today:* USRDS Releases 2007 Report.
Keith Chartier 11/01/2007 http://www.renalbusiness.com/articles/07novfeat1.html

22. *NIH Publication No. 09–3895 February 2009* Kidney and Urologic Disease Statistics for the United States
http://kidney.niddk.nih.gov/kudiseases/pubs/kustats/

23. *American Diabetes Association*
Diabetes Spectrum January 2008 vol. 21 no. 1 5-6
doi: 10.2337/diaspect.21.1.5

24. Prevalence of Chronic Kidney Disease in the United States. Josef Coresh, MD, PhD, et al
JAMA. 2007;298(17):2038-2047.

25. *NIH Publication No. 08–3925* September 2008
NIDDK NKUDIC Kidney Disease of Diabetes

26. *Sci Transl Med 26 May 2010:*

Vol. 2, Issue 33, p. 33-37
DOI: 10.1126/scitranslmed.3001006

AAAS: American Association for the Advancement of Science

Metabolic Signatures of Exercise in Human Plasma. Gregory D. Lewis, et al

27. *Circulation* (June 22, 2010) On-line May 27, 2010
Aspirin for Primary Prevention of Cardiovascular Events in People With Diabetes, Michael Pignone, MD, et al

American Diabetes Association, American Heart Association, American College of Cardiology Foundation

28. *Nephrology Dialysis Transplantation* 2005 20(3):657-658; doi:10.1093/ndt/gfh645
High-protein diets are not hazardous for the healthy kidneys

Manninen, A.H.
Department of Physiology Faculty of Medicine University of Oulu Finland
Oxford University Press
http://tinyurl.com/25bof29

29. *Annals of Internal Medicine*, March 18, 2003, vol. 138 no. 6: 460-467
The Impact of Protein Intake on Renal Function Decline in Women with Normal
Renal Function or Mild Renal Insufficiency
Knight, E.L., MD, MPH, et al

Brigham and Women's Hospital, Harvard Medical School; and Massachusetts
General Hospital, Harvard School of Public Health, Boston, Massachusetts.
http://tinyurl.com/2c5dept

30. *Annals of Internal Medicine*, September 7, 2010, vol. 153 no. 5: 289-298: **Low-
Carbohydrate Diets and All-Cause and Cause-Specific Mortality. Fung, T T, et al.**

INDEX 1: RECIPES

. . .

INDEX 2: HEALTH INFORMATION

• • •

ABOUT THE AUTHORS

· · ·

Robert Schneider, M.D. has practiced Internal Medicine and Clinical Cardiology for more than 30 years, focusing on the relationship between weight, diabetes and cardiovascular disease (heart attack and stroke).

A graduate of Yale University and New York University School of Medicine (Bellevue Hospital), Dr. Schneider then interned, followed by three years of residency in Internal Medicine and a Cardiology Fellowship.

His previous publications include the books WHEN TO SAY NO TO SURGERY and CANCER PREVENTION MADE EASY, over 130 medical articles for online publications, as well as articles in The American Heart Journal. A Certified Federal and State First Responder, Dr. Schneider was a Chief of Medicine in the U.S. Air Force Strategic Air Command, a Consultant to the Connecticut Department of Public Health, and has taught in the Cardiac Intensive Care Unit at Norwalk Hospital in Norwalk, Connecticut. He is Board Certified by the American Board of Internal Medicine, a Fellow of the American College of Chest Physicians, and a Member of the American College of Physicians – American Society of Internal Medicine. He was also a Participating Investigator in the Veterans Administration Cooperative Study of Hypertension and Coronary Syndromes.

Joyce Schneider, a Wheaton grad and a former Newsweek staffer, is a Heart Smart and Diabetes Recipe cook, who's spent decades getting it better with each new finding in Nutrition, Cardiology, and Diabetes Research. She has written FLORA TRISTAN, a biography for young adults, and the suspense thrillers DARKNESS FALLS and STRYKER'S CHILDREN.

Made in the USA
Lexington, KY
24 March 2013